Central Advanced Studies

SOCIOLOGY

Theory, Methodology and Concepts

Central Advanced Studies

SOCIOLOGY

Theory, Methodology and Concepts

Bhuban Mohan Chakravorty

Retired Lecturer, Tertiary College and Community College [London]
MA, Mod. History, Cal. Univ., MA, Pol. Science, Cal. Univ.
Diploma in Education, Institute of London
MSc, Sociology, Southbank, London

New Central Book Agency (P) Ltd

LONDON
HYDERABAD ERNAKULAM BHUBANESWAR
NEW DELHI KOLKATA PUNE GUWAHATI

NCBA

REGD OFFICE

8/1 Chintamoni Das Lane, Kolkata 700 009, India

email: ncbapvtltd@eth.net

OVERSEAS

NCBA (UK) Ltd, 149 Park Avenue North, Northampton, NN3 2HY, UK

email: ncbauk@yahoo.com

EXPORT

NCBA Exports Pvt. Ltd, 212 Shahpur Jat, New Delhi 110 049

email: ncbaexports@ncbapvtltd.com

BRANCHES

2/27 Ansari Road, 1st Floor
Daryaganj, New Delhi 110 002
email: ncbadel@ncbapvtltd.com

House No. 3-1-315, 1st Floor
Nimboliadda, Kachiguda, Hyderabad 500 027
email: ncbahydb@ncbapvtltd.com

Shop Nos. 3 & 4, Vinayak Towers
681/B Budhwar Peth, Appa Balwant Chowk
Pune 411 002
email: ncbapune@ncbapvtltd.com

GSS Shopping Complex, 1st Floor
Opposite College Post Office, Convent Road
Ernakulam 682 035
0484-4021054/53

Shop No. 15, Bharati Towers, Ground Floor
Forest Park
Bhubaneswar 751 001
email: ncbabub@ncbapvtltd.com

Radhamayee Complex (Second Floor)
Opp. SBI, Panbazar, Jaswanta Road
Guwahati 781 001
email: ncbaguwahati@ncbapvtltd.com

SOCIOLOGY • **Bhuban Mohan Chakravorty**

First Published: July 2009
Reprinted: July 2016

PUBLISHER : New Central Book Agency (P) Ltd
8/1 Chintamoni Das Lane, Kolkata 700 009

TYPESETTER : Lasercraft, New Delhi

PRINTER : New Central Book Agency (P) Ltd
Web-Offset Division, Dhulagrh, Sankrail, Howrah

ISBN: 978 81 7381 602 4

Price ₹ 650.00

Preface

The book is intended to meet the requirement of students doing their graduate and postgraduate studies in Sociology, both in Indian universities and overseas. As Sociology is a predominantly theory based subject akin to scientific thinking, emphasis has been laid on explaining issues using the methodology firmly established in the discipline of Sociology.

Our society is changing rapidly and so also is our sociological imagination, especially the method of learning which makes education so different and effective. Sociology covers most of the changing aspects of our society, state and government which have developed under the aegis of new technology and research findings during the last fifty years or so which are now brought under purview. These new inclusions enrich this edition.

The conflict theories of education, the interaction theories which focus on how we perceive society from each others' point of view, new phase of Marxism and feminism, theories of social change, post-modernity and so on. There are 29 chapters and each is unique by its nature and character of content. A separate chapter is devoted to the numerous sociological concepts which is usually absent in other books on Sociology. The reason why they are to be studied separately is because these provide conceptual meanings relevant to understanding individual subject or topic.

A great deal of care has been taken to produce the text in lucid form linguistically, the students would find it worthwhile to read and love it. The next edition however, would be bigger and better. For further reading, every chapter has a list of recommended books at the end ensuring that the readers don't have to search frantically for the right reference books from among the long list of Bibliography.

B. Chakravorty
London

Contents

Part 1

1 Introduction to the Sociological Theories

Historical Context, Definition of a Sociological Theory, Character of a Sociological Theory, Consensus or Conflict, Relationship Between the Individual and the Society.

Historical Context

Sociology is about us and our society and the theory is a construction of our lives with in the framework of a system in which we work, live and survive. Peter Burger suggests that sociology is based on a critical awareness of social life. Social philosophy is an attempt to explain the society how it is organised and for what purposes it exists. Sociology is a kind of social philosophy which enables us to renew the system of society as well as its functional and operational methods based on the needs of people, after all, sociological theory is a systematic idea engulfing all relevant thinking, imagination, behavior of people and their social roles. According to Durkheim, whenever we act, we act towards and in a total social situation which include the abstract general concept of the vast heterogeneous aggregate of customs, law, roles, expectations, accepted ways of doing things etc. which constitute our actual social situations. Sociological theories are thus structures of all our doing with in the social and cultural frame work.

There are numerous sociological theories for us to learn and to grasp about what is going on in our society. Their number is also steadily increasing. I have endeavoured to generally over view most of them and then discuss their perspectives highlighting what they are offering to us. Some of them are macro theories dealing with the society as a whole and some are micro theories dealing with specific issues of society like feminism, minorities etc. Both the categories are important for the society as they present a panoramic view of the whole society which includes all shades of opinion, colour and creed. More or less, all the sociological theories have enriched the discipline of the subject by raising its value and awareness to readers better than before. Logic, consistency and coherence would be the criteria for judging their scientific level of perfection. Those which have delivered resolution and direction in the field of Sociology could also be used for future research work.

Understanding sociological theories is crucial to understanding the subject as a whole. Theories cover both classical, modern and contemporary periods. They include consensus and system theories, conflict and action theories, interaction theories and so on. Other subjects of immense importance are given equal consideration and discussion which are theories of education, phenomenology, social change, modernity, class and caste and so on. Moreover, theories of current issues like racism, feminism, power, globalisation, and post-modernity also have been adequately focussed.

The founding fathers of sociology for instance-August Comte, Emile Durkheim, Lambert Simnel, Karl Marx Weber, and also some post modern theorists whose contributions have enriched the subject of sociology immensely are adequately discussed. Their place in sociology is permanently established. There is no clear cut dividing line between the differing schools of thought; and even though they retain their respective distinctiveness, they can cross each other's domain by overlapping. There is a traditional group-the functionalists who have dominated the sociological scene in the United States for well over forty years. With the advent of Marxism, their influence diminished for a while but as to day Marxism seems to have lost its ground making room for functionalism's reappearance.

Marxism is alleged to have failed to deliver its objectives, so it has been packed away in the East European countries.

Marxism engulfed Europe after the Second World War but it has not stood the test of time. A total renewal of its ideology may resurge its fortune. As old ideas die hard so also perhaps Marxism. Already, the Neo-Marxism is carrying its banner, however with modified perspectives. The fall of Berlin Wall and removal of Lenin's statues, from cities of the East European countries including Communist Russia is the hallmark of its downfall leading to the return of the democratic system in the Eastern Europe with full force. Functionalism does better with democratic and republican systems of government than socialism.

There have emerged several conflict theories to day broadly representing Marxism but with slightly different meanings and objectives which also run parallel to the classical, modern and contemporary sociological thought. A new generation of thinkers have appeared during the last fifty years or so who have widened sociological horizon with their challenging approaches. For example, the Frankfurt school and the Critical theory, the ideology of Marxist Feminism, Radical Feminism, Neo-functionalism and Neo-Marxism with their adaptability to changing social scenario are remarkable examples of a few amongst others. The new breeds have revitalised the sociological thought with fresh research findings paving the way to lead a better life in our modern society.

What is a Sociological Theory

At this stage, it is important to highlight what the sociological theory is about. A theory is a set of ideas which are systematically produced either deductively or inductively or using both the methods and tested empirically in order for it to be valid and predictable. The objective of the theory is to develop it as a scientific piece of evidence and when necessary, use it as a reference to further research work. Some times, a theory can be used to explain a relevant social issue or a combination of issues. A sociological theory is always helpful in critically evaluating or developing any new themes.

As said above, a theory has to be empirically tested before it could be recognised as a valid theory. Nevertheless, there are some theories which are without empirical validation but still regarded as scientific. Their value is well recognised because they have enriched the quality and content of the subject.

Furthermore, a theory to be scientific is structurally constructed which should have the qualities of consistency, coherence and logic either with a macro or a micro appeal. According to Ruth Wallace, an American sociologist, the classical definition of a sociological theory is a deductive one. It lays-down rules about how to classify the things we observe. Then the observations are put forward in the form of propositions. The observers have to classify the subject matter of these propositions. The next stage is to test them logically by the deductive method in order to prove their validity. Once that has been done, then appears an acceptable theory.

There are sociologists who would not accept the deductive method as the right method to testify a theory. According to Harold Garfinkel and Blumer "when we are dealing with behaviour of human beings such method could not be accepted as valid" (Harold Garfinkel and Blumer in 'Contemporary sociological theory. pp 5-7). There are other methods like the inductive methodology which can produce a testable and valid theory. Regardless of the controversy about whether deductive or inductive is the right methodology, the overwhelming opinion is for using both either individually or jointly.

Robert K Merton, an American sociologist holds a different view of sociological theory. According to him, "Much of what is described in text books as sociological theory consists of general orientations towards substantive materials" (R.K. Merton. Social theory and social structure, 1957, p. 141). According to him, any sociological theory constructed on a grand scale, as Talcot Parsons tried to do, could lead to structural problems–the impediments which would restrict empirical validation. In his view, in a highly modern diversified society, trying to achieve a functional unity, essential for a grand theory would end up being too abstract. Any empirical test of the whole theory would not work. Instead, he advocates developing more concrete theories grounded on empirical evidence and addressing specific social issues or phenomena could be the right approach for theory development. Merton calls them, 'theories of middle range'.

Functionalism is a major sociological perspective divided into early and contemporary parts. Marxism and its by-products-the different conflict theories form another substantive part of sociology. Then, we have phenomenology, ethno-methodology, interpretive, action and socio-biological theories.

Sociological theories are the products of sociological thinking which have grown from critical awareness of social life including material factors of society. The thinkers and the research workers collect their ideas and facts from Anthropological sources which unravel the roots of human society.

Social theories are necessary to read and understand social issues which may be in the form of facts, problem or even abstract concepts. Social facts are empirically investigated in order to establish the truth and accuracy of the matter. But they still require theoretical explanations. The question in sociology is why things occur differently at different social situations and why people behave differently in different societies. There can be theories which can go deeper in to the intricacies of social issues, facts and matters that concern us all. Social questions are to be tested and analysed by theoretical thinking in order to construct abstract interpretations that would help explain a wide variety of empirical situations.

Facts and theories are interrelated; facts alone are not knowledgeable; they require interpretations by theories in order for them to generate meanings as well as their effectiveness. Only then, they become sociologically and educationally valuable.

Sociology, as a distinct form of enquiry emerged in the 19th century in the wake of the so-called "twin revolutions"–the Industrial Revolution of England which occurred roughly between 1780 and 1840 and the Democratic Revolutions of the United States of America in 1776 and France in 1789 (Lee and

Newby, 1983, p. 26). These revolutions heralded a radical transformation of society. Social changes began to take place by unidentifiable and anonymous forces-forces which were not akin to forces of nature. Although the early sociologists characterised the changes in different ways, they recognised that the modern world which they saw emerging in their time represented a break from the past. Gradually, a recognisable society emerged which became something distinct from the state.

Human beings are naturally communal and their interests can therefore be met mainly collectively. Despite the unequal nature of social organism, human beings are dependent on each other. Political and Social revolutions can both be beneficial and dangerous. They can give rise to a dictatorship or a totalitarian system. Liberalism, socialism and conservatism have all influenced the development of sociology. Before the rise of socialism under Karl Marx, much of the 19th century was dominated by the conservative forces promoting capitalism, inequality and social divisions but the emergence of Marxism was like a ghost streamlining the social system (Zeitlin, 1971). Liberalism, however was different which enabled sociology to function as a distinct form of enquiry – the result of which was the rise of an intellectual movement in Europe in the form of the Enlightenment. The Enlightenment has been discussed as a separate piece of work in a later chapter.

The key questions sociological theories attempt to answer are the following.

1. (a) What is the relationship of the individual with the society?
   (b) Do people shape society or does society shape people?
2. Is consensus or conflict the main characteristics of human society.

The Individual and Society

Conceptually, individualism is synonymous with free will' whereas, the social system is synonymous with determinism. When an individual has a considerable choice in selecting the requirement of life and have a large degree of control over his/her personal behaviour, affairs and actions without having to depend on the direction and guidance of society for everything including the mode of behaviour then it is called individualism. An individual or individuals are in charge of their affairs and can mould society in the way they think best. Alternatively, it would be the society which would have to guide and mould them to decide their destiny. We are not suggesting that individuals would be totally free to do anything they would like to do by their free actions away from the constrains of society, in which case it would be tantamount to an anarchy and chaos, but saying that the society should not impose unreasonable constrains and control on their freedom of choice, preference and actions.

So the question arises, what is society? Can there be a society without individuals. The answer is a categorical no. Society is not something that was imposed on us by the divine providence or that was created by a single person and followed by all but was created by people when it was felt that there was a necessity for a society with rules and regulations to conduct the members' affairs. The fact is that there was no society before individuals.

In the prehistoric period, nomads used to roam around for food and shelter; there was no society to help and protect them; fighting was a commonplace thing around in the region. British social philosopher Thomas Hobbes described life in the state of nature as 'nasty brutish and short'. They felt that life was at risk in an atmosphere of insecurity because there was no order and no body was in control but everybody was against everybody. It was felt that there should be some kind of order in the area or every body's life would remain in danger. There was concern of how to bring order in the state of unruly people where fighting could break out any time at the slightest of pretexts. Persistent efforts were made to cool down the atmosphere and eventually an agreement was reached amongst them. It was decided that every one would have to sacrifice a part of their sovereignty for the general good of all to a delegated person or persons capable of maintaining order. That they should have a leader considered to be the best, wisest and most powerful of all. This is a contract better known as the 'Leviathan' in which all the rules of behaviour and conduct were laid down. This was the only way for people to escape from the life of violence and insecurity.

This view was of course countered by John Lock, another British social scientist who argued that there was no chaotic state at all. Common sense prevailed all the time in the state of nature. For further reference see the chapter on functionalism.

The diversity between determinism and free will have developed sociological perspectives which can be categorised into the structural or social systems on the one hand and 'social action' or 'interpretive' systems on the other.

The former, in other words known as the 'social system' emphasises the way our behaviour is constrained and structured by social forces. The society is predominant over us which takes charge of building and moulding our mode of thinking and doing our activities. It decides our social values which we try to achieve and roles to play in the society. The society constructs our life and individuals are parts of it and controlled by the society. The society as a whole develops our culture, norms and our functions. In fact, the society becomes the overall guardian of all people.

Social action perspectives, also known as interpretive approaches emphasise the importance of individuals who are in the driving seat conducting their own affairs because they have the ability to exert control over their own actions. So, it is the individual who constructs the society, decide the mode of behaviour, social and individual functions. The individuals take full control and participate in shaping future of the society the way they wanted to see it. They can change the social system, rebuild it if the members want to re-structure a new system and their management. They develop meaningful debate before taking action and directing their behaviour. This is interpretive because people interpret and give meanings to their voices, actions, motives, values, behaviour and situations.

According to interpretive approaches, social roles, values and norms are changeable-they are flexible and not rigid. So the guidelines can be changed if members find them restraining their 'free-will'. Roles are in the same way subject to interpretations and negotiations. the individuals are participants in making new roles by renewing the old ones.

Broadly speaking, neither the social system nor the social action approaches are closed door systems. It is the question of emphasis. The former puts more emphasis on the structure of society and its overall power to regulate it and its members, whereas the social action approaches put more emphasis on the freedom of the individuals to take charge, guide and to renew the society and its functions according to their rational judgement and contribution made fully for the benefit of all in the society.

Is Consensus or Conflict the Main Basis of Human Society?

This is the second key question; Consensus means agreement. A society is run by agreement of people; it can not survive for long if not based on consensus; if there is disagreement about issues and decisions then the society would be left in a chaos effecting the functions of society and jeopardising the interest of all. An agreement is based on dialogue, reason, cooperation, adjustment and social unity. Value of consensus provides a harmony to run the society smoothly.

Conflict is a replacement of the social values achieved through the consensus or agreement approach.

No society is perfect; so the aim of society is to develop a trouble free society as much as possible. But when that becomes impossible, either the vested interested parties or the conservative forces are too powerful which ignore and continue to resist the grievances and complaints of people then the conflicts develop in to some ideological battle to lead to open conflict or to take direct action. Conflict sometimes is seen as the only way to resolve a crisis. Many sociologists think that conflicts are part and parcel of a society which are evolved as a result of the

Dialectical processes and thus inevitable in a class based society. Conflicts may lead to a class based war and in the words of Karl Marx it will be the Proletariat Revolution which will resolve the crisis.

According to Karl Marx, there are two stages of conflict in which to operate called thesis and anti-thesis-each opposed to the other, otherwise known as social conflict which leads to a third stage called the synthesis. Marx foresaw a socialist society to emerge out of the revolution. This revolution would bring to an end of the class rule, and the consequent exploitation of the people.

Comment

None of the system are perfect: Norms and values-the core ideology of the consensus social system are not all that easy to agree upon; they are in most cases forced upon the will of the people by the majority. Consensus becomes coercion-essential to maintain order in the system and if necessary to prevent anarchy.

On the other hand, the conflict approaches rob peoples' rights and in place of exploitation brings one party rule which can degenerate into totalitarianism. Of course, there are a number of different conflict perspectives which can offer more choices, humane and liberal agenda than Marxism which offered less choice and less freedom.

There are interaction approaches, Such as, Neo-Marxism, phenomenology, critical theories etc. which will be discussed throughout the book.

Max Weber, a prominent German sociologist is considered to be both a conflict and an action theorist which I will discuss in a separate section later in the book. The system theory, otherwise known as the consensus perspectives are discussed in the section of functionalism.

This book is an amalgam of many outstanding theories aimed at helping students at Honours and post graduate courses in sociology because, after all, Sociology is a theory based subject and getting acquainted with these important theories is a recipe for success.

References

1. Ruth Wallace-Contemporary sociological theory, pp. 5-7.
2. R.K. Merton-Social theory and social structure, 1968, p. 141.
3. Harold Garfinkel and Blumer-Contemporary sociological theory. p. 5-7.
4. Lee, D & Newby, H. – The problem of Sociology, London 1983. p. 26.

Part 2

2
Positivism – Past and Present

Introduction, Charles Montesquieu, Saint Simon, August Comte, Emile Durkheim's Positivism, Durkheim's Method, Critical Estimate of Positivism.

Introduction

The doctrine of positivism is a central part of social science and arguably stands in kinship relations with the natural science. It aims to extend science to the study of human society by using more or less the same criteria as the scientific laws and to explain the natural environment. Positivism is a concept, which has helped eradicating the sinister influence of superstition, prejudice and retrogressive effects of religious taboos prevalent in many under developed countries causing immense harm to social perception of people for centuries. The aim of positivism is to make people aware of the scientific laws which help evolving our society towards progress and modernising our culture, mode of living, education system, work culture and even ideology and thinking.

Sociology, known as the science of society is an old discipline originating as a distinct branch of science since the nineteenth century. Sociology has its own theories and methodology comparab' to any science subjects. Early sociology was under the influence of philosophy of history and the biological theory of evolution. As the natural science was flourishing during this period it made an impact on the young minds of many sociologists who looked to it as the future science to study the social phenomena. People like Comte, Spencer, Durkheim, Max Weber and others have thus developed methods which could be applied to the study social scenario.

Positivism arose as a response to the scientific revolution of the 18th century. Earlier, in the age of Enlightenment people learned the right to free thinking. Francis Bacon was the first free thinker who used scientific method to study Astronomy. Then, Sir Isaac Newton, one of the great English scientists who lived from 1642 to 1727, discovered the Law of Motion and the principle of Gravitation with which to explain the fundamental relationships in the universal properties. Whereas August Comte looked to science to study human affairs.

Charles Montesquieu (1689-1755), the French political philosopher discovered that 'scientific laws' were operating in the society like the law of nature. In his 'The Spirit of the Laws', Montesquieu wrote about how our society and its functional parts were like matters of science which could be observed as any other scientific matter and its findings quantified. Montesquieu noticed that the society moved from one stage to another by inexorable forces of new ideas which guided it to form its own laws and maintain order. These ideas led to a science of society meaning an organised and an orderly society.

Another free thinker was Saint Simon, also a French man who used the word 'positive' for the first time meaning science is useful to study the human society. He described the society as an organism. To him, the society moved from its religious environment to the positivistic stage as a final growth. According to him, positivism has been rooted in different branches of science and later spread to the socio-cultural organisms and physiology of society.

August Comte (1798-1857) was the most prominent positivist of all who took his doctrine to its scientific level to the extent never reached before. Comte made social philosophy fully scientific. He explained that our society had gone through stages of development to reach its present level known as positivism.

Comte developed the central idea of his thought named 'The law of Human progress or the law of three stages'. These stages are related to the evolution of human thinking concerning their society and how to establish a kind of society they envisaged. In the first stage, otherwise known as the 'Theological-religious' stage, the human mind was seeking the truth behind the cause and effect of the phenomena surrounding them. The natural phenomena such as wind, light, tidal waves, darkness, different sounds, storms etc. which the human beings came across everyday not knowing where they were coming from and who created them.

They took them as supernatural things created by some mysterious forces like gods or creator which were at work behind the phenomena. People could not resolve the mysteries of the earth, so they gave rise to speculations and numerous superstitious ideas and dogmas that dominated their minds believing that these superstitions were nothing but truth. Also they developed a fear complex about the natural power that they would do harm unless worshipped by the people. Also they believed these forces helped them to build a cohesive society. To please the nature, they then began to worship the supernatural forces in order to be safe and happy. Supernatural forces as said above, were often equated with the power of god and any disrespect of these forces could bring doom and destruction.

Later, in the second stage known as 'Metaphysical' stage, people's perception about life and society improved to the extent to link it to the laws of the universe. The universe around them became an object of importance as they saw its relevance to life. In this stage, people cast off their religious prejudices and took to philosophical context to explain and to interpret their social existence.

In the final stage or the 'positive' phase people gave up their vain search for 'Absolute notions', destination of the universe and causes of phenomena. Instead, they dedicated to unfolding the 'Laws of nature' and their invariable relations with people and society. Peoples' mind changed to free rational thinking using the inductive reasoning to explain social evolution and its inter-relationship with the law of nature or natural science.

This progressive development of human mind went concurrent with the development of society including social order and material conditions of human life. They looked to social development critically and scientifically using social facts as matters. The positivists used hard quantitative matters to discover causal relationship between the facts using the deductive method which led to, in the opinion of August Comte,' a positive science of society'. He believed that the society was guided by the invariable laws of nature, in other words known as the natural science. Comte ruled out 'unobservable facts' as inept tools of research, only 'observable facts' which could lead to scientific research that would discover the scientific truth. According to him, observable facts are measurable, quantifiable and their validity is reliable.

Emile Durkheim's Positivism

Durkheim belongs to the second generation of positivist school in which he excelled his predecessor August Comte in establishing sociology on a firm footing and to make it an integral part of the natural science. Durkheim said that sociology should be studied as a scientific subject as the ingredients of sociology are similar to those of science subjects. He argued that aspects of society such as, institutions, values, beliefs and other things are like 'social facts' which are numerically countable like mathematical numbers or scientific matters. He argued, 'consider social facts as things', therefore, they should be considered and treated in the same way as objects, events and processes of the natural world. They can be objectively measured, quantified and subjected to statistical analysis. Theories can be developed based on the cause and effect relationships between facts in social situations which also can be used for explaining the social functions.

It is argued that natural science do not collect 'facts' like sociological facts and have no natural feelings like sociology. But that should not preclude sociology becoming a scientific subject.

According to Durkheim, social facts form a part of our consciousness. Also social facts exist outside of us and can be objectively treated as external things. So, the fundamental laws of natural science can be applied to the study of social facts. Inductive method of generalisations can be used to find regularities in the social facts which is a scientific method similar to the method of observation and experiments used in studying the natural science. In Durkheim's terms, sociology is a 'natural science of society'.

Durkheim, while trying to establish a 'law of human behaviour' devised a technique known as 'multivariate analysis' which could help to check causal relationships between two or more variables within a particular situation. The findings can be compared with similar situations in different societies at different times. If the findings correlate positively with other findings then we have a 'Law of human behaviour'.

Comte and Durkheim believed that real laws of human behaviour could be discovered. Durkheim also believed that the law of human behaviour operated in the case of 'suicide' was the hall mark of his scientific discovery. He tried to prove that the rate of suicide increased at the time of economic 'boom and slump', because these conditions caused uncertainties in the economy which made people suffer stress in vulnerable position more than usual; hence the rise in suicide rate.

Moral facts: They became one of Durkheim's contentious issues conflicting with social science. Durkheim explained that apparently, they looked like human issues with emotional feelings, but discerned that they equated with any other facts or data in social and material world. They are no different, in his words, they can be observed, described and developed in to laws. They can be turned into 'indirect indices' and legally codified to make them usable for positive sciences.

Durkheim wrote in his 'Division of Labour' 1893, the moral issues concerning the labour relations which have been charted for legal purposes. The laws have been developed to apply to the moral issues positively. As indicated above, Durkheim discovered his scientific theory through the study of the 'suicide case'. The investigation was published in 1897 in his book, 'A Study in Sociology' which generally accepted as a piece of scientific methodology. He argued that suicide was not caused by pathological factor but by social factor; it is socially constructed. There may be individual cases where psychology could be responsible for suicide but Durkheim was dealing with the vast number of suicide cases, in which individual case or cases were not concerned. Always, there are exceptions to rules. According to him, suicides are social facts, they are real living and active forces of society.

Durkheim's Method

Durkheim examined official statistics from a number of European countries where he found the suicide rates were fairly constant for a number of years. The second thing he noticed was the presence of significant difference in suicide rates between religious groups with in the same society. The correlations were conclusive. Besides religion, other factors were age, family condition and location.

One of the causal relations was the variation in the level of 'social integration'. For example, in the case of older adults, they were less socially integrated than the younger adults. Earlier, in their adult life when they had families on their own and jobs to go to and social engagements they were fully integrated. They had a thriving family life. But later, every thing was gone even the grown up children were setting up own families else where leaving behind parents lonely. Things got worse when many were befriended and relatives have died as well. Also as retired persons they have lost touch with their colleagues; life for them became meaningless, shattered and disintegrated.

Furthermore, he found that suicides rates were higher with people like protestants, city dwellers, older adults, unmarried people and even people without children in married life. Whereas their opposite numbers like Catholics, rural dwellers, young adults, married people, and families with children had much lower rates. The main reason, according to Durkheim, was that the latter group or groups had more social integration than the former groups. Based on this statistical co-relationship Durkheim justified his suicide theory that it varied inversely with the level of integration of the social groups of which the individual formed a part.

Critical theory of the Frankfurt school attacked the scientific status of positivism as a part of social theory. Peter Half Penny argued that Marx's Dialectical materialism was the only credible attempt ever made to create a scientific sociology. The Critical theorists consider positivism as a form of 'instrumental rationality' which could be technically oppressive.

Karl Popper defended positivism as a science of society which he tried to prove using his elaborately drawn twenty seven theses. Popper emphasised that testing of hypothesises would be required before a theory is confirmed as a scientific law. Nevertheless, he implied that no scientific theory could be absolutely scientific without having the possibility of its being falsified by a new theory or evidence.

He changed the logical methodology of enquiry from inductive to deductive. The inductive method starts by collecting data or facts which are analysed and then the results are developed into testable statements. These are necessary procedures for developing a theory. This is a positive method regarded as scientific by most sociologists including Durkheim and August Comte. Theories arrived at by the inductive methodology are also tested against other sets of data to verify their accuracy. When confirmed they could be assumed as discovered law of human behaviour.

In the early 20th century, inductive methodology was criticised by some scientists as not valid reasoning for scientific procedure. They were more satisfied with the 'deductive' methodology than the Inductive methodology. Deductive approach starts with a theory which is thus tested against the evidence provided. Karl Popper in his book 'This Logic of Scientific Discovery' discussed the 'Deductive reasoning' which is the reverse of the inductive method. Popper's main argument was that whatever method or methods are used they should be able to stand the tests of positive nature of science in the future. The Positivists have been using the 'Inductive methodology to establish sociology as a natural science.

According to Karl popper, prediction about the future can be deduced like the 'Law of Gravity' which was deduced by Sir Isaac Newton. With this theory, the movement of bodies of a given mass and their predictions can be tested against future events.

According to the positivists, scientific theories once established can not be disputed or challenged or proved wrong which Karl Popper was unwilling to accept. According to him, theories can be challenged by a scientist if he had found new evidence to disprove it. This is Karl Popper's 'falsification theory'. So whether natural or sociological, laws do not have to be permanent in nature all the time. Despite this, Karl Popper had insisted that scientists should have to be very objective, meticulous and rigorous in their methodical process all the time in order to get the best result.

A new scientific technique was devised by Karl Popper known as the 'testability' with which facts and theories can be tested before they are established. Popper was a member of the Vienna circle which developed Logical positivism as a scientific doctrine. Logical positivism differed from Comtian in which the former severed close links with sociology and also abandoned metaphysical notions of the latter. Logical positivists took to concrete objective view of facts and meaningful statements only. Positivism went further change when theoretician Hempel tried to unify Logical Positivism with Empirical Method. This gave a unity of methods between social and natural sciences.

Prompted by the alarm of over anti-positivist stance inaugurated by the Interpretive Sociologists in the 1960s, a fresh argument for a 'science of society' was started by the eminent sociologist Bhaskar Roy (1975). Bhaskar is a realist critique of positivism. Realists like him applaud positivist's naturalism but rejected its dependence on empiricism especially the deductive monological model of explanation. (2) Hand book of Social theory, p. 379.

Bhaskar recognises that there are differences between social and natural worlds. Nevertheless, he believes that a science of society is possible. Co-relations between the structures and mechanisms which exist and differentiate between the social and natural worlds can be discerned and solutions found to minimise their differences, because the principles that guide the social and natural sciences are not different but the same.

Sociology as a positive science has come of age and is now well recognised as a branch of science. There are a few reasons why this has happened. Fundamentally, methodology of sociological study has been thoroughly overhauled. Sociology uses scientific methods used by natural and general sciences. It painstakingly strives to become more objective than it was before. Sociology is a value free discipline where personal feeling, attachment or bias have no place. A sociologist has to be detached from the facts, events, records etc. in order to get rationally evaluated in depth and meaningful truth about them which have to be logically tested to be true. Findings in sociology are always open to inspection, testing and evaluation. Sociological imagination is unique by nature, its thinking is its main tool and its perception always opens up new perspectives. Its procedure involves systematic methods of investigation, scrupulously selective on gathering facts, evidence and materials which are to be logically assessed. Sociology also formulates hypothesises and co relates them with the existing theories, research results and checks their validity. So it can be safely said that sociology is a positive science of society.

Further Reading

August Comte – The Positive Philosophy, Bell and Sons, London, 1986.
Charles Montesquieu – The Spirit of the Laws.

Emile Durkheim – The Rules of Sociological Method, London, 1982.
Karl Popper – The Logic of Scientific Discovery, London, 1982.
Bhaskar Ray – A Realist Theory of Science Hassocks, 1978.
Bhaskar Ray – The Possibility of Naturalism 1979.
Jurgen Havermas – Communication and the evolution of society, London, Polity press, 1979.
Abrms Philip – Historical Sociology. Cornell University Press, 1982.

3
Structural Theories of Society

Introduction, Functionalism and Social Structure, Durkheim's Concept of Social Structure, Radcliffe Brown's Concept of Social Structure, Talcot Persons' Structural Functional Theory vs Social Action Perspective, Anthony Giddens' Structuration Theory, Criticism of Giddens' Structuration Theory.

Introduction

When a society is constructed it is aimed to play its part in rendering services to its members which it can do with help of structures. The structure is a framework of functional institutions meant to serve the society with all its paraphernalia. Theories of structures are concerned with how societies are organised, developed and used and what methods and strategies are adopted to respond to the vagaries of life that also include deviance and unsocial elements. What are the aims, purposes and commitments of the social structures to their members and how do they function. Theories also scrutinise individual roles and their relationships with the society in general and their obligation, duties, conforming rules, norms and values etc. in particular. Structural theories are also concerned with educational institutions and their systems, so also the legal system, the human rights programmes and so on. Structural system is more concerned with the Macro society than with the micro society.

Functionalism and Social Structure

A typical example of a structural system is 'functionalism' which serves the interests of the multifarious forces such as races and communities. It believes in the unity of society and so organised structurally to maximise social equilibrium and harmony. The structural pattern involves individuals to commit to its purposes and to become important parts of the organic whole. The structural system once formed is not easily changeable unless social forces both internal and external make do it. Marxism as a macro type which falls in to the structural pattern even though some fundamental differences are traceable between the structures of functionalism and Marxism. Marxism is a unitary pattern in which all institutions congregate to the whole. Functionalism too, theoretically, endeavours hard to reach the holistic stage.

Marxism does not believe in a society which can be trouble free with out radical changes of the economic and the class systems because they are riddled with inequalities and conflicts of vested interests. These are differing statuses, privileges, level of earnings and opportunities. The society is bound to suffer as a result from oppression, exploitation and profiteering which are at the root of social disorder. These conflicts can not be uprooted unless fundamental changes have been forged in to effect its restructure. Marxism provides an ideology that can set up a new form of government and a society better known as socialist form. Marx believed that revolution of the workers could transfer the means of production from the control of the ruling class to the proletariat. This would herald a new ownership of the people who would setup a classless and stateless society.

Durkheim's Concept of Social Structure

Durkheim's concept of social structure is well thought out and firm compared to others. His concept of structure constrains individual actions. He says that social structure 'constrains our activities in a parallel way-setting limits to what one can do as individuals; also it is external to us'. According to him our social structure has been created long before our generation; we are born into it, so also the cultures, rules, regulations, ethics, code of behaviour, education and economic system as they exist have been here before us. Durkheim asked how can we deny them when they were here, but we were not.

Durkheim's structure is a holistic type in which all aspects of social life congregate to the whole. Social structure becomes coercive only when the individuals are to be told or reminded of their commitment to the society. Durkheim's idea is that society moulds and penetrates in to the individual in order to make them effective members of society. So according to Durkheim a solid and a unified society is the objective of the structural society. In Durkheim's view the term, 'Structural form' is to refer to the observable structural continuity (Patrick Bayert, 1998, p. 46).

Radcliffe Brown's Concept of Structure

A prominent British anthropologist, Radcliff Brown argues that the "ultimate components of social structure are human beings. The relations between the individuals and the social structure involve well defined rights and duties for the individuals." (Radcliffe Brown, 1958 p. 16ff). Brown compares the social structure with the human body and says, "Like the structure of the human body, social structure is in constant flux" (Radcliffe Brown, 1952, p. 3-4, 191ff, reprinted in 1971). Brown further explains that like the molecules of the human body which constantly change, society also changes, such as people come and go, or take up different positions and roles in the social structure. There is a continuity of the structure despite changes. Like the human organism which retains its form in spite of changing molecules, the social structure as well exhibits an observable 'structural form' despite changes.

Radcliff Brown insists that his notion of structure is an observable reality. According to him, the general concept of a structure refers to an arrangement of interrelated parts, such as the structure of a piece of music which is an arrangement of sounds, as the structure of a molecule arranged to atoms.

[Radcliff Brown {1958, p. 16ff)]. He denines social structure as the complex network of actually existing social relations.

Talcot Parsons' Structural Function Theory

Talcot Parsons, the American sociologist, differed with Brown about his theory of structure because in Parson's mind, Brown was depicting a positivist stance and reproducing a scientific view of society. To Parsons, Brown's view opposes 'the essential purposes of human action' (P. Baert 1998, p. 48). According to Parsons human action is needed for a functional society. He argued that peoples' actions are goal oriented and constrained.

People's actions are modified in order to make them acceptable to the society. Therefore, there has to be an external code of practice and guidelines to human actions. Parsons drew ideas from Emile Durkheim and Max Weber's concepts of collective conscience and action perspective. Collective conscience is the shared central values and norms of society. Parsons reformulated the 'Action theory' in order to generate and strengthen his 'social system' which becomes a structure of society.' This reformulated 'action theory' of Parsons proposes to sustain law and order, improve economic condition and standard of living, remove poverty and defend integrity of the nation and so on. Parsons' social system came to be known as the 'structural functional system' which provides all the requisite functions of society with in the structural framework. (Talcot Parsons, 1952, The social-system.)

Talcot parsons has described four principal types of social structures based on social values such as universalistic, particularistic, achieved and ascribed values. Universalistic social values are common to every society such as expert craftsmanship which is essential to livelihood. The particularistic social values are those selected from racial, ethnic, religious, caste and class backgrounds. Achieved social values are those accorded to achievement by endeavour and effort. Lastly, ascribed social values are inherited or hereditary such as titles and wealth etc.

Parsons views society as a system which is 'structural functional'. This has four basic functional perquisites. They are adaptation, goal attainment, integration and pattern maintenance. In parsons' view, these essential requirements are to be achieved by a society in order to survive and to progress. These functions are with in the framework of the social structure. Adaptation is a relationship between the social system and its environment such as food and shelter, control of the environment must be maintained. Second, goals of society must be set out and institutionalised into the political system. Goals to be achieved must be adequately resourced. Therefore, regulations must be made in order to achieve the targets. Third, integration is the system of minimising discord, discordant attitudes and managing coordination and adjustment. The differences between individuals and institutions must be reduced by the legal norms and standards. Last, pattern maintenance relates to the social values to be accrued from religion, cultures, traditions, education, languages, normative behaviour, order, stability, social equilibrium etc.

The structural system gets changed when the society changes and sometimes these are legislated for compliance by the public. In structural functionalism, societal norms, values of interaction and relationships including roles, duties and functions of each person is well constructed and designed in order to avoid chaos and confusion about what to do. According to the structural functional strategies social programmes have to be followed by all members with out exception in order to achieve maximum social solidarity and stability. In this system, every individual including all members of the family are considered very important organs of society. Patterns of behaviour, norms and values are all regulated and accepted by the vast majority as standard compliance and inclusive.

Sayer defines structures as "sets of internally related objects or practices." He uses the example of land lord and tenant relationship where the tenant pays rent and follows the rules of tenancy.

Functionalists believe that for any social system to survive a number of functions or needs must be fulfilled; for example, a minimum level of solidarity is needed in the system. Various social practices fulfil some central needs of society. For example, the education of children is crucial to their growth as useful people of society; so also the economic system and the social system which are fundamental to the needs of society. Behaviour of people is structured too. In functionalism, social relationships are organised in to structures which become normative aspects of life. They are value-oriented too. These values contribute to the construction of individual roles. Various institutions are developed to play their roles in the structural system. Values in society, according to Talcot Parsons are to be institutionalised in to the social system. Values such as raising the standard of living, national output, improving social behaviour, eradicating illiteracy and poverty from the society; in Parsons' words people must be value conscious, Social order, for example leads to social stability and common values lead to common goals.

Structural Versus Social Action Perspectives

Sociological theories are broadly divided into two schools as mentioned above. Structural pattern is also known as macro perspectives which constitute functionalism, Marxism and their offshoots such as neo functionalism and neo Marxism. Despite their differences, functionalism and Marxism work with in the structural system believing that the society works as a whole for the best interests of the most. Their offshoot versions almost take similar standpoint but retain their individual differences in strategies.

The social action perspectives on the other hand, are non-structural theories; they prioritise individual role over the structure. The engage themselves in interactions in the process of shaping the activities of the society. They follow some of Weber's ideas of individual action and motives, symbolic interaction's ideas of self concepts and finding new meanings of society, Phenomenological ideas of understanding the world more closely and ethno methodological ideas of categorising the world in order to discover a sense in social life. They all go through the interactive ways to discover the truths about how to shape up a better society worth living exercising individual action and freedom.

Gidden's Structuration Theory (Structure and Action)

Both schools of structural perspectives have strengths and weaknesses in their explanations. So new method should be tried to remove these weaknesses and increase strength. Earlier, attempts have been made by Max Weber to reduce the differences between the two schools amalgamating them under a broad sociological church, say to develop a general sociological theory. This should have also included those remaining out side the broad division. But his attempt failed. Also sociologists like Paul willis, W. Wright, and Anthony Giddens have tried. I will discuss specially professor Giddens' contribution to this process. One distinct aspect of Giddens' social structure is the physical dimension of human action by which he meant the biological frame of the human being and its capabilities to deliver the objectives. According to him, all our social interactions are expressed through the contextual of bodily presence. Giddens argues that human actions produce and reproduce social practices, form and reform them; they are transformational. Further, Giddens conceived of social structures described in his own words, "structures consist of the rules and resources recursively implicated in the reproduction of social systems". (A. Giddens, Central problems in social theory, p. 64]. Rules, according to him are a wide range of regulatory practices which influence action. They could also mean unwritten rules or practices, such as marriages which can take place in many ways. The second element of structure in Giddens' view is resources which can be both allocative and authoritative resources. Allocative resources are the resources of the capitalists or the 'forces of production' and the authoritative resources indicate the distribution of power.

In the primordial society, according to him, social structures were simplistic, their communications were face to face and their bond of kinship was strong. In developed societies, structures are more elaborate, diverse and sophisticated. To day, the electronic system communicate so fast; market forces, currency system, formal property rights etc. lead to social life diverse and disengaged. Class divided societies specially in the cities create and recreate structures through different institutions which generate enormous power and 'authoritative resources'.

Giddens visualised that to be effective, a social structure must combine with agency or action, together they will make the concept of structuralism, by which he meant that neither structure nor action can fulfil their purpose on their own without the help of the other. According to him, action also produces social structures as structures produces social actions. So they are inter-related. In Giddens' view, you and I also help to create structures in different ways. In a society people contribute to make rules and laws which facilitate structural development and they are reproducible too. Interaction processes for example, contribute quite a lot to improving the structural system. Structures once developed can survive for generations but they go changed if other factors such as science, economic development, political system force them to change. According to Bernstein, "the very heart of the theory of structulation is intended to illuminate the duality and dialectical interplay of agency and structure" (Bernstein, 1989, p. 23). Giddens confirms that his analytical starting point is human practices but they are used as recursive. Focussing on the recursive character of structure David Held and Thomson argue that structure is reproduced in through the succession of situated practices. Bernstein continues the argument saying, "agency itself is reflexively and recursively implicated in social structure" (1989: 23). George Rizer explains that Giddens uses his 'agency structure' issue in a 'historical, processual and dynamic way' (George Ritzer 2004:380).

So after an analysis we find the following features of Gidden's structuration theory:

His theory is built on the concept of 'duality of structure' which postulates a relationship between social structure and human agency or human action. In simple terms, agency and structure are just two ways of looking at the same thing. According to Giddens structures are produced by the social action and maintained by it over a long time. Again, without structures social action can not be operative. They are like two sides of the same coin.

The third feature of Gidden's structuralism is the language which as a medium of expression conveys the meanings of concepts, theories, ideologies and so on. Language to be fully accurate and meaningful should be properly constructed using correct grammatical rules like syntax etc.

The fourth feature is his concept of consciousness. Giddens makes a distinction between discursive consciousness and practical consciousness. In the first, he argues that our actions are expressed in words i.e. speech whereas in the second consciousness actions are taken for granted without explaining what they are for. Giddens confirms that the second category only is primarily essential for the structural theory. In other words, 'what is done is more important than what is said'.

Criticisms of Giddens' Structuration Theory

Giddens' theory does not follow Durkheimian pattern which views the structure as external to and coercive of actors. Giddens does not flatly deny Durkheimian perception of structure but argues that 'structure is both constraining and enobling' (Giddens: 25, 163).

Ian Craib has criticised Giddens saying his work "lacks ontological depth". That he fails to get at the "social structures that unlie the social world" (George Ritzer etal 2004:388).

Another criticism of Giddens' structuration theory, according to George Ritzer is that 'it does not have an end result and a direction' (2004:385).

Michael Foucault also has criticised Giddens' 'structure' in terms of 'rules and resources' as not accurately defined. (1977B, p. 170-94). Secondly, he is criticised for failing to interpret Marxism correctly. His account of Marx's 'historical materialism' is interpreted as a kind of evolutionism and functionalism which is according to Foucault a misreading of Marx. (1977b, pp. 177-84).

According to Karl Popper in terms of critical dimension, Giddens' theory of structuralism is unsatisfactory, specially compared with Frankfurt school. (Logic of scientific Discovery, cpt 8).

Margaret Archer criticises Giddens for sticking structure and agency too tightly together. As they are two separate issues quite opposite to each other; the best way to get the best out of them is to maintain a flexible union in which each has a room for manoeuvre. According to her view, Giddenis was trying to show that agency would try to transform the structure to behave like the agency. That could not happen so easily. In her view, structural restraint and agency freedom could not deliver much, because the experiment was still going on; it was not complete. Society would not change at will, at least not on a time scale 'the actors involved might wish'. (haralambos-1995, p. 907). So in her view the theory of structuration has a long way to go to claim a complete success.

There are other critical social scientists who see societies if organised according to the structural system can be damaging to progress because it constrains or limits people's autonomy and their effort to do what they can. Societies are not static, they are rather dynamic and changeable. Structural system can be a problem to change. Many societies have changed caused by the effects of modernity and scientific and technological inventions which cater for a flexible and less structural society in which changes can take place and individuals can manoeuvre but for rigid form of society it would not be possible.

References

Patrick Bayert, 1998.
Radcliffe Brown, 1958.
Talcott Parsons. The social system, 1952.
Anthony Giddens, Central problems in social theory, 1979.
Bernstein, 1989.
George Ritzer, 2004.
Michael Foucault, 1977b.
Karl Popper, The logic of scientific discovery, 1959.

4
Sociology and Natural Science

Introduction, What is Natural Science? August Comte, Science of Society, Emile Durkheim, Suicide Case, Karl Popper and the Reconstructed Logic, Thomas Kuhn's Scientific Revolution, Roy Bhaskar and the Realist View of Science, Is Sociology a Value Free Subject?, Is Sociology Science?

Introduction

The controversy surrounding the question of sociology being a science subject similar to other sciences like the natural science has become a major debatable issue since August Comte had launched his scientific theory of Positivism. His aim has been to establish sociology as a part of natural science. But the controversy had never gone away even though Comte, the French sociologist and also the founding father of sociology, had established the fact that sociology had a similar scientific background as any other science subjects like physics, chemistry, biology and so sociology is a good science as well. The most ambitious attempt to apply natural science methodology to the study of sociology is known as positivism which I have discussed in the previous chapter. According to Comte, if our society is studied scientifically using methods and assumptions of the natural sciences then we would be able to establish a real science of society.

What is Natural Science?

Natural science is concerned with explaining the 'world of nature' or the natural world. As said above, natural science constitutes fundamentally physics, chemistry and biology and any other sciences which research on nature. The purpose of science is to collect information about natural objects and to develop knowledge of science which has to go through experiment and testing for finding the scientific truth. Before all these, an observation of the phenomena is essential to find facts. Then, there has to be a hypothesis relating to the object under research which has to establish first whether the hypothesis is true or false.

The natural science is believed to be based on matter which has certain measurable and quantifiable properties which if put under certain conditions such as heat, would behave in a way as to indicate its properties including the cause and effect. An exact amount of temperature has to be applied to a particular chemical in order to get the correct result. Data can be sorted out and used for further researches. In this way, human behaviour in a social set up can also be observed and objectively measured to know the cause and effect of the behaviour.

August Comte

A theory in natural science is established when under similar conditions specific factors or elements will interact in the same way repeatedly paving the way for a prediction. The natural science uses laboratory controlled experiment to test the hypothesis. A reliable and valid experiment is repeatable and the findings are open to further verification. If all the verifications produce the same result then this becomes a law of science.

Whether the natural science methodology can be applied to the study of social science has become an issue when August Comte undertook it to resolve. Initially, he called sociology a 'Social Physics'. He advocated the methodology of systematic observation and experiment used to find the truth in natural science, to apply to the study of society, which he believed would deliver the 'laws of society' similar to the 'laws of physics or chemistry'. He also said that sociology is a positive science, meaning there are 'social facts' which coincide with other social facts in similar circumstances and interact in ways which can be observed and measured to find predictable results. These results will produce similar identities. If the results are same then you have established a prediction to recur in future. In the positivist structure only 'external social facts' are taken in to account to cause human responses.

According to August Comte, our society has been evolved by the inexorable law of nature which are similar to the laws of natural science. Natural laws are scientific laws acted by logic which can also explain the functioning of society including its evolutionary process. Their conviction rested on the fact that by applying the rules of Logic and using all other essential scientific methods, Sociology can discover the inherent nature, instincts and the peculiarities of human behaviour which are at the root of social science because only the human beings can form a society worth living and only they can formulate the rules and regulations for its maintenance and progress. This is similar to knowing the science subjects which unravel the laws that guide the behaviour of matter. There is no significant difference between the two subjects.

August Comte, is the forerunner in asserting the principle of methods and procedures for scientists to use in their enquiry about aspects of physical sciences. These are essentially the physical matters and their behaviour. The same methodology can be applied to the study and to investigate social science matters. Comte was convinced that only the observable 'facts' could be presented as reliable evidence in the science of society. Unobservable and subjective facts could not be measured and quantified and therefore are to be discarded. Cause and effect relationships between facts must be established so as to discover the underlying laws of social evolution.

Emile Durkheim, a French sociologist also argued that social facts can be treated as good as scientific data. They can be objectively observed, measured and quantified: such as statistical analysis can find out correlations, the cause and effect of human behaviour and their inter-relationships; so Sociological matters following scientific methods and rules can produce similar results if correctly followed, same as produced by scientific subjects. Like Comte, he believed that a positive science of society is possible if correct scientific procedures are followed.

Emile Durkneim

Emile Durkheim has established that, 'consider social facts as things'. Social facts for example, can be like acts, bodies, institutions, beliefs, values, norms of society which can be treated as objects, events, cases, matters etc and can be subjected to statistical analysis. There have been numerous questions about using a human society with its inanimate objects as matters which have no consciousness. Societies are formed, reformed, changed and even removed from earth but natural sciences and their fundamental laws exist there eternally. Of course, there are scientific laws which have been disproved and replaced by new laws, for example, the planet earth like other planets moves round the sun; but it was quite the opposite view in the late middle ages. There are other scientific theories which have been replaced by new theories. According to Durkheim, social facts 'have a reality out side the individuals' and these can be studied objectively as external things. So there is no harm using the natural science methodology to the study social facts.

Durkheim's 'Suicide' case published in 1897 increased society's scientific status. He used positive science methodology to the study his Suicide case. Durkheim published his 'The rules of Sociological Method' in 1938 (The Free Press, New York) in which he developed his methodology to study social science cases. The document discusses 'suicide' in detail. He termed suicide 'as the product of social forces' external to the individual. According to him, suicides are not caused by individuals' psychological problems which may be primary causes but the social factors which prolong to cause the suicide in which the individuals are ultimately driven to.

So, suicides are the social facts and they are the products of 'real, living, active forces which affect the individuals without having any power to cancel. Durkheim found that suicide rates varied according to the peoples' religious denominations, location, age and family conditions etc. Also were found noticeable changes between social groups and societies with in the same country. Difference varied between married and unmarried people, city dwellers and rural dwellers, older adults and younger adults, Protestants and Catholics and lastly childless married couple and married couple with children. Finally, the effects of the climate and seasons also have great influence on the suicide rates.

The causal relations of these factors centred round variations in the levels of social integration. Those groups with lower level of social integration, for example, people being unmarried, lonely people living in the city, old people living on their own, people being Protestants etc. became more prone to suicide than those living as integrated members in the society. Durkheim explained that people who are integrated into society are able to play a greater social role than those without-a social being has a more satisfying social life in which to play the part and to develop interest in work and involve in activities essential for living in a society. But those who did not have a social life, suffered from alienation and rejection to the level of desperation which caused their suicides. For further information, (please read the chapter on Emile Durkheim).

Karl Popper and the Reconstructed Logic

Karl popper has agreed to the positivists to the limit that it is possible for both social science and sociology to becoming scientific if methodological procedures are meticulously followed. And these methodological procedures are known as 'Reconstructed Logic' generally used by the scientists in their empirical researches. The scientists some times go beyond their 'RL' and use other practical methods in order to achieve their cherished goal. Popper, however disagreed that all sociological theories could be considered for 'RL' because some of them do not have sufficient logicality to generate credible hypothesis necessary for falsification.

In his book 'The logic of Scientific Discovery' Karl Popper has advocated the use of 'Deductive' method instead of the 'Inductive' method, even though, many scientists use the latter. In Deductive methodology, a hypothesis or a theory starts with a general view of the premise and then proceeds to testify that view by collecting evidence or data necessary to prove that view. The opposite would be the Inductive method. But in both cases, an element of falsification or nullification of the theory should be agreed to. No scientific theory is scientific without a falsification prospect being a part of it and, in his opinion, this is crucially important.

Emile Durkheim, an eminent French sociologist, in his well read document, 'The Rules of sociological method' has stated that laws and structures of society can be explained by the laws of science. Because, according to him, social matters can be quantified and logically proved. A subject should have a theory, formed from social facts and evidence which after research produce credible and meaningful data free from contradictions and suitable for scientific enquiry. Durkheim argued that a scientific theory is not scientific until it goes through a whole process of collecting data, describing, classifying and analysing them using scientific criteria in order to develop a theory and the whole process is known as 'Inductive'. An inductive method, thus starts with individual data. Then, evidence have to be gathered from different sources relevant to the purpose and have them tested in order to get a scientific result. Whereas, the 'Deductive' method is the opposite of the former, and it proceeds with the general and goes down testing individual cases till a conclusion is reached. Either way, the theory has to prove right logically to acquire a scientific status.

Karl Popper also as indicated above, has argued that a theory to be truly scientific must be capable of falsification, but that can be disproved when a different kind of evidence was found against it. Popper's 'falsification theory' is based on the assumption that a theory can be scientific and able to produce results accurately every time when it is tested but it can be disproved when new evidence is found to falsify it. To him, this is a distinguishing characteristic of science. Any scientific theory incapable of falsification should be treated as unscientific. On that ground, he could not accept Karl Marx's 'Theory of History' as scientific because it could not be falsified.

Thomas Kuhn

The Structure of Scientific Revolution

Popper has accepted that theories of human behaviour can be constructed scientifically because they are capable of falsification. Popper, however has rejected laws governing the evolution of human society; to him, this is 'a unique historical process' (1961, p. 108).

What is Science, is viewed differently by Thomas Kuhn who has argued in his, 'The structure of Scientific Revolutions' (1962), that for 'normal science' to operate, there should be a paradigm which is a framework of concepts and theories different from conventional scientific methodology. Kuhn rejects the conventional views because they are entirely based on the testing trying to prove or disprove hypotheses. To him, change in science does occur but only when a new paradigm is able to replace the existing one. Kuhn calls this a 'Scientific Revolution'. This happens suddenly. A classic example is when the Newton's paradigm in physics has been replaced by the Albert Einstein's paradigm. This is sudden and revolutionary as people's thinking about the world was almost changed overnight. This is the way according to Thomas Kuhn, the scientific revolution takes place allowing 'normal science' to function.

Scientific revolutions are caused by the effects of accumulated evidence which can not be explained by the existing paradigm. Another example of a scientific revolution occurred in the 16th century when the scientist Copernicus declared that it was the sun not the earth that was at the centre of the universe and that all the planets were orbiting the sun. This scientific truth could not be explained by the previous paradigm established by Ptolemy.

Kuhn's view of Scientific paradigms and Revolutions have been disputed by some critics. According to Lakatos (1970), science is not dominated by a single paradigm rather by many. There are paradigms competing all the time and science is the product of all paradigms operating within their historical processes.

Roy Bhaskar – The Realist View

Another view of science is projected by Roy Bhaskar representing the Realist approach to science who has found that differences exist between the social and the natural worlds. Nevertheless, he believes that a science of society is possible. According to the realist view, the structures and mechanisms which exist and differentiate between the social and natural worlds can be discerned and solutions found to co-relate the two. In fact, the principles that guide the social science and the natural science are not different but the same.

Scientific studies take place in two ways. One takes place in the Lab, whereas other studies take place outside the lab. The first one takes place in strictly confined environment like the laboratory conditions whereas other scientific researches take place in the open conditions like the natural surroundings or field studies. That is why, physics, chemistry and also part of psychological studies can be carried out in the closed system where variables can be controlled and results made accurate. Science of Society is studied mainly in the open and results are verified there.

With in the open conditions, variables can not be easily controlled, yet a vast amount of scientific studies take place in the open and their results deliver a lot of important forecasts, clues and predictions. Meteorology is a natural science conducted under open system even though, part of its researches can be done under strict experimental conditions; in the same way the geological studies can predict oil deposits in certain locations using certain mechanisms. Astrology and Astronomy also are important scientific fields in which some predictions can be accurately made if physical and mathematical scientific theories are strictly followed.

According to the Realist view, there can be a social science if human behaviour is studied following the structural and mechanical principles just as the meteorologist, geologist and evolutionary biologists study and explain behaviour of matter and species in the natural world. Mechanisms operate within structures. The scientists would be able to identify these mechanisms and explain how they worked. The social and the natural scientists would be doing the same job but in their own sphere of knowledge; that will be the main difference.

Can Sociology be a 'Value Free' Science of Society?

One key question needs discussion. Can sociology be a 'value free' science of society? This issue is constantly argued about in the sociological circle.

The scientists are more concerned with establishing the scientific status of the subject through their enquiry rather than being concerned with establishing the value system of society. There are institutions legitimately responsible for maintaining the social values acquired through centuries of hard work as well as those new ones for the benefit of society. These are engrossed in ideological and religious matters unconnected with sociological science. Sociology as a categorical positive and normative science should be engaged in purifying its scientific image of society than be entangled in the value building processes. The purpose of sociology is to make an empirical analysis of social institutions and their products-to see their relevance to the purposes of society rather than analysing the values of society.

Different societies have different sets of values, the job of sociology is to test the empirical aspect of social behaviour-how people behave under different stimuli but not to make judgement on their goodness or badness which is a job of the moralists.

Finding empirical value of a social issue is different from identifying its moral and ethical values. While social facts can be subjected to empirical tests, social values can not be likewise subjected to rigorous empirical tests. It is strongly argued that a science of society can be made possible if it is done through objective observation and analysis of social life but which are to be made free from social values, moral judgement and ideology of the observer.

What are those values which sociologists are most concerned about?. Values are beliefs that are good for and desirable for society. Some sociologists argue that moral, ethical and ideological values should be the concerns of sociologists too. In the Western society, safety and security of life is considered important. Hygiene at home and public places is linked to the quality of life; good manners and reason used to settle disputes are values given importance to. Many sociologists think that sociology should be concerned with those values.

The German sociologist, Max Weber (1864-1920), has argued in favour of sociology becoming value-free. In his words, only a 'value free' approach could facilitate scientific development. In his view, a social scientist as an objective investigator must remain neutral about value systems. This view of Max Weber has been further developed by contemporary positivists who believe that sociology should be value-free which should exclude political effects, moral problems and philosophical influences from their work. These affects could jeopardise scientific values and empirical judgements-essential parts of scientific socialism. The scientific methods of natural sciences if transferred to the study of sociology to enhance its scientific status then sociology could not be a value laden subject because it will cloud its work and assessment processes.

There are many tempting issues in society which can attract attention of people like politicians, social workers, religious groups, sociologists etc. These can be effects of arranged marriagtes, adultery, permissive society, caste system, abuse of children, repression of women at home and society. Sociologists use statistics concerning these social issues for research and experiment but not for their value judgement. Sociology is concerned with the empirical aspect of social behaviour, not attempting to say what are the values of good and bad behaviour. Social facts can be empirically tested but values can not be tested. Herbert Spencer viewed society from the organic point of view; he was not concerned with the valuation of society. According to Weber, a biased sociologist would not be able to make a valid judgement. A social scientist has to be essentially neutral, he or she is not allowed to provide recipes for practice.

Is Sociology Science?

Some critics argue that Max Weber would not like being seen as wholly against sociology as a value-free discipline. Arnold Brecht writes "Max Weber never ceased personally to believe in ultimate values, nor did he ever under-rate the importance of such belief for human personality and human dignity". Alvin Gouldner wrote an article called "anti Minotaur" meaning that a sociologist should have some values or else would turn in to a sort of Minotaur-a creature with a human body and head of a bull.

So it comes round to the issue that study of values can not be totally dissociated from the scope of sociology except for some specific matters. Some would say it is an integral part of sociology but others would say it is not; it depends on what kind of sociology you are talking about.

Durkheim, Marx and Weber have worked on tirelessly enhancing sociology's scientific status through their rich theoretical and methodological researches. Some professional sociologists like John Goldthorpe and A.H. Halsey have carried out complex and rigorous empirical researches on sociological issues which go above the commonplace understanding of people; but for knowledgeable people the image of sociology is being increasingly enhanced through efforts of dedicated sociologists.

Sociology do not have to produce results like physics and chemistry to be called science. There are other science subjects like Astronomy, Physiology, Meteorology and some other physical sciences as well which do not produce accurate results as such each and every time and are not required to use laboratory experimentation. Such as, Astronomy which studies and observes the movement of the stars in the galaxy and its physical environment do not require a test to confirm its findings in the laboratory conditions; rather use mathematical and physical and physical calculations to produce scientific truth. Their discoveries have tremendously increased the boundary of scientific knowledge. What determines the scientific character of a discipline is its methodology. Sociology does make good use of scientific methods in the study of its materials which is refined in the process to deliver accurate results; so from most counts sociology deserves to be called a science.

Further Reading

D. Potter et a, eds Society and the Social Sciences (open University Press, 1981).

K Popper The Logic of Scientific Discovery, London, Hutchinson, 1959.

A. Sayer A method in Social Science, Routledge, London, 1992.

R. Bhaskar A Realist Theory of Science, Harvester, Hassocks, 1978.

T.S. Kuhn The Structure of Scientific Revolutions, Chicago University Press, 1962.

E. Durkheim. The Rules of Sociological Method, Free Press, New York, 1964.

Part 4

5

Functionalism

Introduction, The Organic System, Common Characteristics of Functionalism, Appraisal of Functionalism.

Introduction

Functionalism has grown up as a dominant sociological theory in the 20th century, even though its roots go back to the century before. August Comte, the French sociologist philosopher conceived of it in the 19th century followed by people like Herbert Spencer, Vilfred Pareto and Emile Durkheim. Together, they made the concept viable and acceptable to most sociologists. Talcot Parsons inherited the function a list ideas from them and himself became a great exponent of functionalism who enriched its spectrum to a level others did not. Parsons' contributions to functionalism made it an outstanding sociological thought of the 20th century. Earlier, two noted British anthropologists A.R. Radcliffe Brown and Bronislaw Malinowski added their immensely valuable collection of knowledge of early social life of people to the subject. Parsons benefited from this treasure contributed by these noted scholars.

Functionalism has been fully defined in the modern Dictionary of sociology as, "The analysis of social and cultural phenomena in terms of the functions they perform in a socio cultural system. In functionallsm, society is conceived of as a system of interrelated parts in which no part can be understood in isolation to the whole. A change in any part is seen as leading to a certain imbalance, which in turn results in changes in other parts of the system and to some extent to a reorganisation of the system as a whole. The development of functionalism was based on the model of the Organic system found in the biological sciences". A modern dictionary of Sociology, 1969, p. 167.

The Organic Theory

Originally pioneered by August Comte and Emile Durkheim, as indicated above, the society is seen by them in the context of an organism, say a human body. The body of a human being is made up of various organs such as heart, lungs, liver, kidney, nerve system and so on. Each of the parts of the body functions independently but also in unison with other organs. In the event, if any part of the body malfunctions, then other parts are effected by this. As a result, the human body becomes ill and gradually loses its control until the effected parts are properly treated and made well.

In the same way, a society also suffers when an institution, similar to an organ is out of shape, caused by either of mismanagement or defective machinery; its malady could effect other parts as well. For example, if there is a law and order problem in the country, it would effect all aspects of life, in the same way, if the economy or for that matter, the education system is badly managed, there would be problems like inflation, scarcity of goods and services, rising debts of people, rising prices, unemployment and so on, Problems would escalate from one industry to another and there would be utter chaos. So also the education system, when it is run by an inefficient authority, the victims would be the students, who would not only have missed their proper education and left school with out a certificate; but also would find no jobs; life would be a misery and their families would suffer from lack of resources. Standard of living and quality of life would continue to erode to the extent it would be too difficult to catch up with the rest of society.

The analogy of the organic system in relation to the society explains functionalism, which works as interdependent and inter-related system to other parts of society. The needs of the human body such as food, drink, oxygen, love, nourishment etc are required to sustain its functional capacity which are similar to the society's functional pre-requisites. Those preriquisites are norms, values, family roles, integrity, health, stratification, law and order, rules, cultural matters such as religion, education and so on. So members of society must be motivated to play their roles properly or else the society would collapse through lack of effort.

According to Anthony Giddens development of functionalism in the modern phase has been influenced by the two anthropologists as mentioned above, who spent years in distant field work. Radcliffe Brown lived in the Trobian Islands in the Pacific and Malinowski lived in the Andaman Islands of the Indian Archipelago in order to study the daily life of the tribal people there. Anthropologists, before them only worked on the basis of reports and documents left by travellers and missionaries. What was not available were the mode of life of the tribal people and groups; their social, cultural, religious usages, their modes of living, rules, norms and also the nature of the intertribal relations. The British researchers' findings have greatly uncovered these facts from there hitherto unknown. This knowledge added a great value to the functionalist thought.

Functionalism requires that behaviour of people is regulated and structured. Every member of the society has to conform to the structured values and norms of the society; the rules are carefully formulated and strictly adhered to; no one excepted. Roles of people are devised and implemented. Normative pattern of life is expected to achieve a cohesive society in which good social relations would be the motto. Interconnected roles and inter related norms strengthen various institutions with in the society.

The structure of society develops various institutions such as the family which educates and socialises its young members to grow up as useful and responsible members of society. Education helps them to build their careers which in turn would improve the economy. Other institutions comprise economic, welfare, judiciary, education and training systems.

Social functions are multifarious and diversified; nevertheless, the society is a composite whole; nothing happens outside the society.

Common Characteristic

The common characteristics of functionalism are the following.

It portrays society as a system.

It is based on a structure and its functions are fully illustrated and defined.

Functionalism is constituted of various functions of the society which act in unison for the common good.

The institutions of the society are interdependent on one another and the aim is to contribute to the cause of the whole society. Earlier, sociologists of the 19th century stressed the need for independence of each institution but under Emile Durkheim and Talcot Parsons integration of all parts of society for the solidarity of the social unity can not be compromised and would remain pre-eminent.

Parsons developed the concept of structural functionalism in which social solidarity is expected to be a crucial part.

August Comte declared that lack of harmony between the whole and parts of the social system was 'pathological', August Comte, The Positive Philosophy 1896, vol 2. which Parsons resolved by saying that any negative or deviant element would be gradually absorbed into the social system through the process of 'moving equilibrium'. Parsons borrowed the idea of dynamic or moving equilibrium from Pareto who conceived of harmony for the social system.

Functionalists agree that each and every part of a society has to make their individual contributions to the organic benefit of the whole. This means that the primary roles of each and every part as individual unit has to function and deliver their maximum contribution to the common good of the society. They should not depend on the contributions of others. Each unit has to do their best and in this way the society would prosper better than before. But all their contributions and services are to be part and parcel in relation to the common functions of the society similar to different organs of the human body which function for themselves as well as for the rest of the organs as a co-ordinated process. The purpose is to see that the overall functioning of the social system runs smoothly.

Functionalism to be effective and positive requires a set of pre requisites or survival guides necessary to make society stable and harmonious. Even though every society has institutions like the family, the education system, the class system, the economic system, the democratic system etc, yet many societies become near extinct or decay gradually or suffer from internal conflict and corruption with terrible law and order problems. The reason is that they lack survival guides like coherence and co-ordination of the institutions essential to an organised and integrated society.

According to Davis and Moore some societies do better than others. Institutions can be there but are they properly organised? That is the question. Unless social pre-requisites are devised for coordination and integration of the society and simultaneously, social values are developed and reproduced for the next generation to adapt to, the society would not survive for long. The education system for example, should be such as to produce people with common sense, skills, sense of responsibility and commitment to work and to develop society. The whole purpose of education is to produce better people who would be able to generate a good economy and quality of life for people. Social and educational values have to be developed and internalised by the members who also should be inspired and motivated to build a stable society which is to function effectively.

Functionalists believe that religion has an integrative force. It can protect society but it must be compatible to other values which exist with different institutions. Without conformity to ethics, values, beliefs and tolerance, the institutions would fall apart and hasten the collapse of the social system. Durkheim for example, has emphasised that religion perpetuates core social values enabling social cohesion to hold on longer. Functionalism got a fresh fillip from the work of Talcot Parsons and Robert K Merton who reassert that functionalism has been a key factor in the development of sociological theory and research.

According to Anthony Giddens, Robert K Merton has produced a more sophisticated account of functionalist analysis than was offered by the British Anthropologists. Merton's study of the industrialised societies differed from the simpler cultures studied by the anthropologists. Merton analysed the differences between functions and dysfunctions. The anthropologists' study of the islanders included cultures of simple societies which were more functional and integrated in character than the diversified industrial societies which are large and characteristically problematic. They became subject of sociological enquires. The industrialised societies tend to generate dysfunctions caused by continued changes of norms and values in society. Many members fail to adapt to these changes, as a consequence become deviant and anomic.

Appraisal of Functionalism

The organic theory used by most sociologists to explain the nature and functions of a society is found less convincing by critics. In their view, the society is an inorganic institution built by the human beings for their day to day functions where as the organic system in the like of a human body in not built by the human beings but born in the nature which functions by its own laws without the making of the humans. The organs do not think whereas people do. The organic analogy can not go far enough to explain the social actions in society and their similarity to the biological functions in the human body is only referential. Biological functions take place below the level of conscious awareness. Human mind is active with ideas, imagination, thinking and reason. These don't appear to be the case with the organic system which is just a natural system operated by the universal forces beyond any body's control. If the organic system as in the natural world malfunctions, the consequences could be disastrous like the Tsumani flood. Humans can be blamed for polluting the organic system in the atmosphere causing the global warming. The eco system and the ozone layer have been damaged by excessive use of industrial fuel emitting black smoke and pollution-the consequences of which are devastating earth quakes, flood, melting Iceland and rising temperatures and so on.

Also, functionalism has been criticised being too deterministic where as the society is expected to be changing and flexible. Flexibility is necessary for a society to be vibrant. Is it not too much to expect of a social system to function as determined by the authority all the time. What about the emergencies and natural disasters like war drought, famine, political turmoil, change of government, economic fluctuations, social problems like prejudice, racial discriminations, unemployment etc. Without flexibility; these problems can not be dealt with satisfactorily. It also appears that the social solidarity can not be achieved without a high degree of value consensus. According to Robert. K. Merton, the degree of value consensus is determined by empirical test not easy to presume in advance. He argued that in modern highly differentiated societies some form of functional autonomy will have to exist in different parts of the social system. Merton further adds that some institutions regarded as inevitable can not be justified because, same services can be rendered by alternative providers; so the continued existence of those institutions might cause some tension in the system.

Thirdly, Merton finds that many functionalists put undue stress on the question of social cohesion, when they should be aware of division and conflict are a part of life in society. Moreover, societies do not have all the qualities as expected by the social system. Qualities have to be produced to learn and to get acquainted with. Societies generate maladjustment because human beings are different as they have different abilities and interests which can not be streamlined. There is a high degree of possibility that problems would accrue which have to be dealt with straightaway if qualities are to be maintained in tact. Nevertheless, aim should be there to achieve qualities at their maximum level.

References

A Modern Dictionary of Sociology (1969) p. 167.
August Comte – The positive philosophy (1896) vol. 2.
Alan Swingewood – A history of sociological thought, 1991.

6
Emile Durkheim (1858-1917)

Introduction, Durkheim's Indebtedness to his Contemporaries, Durkheim's Theory of Social Structure, Concept of Social Facts, Case Study of Suicide, Durkheim as a Functionalist, Religious Ideology, Concept of the Division of Labour, Social Theory, The Rules of Sociological Method, A Critique of Emile Durkheim.

Introduction

Emile Durkheim was born in France in 1858, studied Social and Political philosophy in Paris and took great interest in the work of Montesquieu and Rousseau. Later, he became a professor of sociology in Sorbonne University, Paris. His area was Scientific Sociology in which he was influenced by August Comte, the founding father of positivism. Durkheim also made a significant contribution to the development of the Scientific Sociology in which he excelled his predecessor. Other erudite, Herbert Spencer, the British natural scientist also impressed him much by his work on the development of evolutionary theory of society using sophisticated social analogies to explain the biological evolution.

Durkheim was indebted to his teacher, Charles Renouvier who taught him the efficacy of holistic approach' as a useful tool to frame the concept of a society. This helped Durkheim construct the structural theory. He also learnt from August Comte the rigorous method of studying sociological issues but added to it his own method of empirical tests in order to increase their scientific strength. He looked at society more critically than his mentor, August Comte who was rather satisfied with a generalised view of society. Also he learnt from Comte's philosophical exposition of social evolution which showed transition from the idealistic to the scientific positive stage of development. In the evolutionary theory, Herbert Spencer too has explained how a society moved from the military to the industrial phase.

Durkheim preferred a different phraseology explaining society's transition, such as: from 'mechanical to organic solidarity'. The mechanical form prevailed when a society was in its formative stage. It showed that life was simpler; and also other characteristics; which helped social solidarity to be easily achieved. In the industrial stage, society was differentiated by the 'Division of labour', sophisticated relationships and structural complexities. The society was organic-each unit had to depend on the next unit and vice versa. In short, society in the organic stage became interdependent. As mentioned above, Durkheim studied society more closely scientifically based on empirical tests than any of his predecessors. A great piece of scientific work he produced was about the 'suicide' issue in which he tried to show which countries and areas had produced more suicide cases compared to countries which had fewer cases, using numerical, climatic and economic variations of these countries or areas. His methodology earned him a status of a scientific sociologist. Durkheim also differed with Herbert Spencer in the context of society getting more solidified after industrialisation. It also becomes more modernised. To Spencer, moral bonds rather slackens with modernisation.

Durkheim has adumbrated numerous ideas taken from other scholars which rather has strengthened and enriched his work than diminished it. The net result was a dignified philosophy he created for all. His treatise, for example, 'The Rules of sociological method' is another example of his remarkable scientific achievement.

Emile Durkheim's Social Structure

Durkheim's concept of social structures is external, constraining and general. According to him, they are like 'social facts'-things that should be treated like scientific matters. 'Social facts' are usages, institutions and moral values of a society. Social life, according to Durkheim congregates towards the whole. His approach is 'holistic' in which all aspects of society contribute to the growth of the whole society rather than parts. Durkheim's society moulds and penetrates in to the individuals in order to make them effective, useful and reliable members. So, social structures sometimes can be coercive should that be necessary; if not, malicious elements would do harm to the society. Constraining social behaviour is required in order to restrain questionable individuals from jeopardising the solidarity of the society.

Social structures precede us and they are constraining. Society lives with the people and according to Durkheim the members can make, remake as well as remould the social structures. Social behaviours are structured too and so also the language we speak. Social relationships are organised into structures and they are value oriented and normative in nature. Whatever the kind of structure, each one of them is allocated a specific role to play; this ensures that a structure becomes functional. For example, in a family, a father is also a bread earner apart from parenting; similarly, a wife is also a mother whose primary role is to feed children and husband and also to educate children how to behave in the society. In the same way, the children have their own allocated roles of how to behave with all and to respond to each member within the family circle as son and daughter and brother and sister. The members of society must strictly adhere to the standard norms of behaviour.

Durkheim rose to fame when some of his great works such as the 'Rules of Sociological Method', 'Division of Labour', 'Suicide' and his treatise on 'The Elementary Forms of Religious life' were produced. Martin Albrow praises him in the following words, 'For much of the 20th century sociologists followed the doctrine of Emile Durkheim. His doctrine has been to explain 'the Social' solely by the social' (Martin Albrow).

Durkheim's Concept of Social Facts

Important to everything what Emile Durkheim wrote, 'The Rules of Sociological Method' stands out clear as a testimony of his great contribution to the scientific school of Sociology. First published in 1895, Durkheim outlined in it the logic and method required for scientific enquiry of social issues and problems. He wrote, 'social facts should be treated like things' or objects as they are in the natural world. He tested social facts empirically in the case of 'Suicide'; which became an important piece of case work in sociology.

As indicated earlier, Durkheim perceived sociology differently from August Comte. Comte's work on sociological science in his view was too speculative and vague. Anthony Giddens, also confers, "Comte had not successfully carried out his programme – to establish sociology on a scientific basis" (Anthony Giddens, sociology 2nd edition); but Emile Durkheim did. To become scientific, Durkheim argued, sociology must study 'social facts'. To him, 'social facts' are external matters to the members of a group or society. Members abide by all kinds of obligations such as laws, practices, norms, customs, values, fashions and so on because they can not live without conforming to these obligations; so they must comply with them like the 'Rule of Law' in an organised society, which must be obeyed as well.

The 'Rule of Law' produce inexorable values to them, even though these are not made by them. When translated, these obligations become 'social facts' and also part and parcel of the collective system of society. They also become synonymous with the conventional ways of life which the members adapt to once they are born. They are taught by the family how to become civilised beings and also in a greater sense by the structures of the society such as the agents like schools, play centres, religious institutions and so on.

Durkheim wrote, "Social facts are collective ways of acting, thinking, and feeling". To him, "Social Facts, are passed from one generation to another and received by particular individuals in a more or less complete form". Durkheim, however, denied that social facts are reducible to individuals and their properties but recognised that individuals and their efforts are also counted as elements of social sciences as atoms in physics. Durkheim also recognised the value of 'collective representations and collective consciousness' – these are expressed in the form of rules of morality, religious beliefs, innumerable precepts of law, and practices of society. They are expressly obligatory, even though 'social facts' are constrains upon individuals and imposed upon them. He argued that individuals can be a part of a collective contribution to help and create general consciousness. Durkheim made it clear that his kind of society is akin to Macro-Form and therefore, should be structurally based.

Durkheim explained that there are exceptions to social facts when certain categories of people fail to conform to the social facts. He suggested that in exceptional cases they can be tried by law courts and punished accordingly. To his surprise, Durkheim discovered that a large number of people have failed to conform to the established norms, laws and regulations. After, thorough research he came to the conclusion that it was the society which should be blamed for failing to bring members up to the required standard of society through their educational and cultural programmes. The members should have been educated how to conform to and to cohere to the social values. If the society had failed in their responsibilities then it should be called upon to question. He used a word 'anomie' to categorise these people who fell from the ethics, norms and values of the society.

Durkheim's Case Study of 'Suicide'

Durkheim's most famous monograph 'Suicide' is a classic case of empirical study which he investigated inductively covering all available causes of suicide. He found that these causes do not explain conclusively anything in terms of the true cause. Mental illness and depression for example, which women suffer most compared to man; but the statistics show that men outnumber women in these categories of suicides.

To find out causes of suicide, Durkheim analysed biological and genetic make up of racial groups. The facts indicate that they can not be good causes for committing suicide. Then he looked into the 'cosmic' or environmental reasons, such as the climate, weather, day or night, summer or winter season and so on. Long night and short day time in Sweden's long winter season can make people gloomy and miserable looking no doubt, but suicide rates are fewer there in winter months than in summer months specially in daylight during June, July and August. Durkheim therefore dismissed all available causes for high suicide rates as real.

The prevailing notion in the society was that suicide was an individual act. Individuals who have been suffering from depression caused by personal failure in life, such as breakdown of marital relations, loss of jobs, death of the near and dear ones in the family, court ruling, burden of debt or whatever potent cause there could be in life of the individual. But Durkheim was least interested in individual cases which in his view, should not be used to generalise the public issue. There must be some potent cause or causes which affect the whole society rather than a few individuals. Durkheim also dismissed the claim of psychologists that suicide takes place on account of pathological causes like mental derangement, insanity, failure to cope with life etc of the individuals. Durkheim insisted that cause or causes lie hidden in Sociology not in psychology.

Eventually, he discovered that, social circumstances are more potential reasons for causing high suicide rates than any other factors specially when the circumstances reach their extremities. He was interested in taking suicide statistics from countries where suicide rates are higher. These could be used as samples for research purposes. European countries have variations in suicide rates; so also their number which varied according to religious background. For example, the Catholics have lower suicide rates than their counterpart–the Protestants in their individual countries. The Jewish as a religious group had a lower suicide rate than the Catholics. Durkheim collected these co-relations from different European countries and tried to find their causal relationships using the multivariate method.

So, Durkheim has divided suicides into four types such as egoistic, altruistic, anomic and fatalistic. Egoistic suicide takes place when some members of a society are detached from the mainstream social life caused by 'relaxation of social bonds' and lack of integration programme, then, they are thrown into despair. This is a fault of the society or the religious group or groups in which they are members who have failed to integrate all their members. Individuals should not be blamed for that. For example, the Catholics constitute a homogeneous community whose members have to follow strict rules of conduct pertaining to religious and moral obligations, as a result they can integrate more into the social bond compared to their counterparts – the Protestants who are relaxed in their religious obligations and are free to interpret their religious vows than the Catholics. So they have higher suicide rates than the Catholics. Altruistic suicide takes place in many societies where some members having had failed to achieve their objectives, commit suicide. Or that, some members in order to save the honour of the family or the group in which they are strongly integrated commit suicide if not, they would face ignominy and disgrace in the society and would remain as shameful burden on the family as well. For example, Harakiri practice in Japan and the Suttee in India are glaring examples. The former plunges a knife into the stomach and kills himself to save his or family's honour. The Suttee in India is another example, in which a married woman burns herself to death in the funeral pyre of her dead husband as an act of loyalty.

Anomic suicide takes place when social order breaks down and normative regulations fail to guide the members to remain on course. Many get confused knowing not what to do. This is an anomic state when a tendency to commit suicide dominates their mind and many actually do it. Some times they do it in an organised way involving many individuals. Although Durkheim has not written much about the Fatalistic suicide occurs when the society restricts individual freedom too much. In his view, persons whose futures are 'pitilessly blocked' and their 'passions violently choked by oppressive discipline', then the fatalistic suicide occurs.

Durkheim as a Functionalist

Ruth Wallac confirms that, "Emile Durkheim is certainly the most important sociological forerunner of modern functionalism". He was also a structuralist as confided by his fellow philosopher Nisbet, "Durkheim was a prominent structuralist in French sociological thought". Functionalism, as Emile Durkheim perceived was about institutional functions in the first place, but with in the framework of an integrated society. According to him, society integrates by moral consensus rather than by fear or force as was suggested by the 17the century British political philosopher, Thomas Hobbes. Durkheim argued that various parts of society would have to work together to build a social system in which to maintain the social order. Some of Durkheim's most important ideas are formed from his lifelong pursuance of the concept of 'integration' in which he had indicated that individuals are part and parcel of society. Durkheim has also denied allegation that he undermined the contribution of individuals to build the social system but maintained that the individuals should always come as a grouping in order to make their contributions recognised and accepted by the people as a whole.

Moreover, he emphasised that there is nothing wrong for institutions to work independently as long as they remain committed to the whole. Durkheim of course, has placed the society above everything else because to him, the society has a reality of its own and also is above the individuals who comprise the society. They have to abide by the accumulated values, beliefs and morals of the society which are passed on to them from the previous generations. This valuable heritage should not be thrown away. In that sense, the individuals are constrained by the obligations which automatically befall on them.

The individual conscience is shaped by the moral values, beliefs and so on which should be integrated in to the conscience of the whole. Durkheim was preoccupied with the functions of society which centred round his concept of 'social order'. To achieve social order, there has to be a 'collective conscience' of people based on the accumulated values and cultures of the society. Social order will constrain individual selfishness for the sake of greater good and for social conscience to grow.

Durkheim's Religious Ideology

Durkheim found religion 'a regenerating force'. Its inherent values of oneness and faith help its believers to integrate into the social group and develop the 'collective conscience'. Durkheim wrote his views on religion in a famous document, 'The Elementary Forms of the Religious Life' published in 1912 in which he presented the functionalist view of religion.

In his view, religion is based upon the 'sacred and profane'. In others words, religion is a unified system of beliefs and practices related to sacred things but those which divide society such as non-sacred profane things are forbidden. To him, society is the real object of religious veneration. Also the society,is more important and powerful than the individuals. Religion promotes social solidarity. Durkheim also saw the importance of 'collective' worship as a source of gaining genuine fellowship among believers of the same faith.

This book on religion is one of Durkheim's most important works. As said earlier, social solidarity and functionalism are also held together by religious values too. In particular, it strengthens the perception of functionalism as embodied in his book. Ruth Wallace praised it, "As the most important contribution to functionalism". Religion has been described by Durkheim as 'an integrative force' which promote social solidarity and its cohesion. In his view, "Society is therefore a religious entity".

Steven Luke points out, "Durkheim's dichotomy between the sacred and the profane derives from and is explained by the basic and the multiple of dichotomy between the social and the individual; that is at the heart of his thought". Durkheim has put emphasis on 'cult' saying that it plays a pre-pondering role in all religions. Rituals also serve to bring members together in a reaffirmation of their collective identity. In the same way, collective effervescence-an emotional pitch which reaches in religious ceremonies also contributes to social solidarity.

Durkheim praised the primitive religious thoughts being contributory to the later growth of Greek and Western civilisations. Next to religious thought, Durkheim found altruistic values of the public school education such as their discipline, order, rules, obedience, ambition and respect for hard work etc are all equally good like the religious values. They could also be useful substitutes for functionalism.

Criticism of Durkheim's Religious Ideas

Many critics fear that Durkheim's views on religion may create a 'faith society' which may be contrary to the principle of a multi-faith society or a society of many cultural and sub-cultural groups. In modern world, some of Durkheim's religious ideas are not tenable because in a secular society religion is set aside as a private institution. It has no primary function with individuals or society at large except in specific terms. Nevertheless, there are some fundamentalist countries which want religion to be made the state religion. But, there is some usefulness of Durkheim's religious ideology in societies of non-literate status or even small community state.

Durkheim and Talcot Parsons Compared as Functionalists

In the sphere of religion, Durkheim and Talcot Parsons technically differ but not fundamentally. Their concerns are about social cohesion, integration and social system. Functionalists have subtle differences amongst themselves on many issues but in essence they are professing more or less same things – all are pursuing social integrity and a structurally based social system. Durkheim emphasised the importance of core human values required to strengthen social cohesion and these originate in religious values practiced through centuries. Much of the core human values were formed in primitive societies as these grew continuously alongwith the social evolution.

As a radical functionalist, Durkheim decried the concept of 'Inherited Wealth'. To him, inherited wealth adds an undue advantage to those already rich. In his 'Division of Labour', he exposed the rich who tried to increase their power and privilege aided by wealth not earned by them but inherited as a result of their birth.

Durkheim was not against those who create wealth by dint of hard work and enjoy the fruit of their labour but not otherwise. Durkheim was inspired by the eighteenth century great French Philosopher Jean. J. Rousseau who was a beacon of the French Revolutionary thought. His solution to the inherited wealth was that if it could not be abolished then it should be heavily taxed in the form of an inheritance tax.

Emile Durkheim's Theory of 'Division of Labour'

Durkheim startled the sociological circle with his version of social evolution which in his view began in the primitive society and progressively moved up to the industrial phase in modern times. This evolutionary period is neatly explained in his treatise 'The Division of Labour', first published in 1893 and has presented two patterns of society: one existed in the primitive period and the other in the industrial period. Life in the former was' mechanical' and life in the latter was 'organic'. Mechanical life was simplistic but organised and based on common belief and trust mostly dictated by religious values like Totemism. Achieving moral consensus and social solidarity were the main concerns of the society at that stage.

To him, life became more complicated and diversified in a later stage, caused by agricultural and industrial revolutions. Urbanisation followed the economic revolution which in its turn started the revolution in ideas bringing too many changes in society as it became more 'organically' oriented.

This brought fresh concerns for social relationships and their allegiance to the central authority. In the 'Division of Labour' Durkheim explained that work in the society became diversified into different roles to be performed by each individuals. Tasks became more specialised, skill based and economically targeted. Individuals who perform efficiently and prefer to take up responsibility are considered for higher reward than those who don't show much interest in work. Organic solidarity began to develop more in areas of industry where division of labour was structurally implemented.

The 'Division of Labour' must be perceived on its own perspective than in the common sense. Durkheim studied 'division of labour' as a social institution rather as an economic institution; of course, economic institutions are only parts of it contributing to the organic whole. The true significance of the role of 'division of labour' lies not in its effect on the growth of wealth, which will be obvious in an organised society as envisaged by Durkheim but in the inter-relationships of different parts-most importantly the individuals and their composition in the society. 'Division of Labour' would promote social solidarity, thereby restraining unbridled freedom and selfish interest of the individuals.

Durkheim's Social Theory

The social theory of Durkheim comes out clear in his 'Division of Labour'. As stated earlier about his concept of 'collective conscience' or conscience collective, in Durkheim's view, we live with two consciences-one individual and the other one common or collective. The individual conscience is selfish and egotistical which leads to interests outside social solidarity. The collective conscience becomes the source of moral solidarity essential for traditional societies to survive and to move forward. People who live away outside social solidarity or collective conscience are known as deviants who can cause immense harm to themselves as well to the society. To counter deviance as a way of life, Durkheim proposed regulation of society and introduction of good education system to infuse social awareness among deviants. Durkheim was perhaps the first sociologist to analyse 'deviance' as social pathology in terms of broad sociological theory. To him, deviance is universal, relative and functional. Deviance is produced by the society because it has not offered 'special needs' programme to educate these people. Their requirement was not addressed to. That is why, they could not conform to social rules and norms and became victims of circumstances.

To Durkheim, there is a normal level of tolerable deviance quite different from the abnormal level which reaches at an unacceptable level. Most sociologists would accept the universal deviance as a normal part of society but not the abnormal one. Relative deviance is some thing that differs from country to country. It is culturally based. For example, divorce, drinking, child abuse which exist almost in every society but varies in terms of level, type and pattern of abuse. Deviance is generally regarded as socially dysfunctional and a social pathology.

But he also argued that deviance can be in a limited way functional to society; People learn from their mistakes; many learn from the predicament of the deviants and restrain themselves from deviating into decay and degeneration. Many deviants fight to recover from their position of social misfit; many also learn seeing people change and improve to lead a normal life. So this can be exemplary. People disapprove of deviance by strengthening conformity to society and measures taken to eradicate it.

The Rules of Sociological Method

Important to everything what Emile Durkheim wrote, "The Rules of Sociological Method" stands out clear as a testimony to his claim that sociology is a science. First published in 1895 it set out the mode of investigation required to make the sociological method scientific. 'Social facts' according to him, should be treated like things or objects as you can see things in nature. He tested social facts empirically to discover the true causes of 'suicide' and these became his most important discovery in sociology, even though his method faced criticism from fellow sociologists.

Durkheim's social facts are 'external to the members and constraining'. These can be laws, social practices, norms, customs, rituals, fashions and so on without which the members can not live in an organised society. People have to conform to the established ways of life or else life would not be worth living. These social facts have inexorable values even though the living people to day have not made them but made generations before. Social facts are part of the collective system and they are also conventional modes of life. A new born baby gradually will have to adapt to these modes in order to live and to socialise. These conventional modes are also common to many values adapted to societies in the wider world. Durkheim wrote, "social facts are collective ways of acting, thinking and feeling". In his view, we learn what is expected of us quite early in life and these expectations become part of our own personality. They are, Durkheim maintained, "are passed from one generation to another and are received by particular individuals in a more or less complete form". The individuals have no choice but to accept and abide by them even though they are constraining to their freedom but they will have to obey them.

A Critique of Emile Durkheim

Despite his outstanding contribution to sociology, Emile Durkheim is still being criticised by a number of sociologists concerning his basic concepts of sociological thought. At first, he was criticised being too obsessive, conformist, deterministic and short sighted. His claim for scientific positivism was doubted by the fact that he was not rigorous enough to raise the level of scientific status of the 'suicide' case which is claimed it to be his best scientific achievement. Also, he was criticised being obsessed with the religious factor as the main cause of committing suicide. Professor Halbwachs (1930) argues that Durkheim overestimated the importance of religion in determining the suicide rate. He further argued that differences in standard of living in the rural and urbán situations have more impact on the suicide rate than the differences between the Catholics and the Protestants.

According to some of to day's sociologists, such as Steve Taytlor, Durkheim adopted a realist rather than a positivist view of science.

Critics like Jack P Gibbs and Walter T Martin (1964) maintain that suicide should be studied using scientific methods and statistical data. But they argue that Durkheim has not entirely followed the positivist method which should have been more rigorously followed as mentioned above. They also believe that Durkhein failed to define the concept of 'integration' sufficiently precisely and in a measurable way. So he lacked his positivist stance.

Interpretive sociologists too have made sharp criticisms of Durkheim's suicide case. They tend to reject many of the basic principles of Durkheim's approach. J.D. Douglas, for example, a prominent interpretive sociologist (1967), particularly criticised him for using official statistics to study the suicide case. The validity of these data, according to him is very questionable because these are secondary source statistics often gathered from accounts of families of the diseased persons. Durkheim treated them as accurate without raising doubts concerning their validity and reliability.

It can be argued that Durkheim's view of human nature is unrealistically pessimistic because he has put more emphasis on the moral regulation of society than the human thinking and their personal moral values. If the society is capitalistic or for that matter socialistic, we are restricting human values to a limited ideological bent of mind and constraining free thinking. The biological nature of human mind will thus be subjected to external control. So it would be unproductive and deterministic. Secondly, if the social facts are selective – only taken into account of those few facts-conducive to the empirical tests, leaving a vast array of evidence unaccounted for, then it would make the study unscientific and unrepresentative too and any results obtained would be limited by their veracity.

References

Durkheim, Emil. The Division of Labour in Society, 1933.
Durkheim, Emil. The Rules of Sociological Method. 1964
Giddens, Anthony, Capitalism and Modern Social Theory. New edn 1992; A Discussion of the Writings of Marx, Durkheim and Max Weber.
Swingewood, Alan. A Short History of Sociological Thought, 1991.

7
Talcot Parsons (1902-1979) Contents

Introduction, Parsons' Organic View of Society, Parsons' Theory of Social Evolution, Parsons' Concept of Social System, Parsons' Concept of Social Prerequisite, A Critique of Talcot Parsons, Criticism of Parsons' Right Wing Views on Poverty, Parsons' Concept of Social Differentiation, Parsons' Concept of Educational Perspective, Other Criticisms.

Introduction

Talcot Parsons is an iconic figure in sociology; more so in the history of functionalism. He is credited to have introduced the concept of 'structure' in the functional theory' and developed the much acclaimed theory of the 'social system'. Born in the United States, Parsons graduated in sociology from the University of Amherst and studied extensively about the subject of Positivism and its founders August Comte, Herbert Spencer and Emile Durkheim. They are the pioneers who viewed sociology as a part of natural science. As the first founder of sociology, August Comte visualised the subject as the last frontier in the domain of science after Physics, chemistry and biology. Parsons is well known as a fundamental thinker whose domain was vast. As we go along, we will see his manifold ideas in sociology including many new concepts he introduced literally to give a full shape to the subject of sociology.

Parsons, came to Germany to study German socialism and having had completed a thesis on 'Capitalism in recent German literature', he was awarded a PhD degree. He arrived back in the

United States where he was offered the chair of Sociology at Harvard. His reputation as a teacher soon made him the president of the American sociological society. In the mean time, Parsons was thinking of building a new society in the way he perceived – the evidence of which can be found in his social system. This would be an ideal society entirely different from any contemporary ones strictly based on his sociological ideas. Unfortunately, the plan could not get through to make an impact; so it was dropped.

Parsons' Organic View of Society

According to his Organic perception of society, Parsons envisaged that a society should be harmonious, integrated, conscientious and morally bound by the norms and values agreed by all the members of the 'social system'. The objectives are to achieve equilibrium and stability without any conflict in society. He found himself in accord with the general functionalist view that a society is like an organism – biologically and functionally similar to a human body. As all parts of the human body such as the heart, lungs, kidneys, liver, brain, nervous system etc. can work in tune with one another and be able to deliver a smooth function of the body, then, why not the society with its different institutions but all coordinating with one another and aimed to function smoothly, peacefully and harmoniously. According to Parsons' conception, societies are 'self-regulating systems' based on the principle of change when required and all institutions readjusting to changes for their survival in a changing world. If any part malfunctions, other parts in the system are effected as a result, like the human body which suffers as well from wear and tear. With right measures taken, the society would come back to normal. The human body too becomes fit and functional after necessary treatment.

Parsons also discovered that the society is evolutionary by nature more or less like the biological evolution. As Spencerian, he adapted to the view that all societies evolved from a simple to the primitive and then to the agrarian form and eventually moved to the phase of complex urban society. The question arises then, whether a society whilst passing through the evolutionary phase passed peacefully guided by reason and moral commitment, or did it go through a violent, chaotic, strife torn and bloody situation. It may be a case, that as the society was in a primitive stage, a state of nature prevailed, which presented a peaceful atmosphere in which to live; people were less greedy and not in the habit of owning material possessions including land because, there was no need for acquisition of property – land was available in plenty and commonly held, so there was no need to possess it. Life was also transitory; people were moving constantly from one place to another in search of a better environment, fresh food and drink.

The 17th century British political scientist Thomas Hobbes however, presented a dismal picture of society which, according to him was full of strife and violence. He argued that in the state of nature, there was no formally organised body to control the chaotic situation. According to him, life in the state of nature was 'nasty, brutish and short' and every body was after every body. The society passed through a period of gloom. Order was only restored when an agreement amongst members was reached to the effect that everybody would have to sacrifice a part of their sovereignty for a greater cause i.e. common good of all; then an orderly society could prevail. A people's 'Contract' known as Leviathan was charted out with which to elect a ruling authority under an elected leader who would be responsible for bringing order in society. The leader was allowed to take coercive action if necessary, against law breakers. Parsons subscribed to this view for some time but later conceded to Emile Durkheim's view that society was not passing through a chaotic phase as presented by Hobbes rather people were bound by moral commitment to lead a peaceful life in which reason and moral impulse played a role rather than violence and aggression.

Parson's Theory of Social Evolution

Parsons' theory of social evolution is a novel expansion of the general evolutionary concepts. Parsons' theory is described through his unique criteria of 'evolutionary Universals' which operate in different forms during the period of change: For example, 'vision' is a universal criteria which is potent in the biological environment including the animal kingdom. Sighted organisms evolve and survive much better than unsighted species; therefore, vision has a great evolutionary value.

Secondly, language, as a form of communication is an essential mechanism to the progress of human society. But the animals have their mode of communication different from the humans, expressed through their body language such as emotion, reaction, barking, chirping, howling, aggression and fighting. To Parsons, communication as an evolutionary universal is an essential tool for a society's growth. No society can move forward without language skills.

There are other universals, no less pertinent to those said already. They are religion, kinship and technology. Together, they make social evolution possible. Parsons' social evolution, as said below, passes from a simple societal stage to the more complex stage. Low level differentiation indicates which society is a simple one and different from the more complex ones Parsons calls it the 'constitutive symbolism' which represents the earliest forms of society with religion as a fundamental symbol. However, it effects or influences the rest of the social life of the primitive or nomadic people. Constitutive symbolism, according to parsons, is thus, a set of symbols ingrained in religion which permeates virtually all aspects of life. The aborigines of Australia are closely knit societies bonded by kinship relations, nevertheless, religious beliefs inspire their activities.

This state gradually advances into the next phase of social evolution which produces some kind of stratification system based on class and ethnic characteristics; social functions and economic activities get diversified and religion becomes institutionalised. Parsons' evolution gets further diversified, structured and organised in the following manner.

In his words, societies are intermediate when they are premodern types, acquiring some literary, agrarian and cottage based industrial skills. Politics grows into leadership and takes charge of localities. Regional administration is formed to run the economic, civil, and legal functions and also to maintain law and order in the developing urban communities. Democracy is still a far cry but some kind of consensus and political will continue to grow. Parsons stresses that at this stage new universals are formed to equip the society with skills to move ahead; such as, bureaucratic organisation, monetary system, legitimisation of politics, specialisation of the legal system, protection of civil societies etc. These are being devised in order to integrate people in to the body politic.

Lastly, Parsons' social evolution reaches its final stage when the society is fully industrialised and differentiated according to peoples' needs, abilities, competences and skills. Differentiation takes the form of division of functions of social and national activities in to departmentalised system, accountable to the political authorities. Religion also has established itself in to a self governing institution.

Parsons' Concept of Social System

Parsons is best known for his 'System theory' as indicated earlier but he has also contributed theoretically to other fields of knowledge. They are known as his sub-systems, such as, theories of action, poverty, sickness, socio-biological personality, education and so on. Taken together, they have contributed to his design for a 'Grand Theory' applicable to a larger (macro) society covering wide range of social groups spanning diverse cultures, beliefs and functions.

Parsons said, "The concept of system in the action field as in others has been central to my thinking from a very early stage". (Talcot Parsons – On building social system theory, 1967, p. 849)[1].

As an evolutionary thinker, Parsons has developed a 'social system' which is both complex and dynamic. It aims to achieve stability, equilibrium and a durable consensus of people which according to him would promote new values as it would protect the old ones. In his words, "social system consists in a plurality of individual actors interacting with each other in a situation which has a least, a physical and environmental aspect, and actors who are motivated in terms of a tendency to the optimisation of gratification and whose relation to their situations including each other is defined and mediated in terms of a system of culturally structured and shared symbols". Talcot Parsons – Social system, 1951, Free press, New York, p. 5.

Parsons' social system incorporates within it the framework of a 'structural functional' form. It is the by-product of the social system. Sociologist Alex Callinocos confirms this in his statement, "The social system represents the first full statement of what Parsons calls it structural functionalism". Alax Callinocos- Social theory, A historical introduction, 1999, Polity press, p. 240.

The central concept used by Parsons to explain the pattern of social evolution is the structural differentiation which refers to the tendency of social institution to become more specialised. This structural system is functionally more specific and specialised to deliver wide range of activities and services such as role allocation of individuals and distribution of rewards, value laden social institutions like the economic, educational, civil service and political systems etc. which are major aspects of a social structure. They have to function with in the integrated social structure. A society or an organisation to exist must have a structure before it can deliver any functions. Theoretically, the structures and the functions of society can be separated but in realty they are inseparable.

There is no place of individualism in Parsons' social system but has a place for all individuals who would play their parts and contribute to building a society. Nevertheless, an individual plays two roles, one as a member of the family and the other as a member of the community. In both the roles he or she has to follow the rules of society which will guide them to achieve all the goals of the social system.

Parsons' social system depends entirely on certain pre-requisites. Together, they are called the AGIL, in other words; adaptation, goal attainment, integration and latency – pattern maintenance. To Parsons, equilibrium in society is achievable if all the prerequisities can function fully and efficiently and in cooperation with one another in order to deliver the objectives. Parsons defines it, "that social life has a tendency to be and to remain functionally an integrated phenomenon so that any change in one part of the social system will bring about adjustable changes in other parts". George. A. etl, A modern Dictionary of Sociology, page 133. Earlier, he has explained that his social system is held together by three sub-systems, namely, personality which represents individuals' internalising motivation, moral values and beliefs because they are also integral to a fully developed vibrant society. His second sub-system is a social system in which individual roles and positions are structured. And the third one is a cultural system in which to develop art, literature, knowledge etc.; in other words, the core values of the society.

Parsons' AGIL

Adaptation: social evolution is continuous; it brings changes in economic activities, political and educational thoughts, in human relationships and so on. A society has to be adaptive to changes to new ideas and findings in order to survive and to lead members to educate and to learn from the changed environment. Any society which fails to learn and to adapt to changes remains primitive and gradually dies-out. Many aboriginal tribes became extinct as a result of their inability to adapt to changes. A society in order to grow must regulate for the use of its scarce resources so that it can survive longer or else poverty and lawlessness will cripple the society with obvious consequences.

Parsons identifies two broad patterns of cultural change similar to the ideas of the German sociologist Ferdinand Tonnies who categorised the social transition from the community (Gemeinschaft) to the modern (Gesellschft) kind. Parsons followed Tonnies concept to form his own 'pattern variables' and categorised them into group A and B respectively. The group A represents traditional values of simple societies, where a person is seen caring rather wholly for the community instead of himself. Group B represents advanced societies where people put emphasis on their personal development more than the community's interest. Parsons emphasises that to move from group A to B requires an industrial development and hard work of people. People, who are not born with a prescribed status will have to earn this in order to improve their lot. Moving to group B is a process that can happen to any advanced industrial society which is both essential and a natural way to continue to survive but lack of effort and a proper target would cause a society to decay and decline. Many primitive societies have disappeared because they could not keep up with pace and changes. Parsons accepted that many rural communities had survived just marginally because of emotional support they accorded to one another during the period when they lived through underdevelopment, poverty and hard life.

Durkheim also following Tonnies typology had analysed societies into primitive and modern types. He identified social solidarity in the primitive level which he called mechanical solidarity. In this type strong collective conscience developed whereas organic solidarity developed in the modern phase when the collective conscience became weak owing to the rise of individualism.

Having had seen both the typologies, Parsons decided to hold the middle ground. He lables the pre-modern societies as expressive and modern societies predominantly impersonal which is identified in his social system and calls it instrumental. Parsons' five fold pattern variables are elaboration of the traditional to modern typology. Parsons depicted the doctor's role as predominantly instrumental because of the high skills and level of technical competence required for the job. Therefore, this is also doctors' 'achieved status'.

The Second Social Prerequisites is the Goal Attainment

A society should have certain goal directed activities which are to be set out either by the Govt or by private institutions or by both, in which people would find their specific roles to play. The objective is to achieve maximum economic, educational, political and social goals. The Govt should also pass laws to regulate professional behaviour in order to prevent distractions and disruptions on the way to achieving the objectives.

The third prerequisite is 'social integration' which has been the hallmark of Parsons' social system. This has also been the prime objective of his predecessor, Emile Durkheim. The process of integration will take place when other processes such as communication, conciliation and resolution act in concert with general agreement. Politically, integration establishes 'The Rule of law', and enhances the sense of justice, toleration and peaceful co-existence.

The fourth prerequisite is the Latency or Pattern maintenance: Agreed social system based on consensus has to be maintained and protected as long as possible. The social system constitutes the functions of the family, religious values, educational objectives and all other social norms, ethics and goals. These values are internalised into the ideological and cultural pattern of individuals in the society, for them to follow and to preserve. The families and the communities will educate their members with those values who in their turn would transfer them to their next generation. Meanwhile, new values on the way, worth preserving should be adapted to enrich the existing stock. This is the way, the society would develop and create a cultural heritage.

Parsons' social system further consists of sub-systems like Kinship, stratification, power and religion. Kinship is the main socialising agency; stratification is the differentiated social status of people in the functional structure who get rewards based on achievements. Power is owned by the society rather than by individuals and religion is a core value as discussed above.

Parsons' functionalism tends to acquire total coherence possessing an inbuilt equilibrium with cooperation from various groups and organisations such as sects, government organisations, churches, social strata, economic organisations and so on. But at the same time these sub-systems generate social inequalities, abnormal types, conflict and deviance. Individuals who can internalise collective goals are thus socialised which augment social order. But those who can not, Parsons would consider them as negative forces but they could be absorbed gradually into social equilibrium which is a dynamic force. It has capacity to change as required for the purpose of building a stable society. His equilibrium becomes thus a 'moving equilibrium'. Parsons' social system aims to achieve a full equilibrium. So he wrote, "Many complex processes are necessary to maintain the functioning of any social system; if its members do not care, the society would soon cease to exist"[5]. (Talcot Parsons – Societies – Evolutionary and comparative perspectives, 1966, p. 21.

A Critique of Talcot Parsons

Parsons' social pre-requisites have been attacked by the right wing groups, cultural deviants and modernists. In fact, the sanctity of the family system so precious to Parsons is found gradually dying out. Many families are struggling under stress and affects of modernism. There are now split nuclear families; even they are not immune from breakdown of relationships and the result of which is the suffering of the children.

Forget by economic liberation, the impact of technocracy and modernism on life most families are now changing to new norms and values quite different from traditional ones. Hedonism and self aggrandizement have become the norms. Economic liberation has enabled women to make choices, if necessary to live alone or with friends. Protection by law, emergence of new morals, ethics and vast array of social and political ideologies to choose from have given memebrs plenty of freedom ever imagined before. Breakdown of marriages has reached an alarming rate in every industrially developed society; the rise in single parent hood, the demise of the father figure from the family and replaced by only mother figure who, has been increasingly becoming a reckonable identity of the child. To day, the family system is in a mess; it has entered into a danger zone when it includes every thing you can think of from living together' to marrying some one from the same sex. Despite being subjected to criticism both Durkheim and Parsons are convinced that the premier values of society were still being generated by none other than the traditional family system. The system was going to stay in the society and therefore should be preserved.

On the subject of poverty Parsons airs right wing views; whilst annotating on the subject, he presumes poverty results from a 'social structure' like many other social issues like the 'suicide'. Poverty is a historical fact well established in our midst since time immemorial. It has brought miseries as well as challenges to those who got stuck in to the rut. By dint of hard work, education and training, many poor people have eradicated poverty from their lives. Also many have become very rich over the years. According to Parsons, those who try to change their life, they can do so themselves with help being made available; that is true, but it is also true that still many more are trapped in the 'cycle of poverty' who could not avoid it. To Parsons, poverty can be beneficial because it brings challenges to the poor. The educational and training opportunities being made available for people by the democratic governments of to day are the real hopes for recovery but effort must be made through hard work to open up new avenues of life and to eradicate poverty once and for all.

Parsons overestimated the fact that poverty can be a challenge to the poor people. Many poor people have accepted poverty as a fact of life which can not be altered. They think that they are born with in it and would die in it, no body could change that. In fact, many people are dependent on it; even if opportunities are offered, they would not have the mentality to accept them because of lack of work culture. In order to motivate people to develop a work culture, there should have to be a full programme of education and skill training; also, out-reach workers to try to contact them and to explain their task. They should be motivated to undergo a job training scheme in which to learn how to start a first work in life. At the end of the training, relevant jobs must be offered followed by a proper monitoring system to record their progress..

Parsons' social system is also based on the foundation of four sub-systems. They are economic, political, kinship, cultural and community. The economic sub-system comprises of financial institutions such as banks, building societies, factories, trade-unions etc. They allocate roles and their respective duties and responsibilities and stipulate service conditions such as norms and standard and so on. The political sub-system is made up of political parties, govt civil service, electorates etc. and the jobs are done by M.PS, ministers, counsellors, Mayors and so on. The kinship is made up of families, their siblings, and relatives and the roles each member plays as husband and wife, father and mother, son and daughter and so on and the standard norms require to include love, affection, care and well being for all. The last sub-system is the cultural and community organisations such as schools, colleges, churches, temples, synagogues, mosques and many more meeting places in which to play different roles as teachers, preachers, students and so on as allocated by the society.

The social system has been made abstract by elaborating the perspectives of cultural, social, personal and behavioural aspects of the individuals who are required to internalise into them the social and cultural values and norms of the society. They are required to do so for them to enhance their personalities and to become more positive, productive and useful members.

Parsons' social system incorporates with in it the framework of a 'structural functional system'. It is its by-product, Sociologist Alex Callinocos confirms this, "The social system represents the first full statement of what Parsons calls it structural functionalism"[6]. Alex callinocos – Social Theory – A historical Introduction, 1999, Polity Press, p. 240.

Role allocation is an integral part of the 'structural functionalism' which becomes more varied and functional along with industrial change. The 'division of labour' in an industrialised society reproduces jobs of incredible variety creating more and more diversified roles for all concerned required by the structure. In this way, the structural system gets further widened; and responsibilities, norms and behaviour of members get regulated. Parsons also mentions the phrase 'structural differentiation' which grows when social institutions become more specialised, such as many functions of families are taken over by specialised agencies or institutions like nurseries, Schools, health, social services, welfare bodies, Leisure centres, security services etc.

There may be too many constrains on achieving the objectives such as lack of resources for example, in pursuing an educational career, or diffecult family problems, lack of transport facilities, infrastructural problems etc., for performing goal directed activities. So the normative rules should be such as to focus on progress rather than hinder it. If that requires expanding infrastructural network, that should be done.

Parsons has explained the social evolution from the simple primitive level to the complex modern life as already indicated earlier. He emphasised that 'adaptation' was the key driving force to social evoltion. The society must move forward towards industrial phase of development, or else it would slide into decay and extinction like many which disappeared from the evolutionary process. Parsons has accepted that some rural communities have survived marginally because of emotional support they had accorded to one another in time of crisis even though they lived in sickness and poverty.

Parsons' Social Differentiation

Social evolution according to parsons leads to social differentiation in terms of social classes and education system. The social roles are allocated according to the ability and potency of the persons. The education system allows class divisions to grow with in it and develop economic disparity. Differential role allocation and differential rewards become the norm which inhibit social integration. Parsons argued that social differential would be less severe after the generalised values were introduced for an equilibrium society. Also he admitted that the beginning of the evolutionary process could be hazardous but that would standardise once the functional system was put in place.

Parsons' Education Perspective

Parsons argued that in modern industrial society education performs a crucial socialising function. Family and school are at the behest of the child's future. Primary socialisation takes place at home, later, the school takes over. Nevertheless, family still remains a potent factor in the child's upbringing and maintenance which cast a lasting influence in his/her whole career. School acts as a bridge between the family and the society. The child is transferred from the particularistic standard at home to the universalistic standards at school and wider society. So, also the child's ascribed status at home will not be recognised for long in the outer world when he or she has to strive for acquiring the achieved status based on role play. At home, the child is judged and treated according to his or her particularistic standard whereas in a wider society the child is treated, according to Parsons, by the universalistic standards applied to all irrespective of their backgrounds.

Parsons saw the school classroom as a 'microcosm of society' like Durkheim who saw it as a miniature society. The school prepares young people for playing their adult roles. Parsons like other functionalists stress on high academic achievement and acquiring value consensus for the maintenance of society. Parsons also stress on the necessity for 'differential reward for differential achievement' – the principle is all have an equal chance to achieve the maximum. Parsons also believes in the selection system in school based on ability, interest and effort which make all the difference between high and low achievers. In other words, the school is like a springboard from which to begin their career for the future.

Parsons has been criticised for advocating the values of the minority which are middle class values. The society has different sets of values, but Parsons' ideology undermines the values of the majority who are poor and uneducated. He is thus criticised for promoting discrimination. Parsons' principle also advocates a 'meritocracy' principle of the school – that all pupils have an equal chance in education to shine but ignored the fact that the middle class children had a better start and chance in life than the working class children who had come from a poor background. Education is also a cultural factor where the middle class children fare better because they are already brought up in a culturally stimulating background in which they had formed rudiments of their career. These opportunities were not available for poor children in which to grow like their counter parts. They also get middle class jobs after education. Students from poor background tend to leave education early because of chances to higher education were fewer. These all constitute the fact that Parsons' educational sociology is based on the criteria of selection.

Other Criticisms

Fulcher & Scot (1999 in page 52) point out, "One of the strongest criticisms of Parsons has been that he failed to analyse action as thoroughly as structure and function". 'Action' as a theory should have got a better deal considering it as a major concept which is at the same time an integral part of the structural system introduced in functionalism. Also, in explaining the sex-role differentiation in the pattern variables Parsons gave prominence to men than women. He writes, "The instrumental leadership role must be accorded to the husband-father on whom the reputation and income of the family depend"[7]. T. Parsons – Essays in Sociological Theory (954, pp. 422-23). Feminist activist took this as a male oppression on mother. Parsons' 'expressive role' little accorded to women as agents of children's up-bringing is also criticised as an attempt to confine them to the bounds of family life and limit their role in the public sphere. Parsons is also criticised being deterministic and complacent about the social equilibrium. He minimised the effect of negative forces that exist in society such as poverty, unemployment, famine, deviance, prejudice and discrimination. Parsons also is seen to have failed to appreciate the usefulness of symbolic interaction and conflict perspectives.

One of the other criticisms he faced was that Parsons' attempt to construct a 'grand theory' in sociology embodying all the different perspectives he developed into one did not succeed even though his method was holistic – converging into the solidarity of the 'social system'. He was also credited to be a macro theoretician engaged in many areas of sociological knowledge. Parsons dominated American sociological field for over twenty years up to the early sixties but his influence declined when new interactive and other scientific theories occupied the ground he left. But it did not take long time to see his influence resurfaced in all its facets amongst emerging sociologists in the eighties when he was gone.

Nevertheless, Parsons still stands out as a leading sociologist of Western Europe. The social system he introduced exists in many forms in many countries but the structural functional system has occupied a permanent place in the civil administration of all governments. After thoroughly analysing Parsons' contribution to sociology Jurgen Habermas has commented that "any theoretical work in sociology to day that fails to take account of Talcot Parsons could not be taken seriously"[8]. Jurgen Habermus – An essay on T. Parsons – Sociological Enquiry 51, 1981, pp. 173-74.

Questions

Describe how the integration of society is possible in Parsons' theory of Social System? What is Social Action? What are its main elements?

References

1. Talcot Parsons: On Building Social System Theory, 1967, p. 849.
2. T. Parsons: Social System, 1951, p. 5.
3. Alex Callinocos, Social Theory – A Historical Introduction 1999, p. 240.
4. A George etl – A Modern Dictionary of Sociology, p. 133.
5. T. Parsons: Societies – Evolutionary and Comparative Perspectives, 1966, p. 21.
6. Alex Callinocos – Social Theory – A Historical Introduction, 1999, p. 240.
7. T. Parsons: Essays in Sociological Theory, (954), pp. 422-23.
8. Jurgen Habermas: An Essay on T. Parsons' Sociological Enquiry, (51) 1981, pp. 173-74.

8

Robert. K. Merton

Introduction, Merton's Relations with Early Functionalists, Merton's Functionalism, Manifest and Latent Function, Functional Alternatives, Merton's Middle Range Theory, His Theory of Deviance, Categories of Deviance, Appraisal

Introduction

Robert. K. Merton is one of Talcot Parsons' Harvard university students who carved out a niche in sociology by introducing the 'Middle range theory' in the discipline. He was educated with a genre of prominent sociologists like Sorokin, Harold Garfinkel and others in the Harvard University under tutelage of Talcot Parsons. Sorokin, Emile Durkheim, and George Simnel also cast an influence on Robert K. Merton's theory. Merton argued that using Emile Durkheim's conception of religion he has developed social cohesion, an important element of functionalism specially the latent functions. He studied Science and Economics of the 17 century England and also wrote a thesis for his PhD awarded by the Harvard University. RK Merton wrote some important books of which the Social Theory and Social structure and the Sociology of Science are particularly useful. Merton also developed some concepts like Self fulfilling prophesy, role model, deviant behaviour and focus groups.

Merton's Relations with Early Functionalists

As a functionalist, Merton criticised Talcot Parsons' functional perspectives as erroneous. He argued that his postulations could not be defended scientifically, for example, the postulations of functional unity, universal functionalism and their indispensability have not been empirically tested. Merton's 'middle range theory' is more compatible with empirical research than the macro theories of Talcot Parsons. Sociologist Paul Lazarsfeld also helped Merton in his effort to develop the 'Middle range theory' using 'Quantitative Methodology'.

Robert K Merton's Functionalism

According to Merton, functionalism in particular and the sociological theory in general have been enriched as a result of his new ideas. He has influenced the young generation of sociologists in their effort to learn sociology in a more sophisticated way than was done previously. His work has helped to study aspects of industrialised societies more minutely than before. Earlier, cultures of simple societies in the primitive phase of development were studied by anthropologists whose main preoccupation was to investigate the basic traits of life of these people; where as, life in the industrialised societies studied in the 20th century is not that simple but complex and diverge. Cultures are different from one country to another which present horrendous complexities as these are influenced by different religious, economic, educational, class and political systems. Any study of life under those complexities would not be easy to comprehend. According to Anthony Giddens, 'Merton produced a more sophisticated account of functionalist analysis than was offered either by Radcliffe-Brown or Malinowski' and particularly readapted functionalism to the study of industrialised societies'. Anthony Giddens, Sociology, 1993.

Merton's Manifest and Latent Functions

Merton distinguished the functions of society between manifest and latent. The former represents those functions as expected or intended by the members of the society. They know that these functions would take place and so were prepared for them. They would only be surprised if these did not take place; whereas the latent functions are un-intended functions which can take place only as a consequence of the former for which they were not prepared. Merton argued that it is the job of the sociologists to trying to uncover the latent functions of social activities and institutions.

Functional Alternatives

Merton has also devised alternative functions known as the substitutes which could instead deliver the sort of functions advocated by Talcot Parsons in the form of 'functional prerequisites'. For example, functionalists like Emile Durkheim and Parsons have found religion a useful tool to heal disorientation of deviants and anomies who could recover from their depression, obsession and frustration in life using religious and educational therapies. Merton argued that use of religion as a therapeutic device could be substituted effectively by the alternative therapeutic devises like counselling and reasoning which can make them understand the values of normal life in society. Secondly, people in their predicament could be educated in the vocational field and trained as skilled and useful workers of society. Education can liberate the minds from religious superstitions. It can also motivate them to become work-oriented, independent and self reliant which would help them recover from depression, obsession and frustration.

Secondly, functionalism took a different turn when Merton refined this perspective substantially. He argued that it may be the case that some times, the societies exhibit 'functional unity' as a symbol of thé nation conceived by the functionalists but it could not be guaranteed that it would always be the case. He mentioned that in a modern society, which is preponderantly pluralistic with diverse religious faiths which can cause friction and disharmony than unity. Merton has doubts about social unity, unless extra measures are put in place to combat conflicts and tension arising out of the religious teachings and propaganda. He suggests that any tension and unrest arising out of those causes should be investigated and proper actions taken. According to him, it would be wrong to assume that functional unity if achieved at all would prevail for long. It many be possible that in a highly modern differentiated society, a relatively high degree of 'functional autonomy' may exist partially in some parts of the social system but that should not be taken as a lead to hasten unity in other parts of the country.

Merton argued that functionalist approach should take guard of the fact that any part of society may be functional, dysfunctional or non-functional. He said that 'universal functionalism' was a premature concept which should be revised as to recognise the existence of non-functional groups with in the society. To make these groups properly functional there should be adequate actions taken to motivate them accept the functional values of society. According to him, the non-functional groups should be explained the values of social cohésion and integration. If persuasion failed then the society had a right to take direct coercive action against the recalcitrant forces for the sake of improving the situation.

Merton's Theory of Middle Range

According to Merton, the term sociological theory, "refers to logically inter-connected sets of propositions from which empirical uniformities can be derived". Craig Calhoun et al 386. He argued, 'Like so many words that are bandied about, the word 'theory' threatens to become meaningless'. Ibid, p. 386. To him, the Middle range theory is principally used to guide empirical enquiry on sociological issues. It is intermediate to general theories of the social system. Merton also criticised attempts being made by general theories to integrate different parts in to a cohesive whole, but failed even when they had been empirically tested. In his mind that would be an impossible task. Because of this reason, Merton would not accept Talcot Parsons as a grand theorist.

Nevertheless, Merton is a functionalist and he is loyal to its central concept but he tried to make his theory reliable and acceptable. The general functional proposition is that all parts of society are inter-connected to one another to the extent that they would work together for the benefit of the whole society and a change in one part of the society will bring change to other parts as well. Merton could not accept this proposition because of its inherent fallibility. In his view, a status like this can not be guaranteed for ever. Change in one part may not bring change to other parts automatically.

He further adds that in a pluralistic society, social solidarity and cohesion even if achieved through a vigorous policy making may falter any time. Merton argues that 'social differentiation' remains constant because of role allocation and specialisation of functions. Despite efforts to integrate all people and classes, full integration becomes impossible because of the multi-cultural, multi-faith and multi-class systems in society. Even a generalised value consensus according to Merton would fail to achieve the objectives of social integration. He continues that some institutions will remain autonomous, regardless of what improvement has been made in the general functions of the society. At the same time, there is also likelihood that some people would prefer to follow a negative role of life style rejecting maim stream ethics and values which means that they would remain dysfunctional in society and gradually slide into the state of 'anomies'.

Merton's 'Dysfunctional Society'

Merton further explains the nature of the 'dysfunctional society'. He characterises the 'dysfunctional society' as anemic-meaning when people fail to reach their goal of life by normal means of effort and endeavour, they then take to negative role to compensate for the failure of their aspirations. Merton of course, explains the factor of 'relative deprivation' as one of the many causes of crime. In his view, relative deprivation is a situation between 'rising aspiration and persistent inequalities' in a society. As a result of this, some people suffering from disadvantages would not be able to make their aspirations fulfilled; so at the same time they would not give up their aim of life too but try other ways and mean to reach alternative goals. Other ways and means would mean mischievous acts like crimes and so on.

Critics argue that Merton's Middle Range theory is only operational in a limited society or micro community where only simpler organisational structure prevails. In to day's society, this system will not hold good in a large society because of multinational companies which would not like to invest their resources in small communities because it would not yield good returns for their capital.

Lastly, the Middle Range theory however, looks good for small societies because these can be suitable for scientific experiments and tests-results which can be applied to specific cases in both micro and macro societies. The values of the middle range theories thus should not be overlooked so they are to be preserved and used, not abandoned. Macro theories are quite legitimate for the larger societies in which the companies would invest more, but at the same time the middle range theories are also important for the society.

Dysfunctions of Bureaucracy

Merton criticises Max Weber's 'bureaucratic ideal type' saying that several elements inherent in that type could lead to harmful consequences. R.K. Merton, social theory and social structure, 1957. This he called 'dysfunctions of bureaucracy' because, when bureaucracy serves the public generally but not individuals in particular, which might cause sufferings to some individuals because of their grievances have not been met; so it is dysfunctional. It is true that the bureaucracy is a public institution meant to serve the whole public but what about any individuals whose grievances have not been met. The rules and regulations are made for the good of all. Theoretically, that is true but according toe Merton, bureaucracy leads to incompetence if some people are getting the raw deals based on their decisions. That is the drawback of the bureaucratic system.

When every individual is tied up to the system for the cause of the general good that is a sure case of sacrificing individuality. This is a low of individualism to which no answer is given. Merton calls Weber's bureaucracy as the 'faceless impersonal bureaucratic organisation' which might lead to a conflict between the clients and the bureaucrats. In particular cases, individual problems or special cases might not get due attention as required. The bureaucrats have little time to deal with individuals' special problems. So he or she is done by the general rules like others but which might not be just for them.

He finds the harmful consequences of bureaucracy as real and genuine. Weber has created a system which as a consequence would lead to the obsession of officials trying to strictly adhering to rules and procedures in the name of discipline and efficiency. This is bound to fail the officials aiming to achieve the true purpose of bureaucracy which implies that the all the clients are to be given a 'fair deal'. And 'going by the book' also causes delay and delay causes inefficiency which leads to the suffering of the people. Merton further argues that in bureaucracy 'initiative and innovation' are sacrificed for the sake of bureaucratic principles. This could present a situation in which the existing rules might not be enough to cope with the new and unforeseen situations. So, Weber's bureaucracy while aiming the develop an organisational efficiency is also developing dysfunctions on the other at the same time.

Merton's Theory of Deviance

Merton has developed the concept of deviance as a part of explaining the 'dysfunctional society'. He accounts deviance as a product of a 'differentiated society' where people are structurally placed in different positions. Theoretically, everybody is entitled to share the generalised values of society but some can not derive as much as others because of their inadequacy. They are not good enough to equal with others and enjoy a fair share of everything because they had less opportunities to develop like others. They remain at the bottom of the ladder and fail to achieve the goal of life which in the words of Merton are the fame and fortune-the so called 'American dream'.

The general concept of deviance can be defined as any behaviour in a social set up which does not conform to the given norm accepted by the large majority of people is an act of deviance. Conceptually, it is complex and prevails differently in different situations far and wide. Some people have good behaviour accepted by others as perfectly normal in a society but not accepted when they behave in different circumstances. In the pub for example, most drinkers behave alright even when they are drinking, but some are not; after a few drinks they behave noisily. They use offensive words in the middle of discerning drinkers without even feeling embarrassed as because they could not distinguish between if they are being offensive and careless; if they are white people-some may tend to joke and be abusive particularly towards non white people, some may not even tolerate their presence there. This is perfectly a deviant behaviour. They curious thing is that they are not ashamed of their disgusting behaviour and not remorseful even later. Worse of all is that they sometimes come out of the pub and start fighting friends if they objected to this type of behaviour or if nothing else they can do, pick on bystanders and abuse them.

There are petty deviants every where-from shoplifting to bringing office stationary home for personal use, stealing books from the library etc. Deviance can be both individual and group behaviour. There are many sub-cultural groups in most urban societies which verge between the racial and communal or extreme religious groups, whose activities are an affront to the society. Many try to establish their power and control in society through deviant behaviour; for them to feel strong and in control of the situation like other successful groups. They also like the rest of society take them seriously and show some respect.

According to Merton, those who don't make it in life try other ways-the negative and deviant ways. Merton learned from Emile Durkheim the concept of deviance – one of its kinds is 'anomie'. Anomie is a state of mind when people are confused about them not knowing what to do and what is happening with them in society. They are in a sort of mental estrangement. There are many causes of crime but according to Durkheim, crime takes place when the society ignores adjusting with the changes taking place but sticks to obsolete rules and regulations which only benefit a few against the interest of many. This results in the growth of the 'anomie'. Some people would feel disoriented and anxious in the absence of proper guidelines; and when they are confused and unable to guide themselves they commit crime like suicide. Durkheim constructed his theory of 'suicide' along this line.

Merton modified the concept of 'anomie' to refer to the strain put on individuals. According to him, the American society offers people the choice of either hard work, get by, do well and prosper or get no where. Many people who can not prosper by the legitimate rules of society try other ways which are illegitimate and unfair means.

Merton identifies five possible unfair means-using them at least would take them some where in their career. The first and foremost is the deviant group known as the Conformists, who follow the conventional ways to meet the requirement of success but when they fail to reach the top target in the career they give up. At least, they get somewhere but not enough to pull through. The civil servants and other white and blue colour workers fall in this group. They lose hope seeing the career ladder is too high for them to climb; so they take to deviant ways of working to rule-no more no less. They come late to work, fall sick and go out in the street for stroll or window shopping, chat with colleagues in similar situation, plan to take union action for more pay and better working conditions. The idea is to shake boredom off their head by doing less in lieu of more money and in this way penalising the authority. This is vindicative and cheating-a kind of deviant act.

The second category of deviance is known as innovators who try hard to follow the socially accepted values but fail to maintain the standard. They fall for the illegitimate means to succeed. This kind of deviance is spread amongst the working class people who can not reach the level of educational standard nor have appropriate contacts required for success in jobs and promotions. As a result, their mainstream routes to success are largely blocked. Then, they search for alternative means which are no other than innovating criminal acts to get more cash.

The third category of deviants, according to Robert K. Merton is known as the ritualists who have given up hope of success by following the normal course of career. These people come largely from the lower middle class workers. Many of them would not be accepted in other occupations as well because of their failure in their present jobs and they are rotting and stuck in their present employment unable to find way out. So they carry on hopelessly in their work as long as they can.

The fourth group is known as 'retreats' who are not anti-social but are a pathetic group bereft of conducting a socially accepted normal life or follow up an institutionalised mean of success. They are harmless to others but living a harmful life to themselves. They are 'drop outs' of society – may come from any strata such as vagrants, vagabonds, outcasts, pariahs, drug addicts, drunks, tramps and so on. They have no way to recover from this condition unless help came from some where. They are aimless and hopeless people with no future. They are defeated and resigned completely. They are deviants because they have no interest in work and have nothing to look for their life.

The last group, according to Merton is known as rebels, who have rejected the institutionalised means of reaching the top but took to criminal ways for fulfilling their career ambition. They seek power to become great by criminal notoriety; and acquire firearms form urban guerrilla groups, and become terrorists. If they succeed, some of them even would like to overthrow a legitimate government and set up dictatorships. They build up revolutionary groups to achieve power and success. In Merton's view they originate from a good class background but failed in career development and are now hungry for power, they are not from the depressed part of society.

All this show that a structured and a cultured society can generate deviance. Excessive pressure put on for success also can cause an 'anomic' condition.

Appraisal

Merton as a functionalist has enriched its perspectives by the introduction of the 'Middle Range theory'. It is one of the scientifically constructed theories amongst others in functionalism.

He was a severe critic of functionalists with special reference to Talcot Parsons and in particular of the bureaucratic theory of Max Weber. He has identified the limits of Parsons' general theory by pointing out that 'every aspect of the social system performs a positive function' which he thinks 'is not only premature, it may well be incorrect'. What Merton wanted to see was that functional analysis should proceed from the assumption that 'part of society may be functional, dysfunctional and non-functional'. Also he disagreed with Parsons' postulate that some social institutions such as 'Religion' is indispensable to society. According to Merton, communist societies do not think so – it is not indispensable. What is indispensable is the economic infrastructure.

Merton's functional alternatives have been criticised as not perfect. His suggestion to combat deviance by therapeutic and educational remedies are found to be ineffectual in many cases. Having applied these procedures to the deviants, it was found that there were still many who by passed and ignored them. For instance, in education there is a requirement of certain standard of behaviour, attendance and performance that students should deliver before they could be called educated. But that did not happen to be the case with many deviants. Some of them felt education was a mockery of them. Problems in educational methods continue unabated as before. Unless new and innovative measures are devised, behaviour and attitude problems in education would never die away.

Merton's theory of middle range would continue to hold good but that would not mean that the big macro theories would be replaced by the middle range theories. Macro theories are quite legitimate theories for larger societies; so they will continue to hold good.

Even then Merton's theory of 'Deviance' has been praised by sociologist like Hunt who wrote in his published essay in the 'American sociological review' which established merton "once and for all as a major figure in sociology". (Hunt–How does it come to be so p. 52).

Reference

1. Craig Calhoun et. al – Classical Sociological Theories, 2002, p. 386.
2. Ibid – 2002, p. 386.
3. Hint – How Does it Come to Be So: An Essay Published in the American Sociological Review, p. 52.

Part 3

Part 3

9

Max Weber (1864-1920)

Introduction, Weber's Theory of Social Action, Protestantism and Capitalism, Stratification Theory, Weber and Karl Marx, Weber's Theory of Democracy, Weber's Theory of Bureaucracy.

Introduction

Max Weber like Karl Marx, was not considered a professional sociologist because a lot of his work was outside the domain of sociology. This caused a confusion in the minds of his critics, about whether he was a historian, an economist or a sociologist. In fact, he was a sociologist of a rare breed and belonged to the tradition of the Positivist School. He was also regarded as one of the founders of sociology and ranked amongst other illustrious figures like August Comte, Emile Durkheim, Karl Marx and Talcot Parsons. Besides making a substantial contribution to sociology he also contributed equally to other fields of knowledge deserving a place in the intellectual circle. A close look at the depth of all his work will unravel clearly the range of his thinking, displaying characteristic versatility and originality in those areas. Sociology was his special area in which he was trained in the University and in no way less significant than others.

Weber was a historian as much as an economist. He has been an empiricist and often referred to as a positivist because he belonged to several academic traditions. In his words, he called himself, "We political economists", and in his 1895 inaugural lecture at Freiburg, he mentioned, 'he is one amongst the disciples of German Historical tradition'. In the 19th century

Germany, History and Economics were combined into one discipline. Born and educated in Germany, Weber became a professor of sociology there but soon after left the job and got involved in serious studies and writing. He wrote volumes about the German economic system. In his words, "The disintegration of the Roman Empire was the inevitable political consequences of a basic economic development; the gradual disappearance of commerce and the expansion of a barter economy". Max Weber-Political Writings, Cambridge 1994 page 24.

As indicated above, Weber left his mark in the field of sociology. He made major advances in combining history and sociology in order to develop a social theory. He spent years in researches in the sphere of Industrial sociology and made it abundantly clear that sociology is so relevant to the issues of the contemporary world that could not be ignored. He also prepared research designs and methodology for studies. He searched thoroughly to find out the effects of factory production on the behaviour and life styles of the workers. He explored into the psychological effects caused by the occupational hazards – such as bad environment in the work place and their impact on the workers' perception, motivation and life chance. In 1909, Weber published a special article, 'The Agrarian Sociology of Ancient Civilisation'. His idea was to discover what role did capitalism play and with what effect in the civilisations around the Mediterranean basin. His agrarian sociology posed many questions such as, for example, modern capitalism developed in the western world but why ancient capitalism died away without leaving a trace of self-ingrained sustained economic system?

Weber is a prolific writer whose work covers General philosophy, economics, comparative history, religion, law, bureaucracy, stratification and so on. In the economic analysis, he came very close to Marx's ideas, who discovered that the society was divided between the bourgeoisie and the proletariat classes, whereas Weber found it divided into four classes. Sometimes, Weber is regarded as a 'shadow of Karl Marx' because he believed that the ordinary people were being exploited by the capitalist system similar to the version explained by Karl Marx. Like Marx, Weber saw class in economic terms as stratification results from a struggle for scarce resources. According to him a person's class situation is basically his market situation. A person belonging to a particular class has only chances in life available to that particular class. A working class person has very little chance of going to a higher job, so also his children will have literally no chances of access to higher education.

Weber also wrote about the cultures and religions of India, China and south East Asia and how their social systems grew from these values. He found Hinduism as the oldest of all great religion with many thoughts and branches spread throughout India and abroad. One of its offshoots was Buddhism – a doctrine, initiated by a Hindu Prince Siddharta Gautama who was sick seeing the sufferings of life occurring from the incarnation cycle which no one could avoid unless adapted to a strict course of dedication to self discipline and meditation. This could help attaining a complete renunciation of the world. Severe austerity and penance were needed to practice, if successful, the result would be a total freedom of the mind far away from the transitory state of life. The peak of one's enlightenment would be the attainment of the ultimate truth and supreme spiritual fulfillment – the Nirvana. Siddharta attained this state of Nirvana through years of meditation, austerity and penance and brought to earth a mode of faith that made him the Buddha – a great sage of wisdom and enlightenment.

Weber was particularly interested in comparing western culture and society with the values of the Eastern cultures of India, China and Southern Asia as mentioned above. He studied the social systems of these countries which produced valuable knowledge to contribute to the general sociological thought. This had enriched the mainstream school as well even though he was branded as a social action theorist. Actually, he was a Marxist, a functionalist and an Inter – Actionist. He was all in one.

Karl Marks believed in the 'economic relations of production' as the sole cause of social division which led to social conflict and eventually to the outbreak of the Proletariat Revolution. Weber found other factors as well for a revolution such as ideas, motives, beliefs, historical issues, etc. which were behind the French Revolution of 1789. Weber did not believe in the Proletariat Revolution as such, as Marx did. He found multi-dimensional factors to cause social conflict, leading to social changes, mentioned above. To Weber, class conflagration and revolution were unnecessary. The causes of social, political and economic unrest could be resolved through negotiations and other peaceful means.

The Theory of Social Action

Perceiving society, Weber believed in the individual right to act in the growth of society. He further found that with out the society the individuals would be lost in the wilderness. So he tried to establish a link between them. In other words, social action is a sum total of the actions of the individuals. In the structural system, the individual is treated as a part of the whole in which the society dominates and creates the roles for the individuals. The individuals have no choice above those roles as fixed by the social system and structured by the society. In the social action theory structures are less significant than the individual action or actions. Weber was keenly interested in the motives, intentions and purposes of the human beings which cause the growth of issues and factors that change ideology of the society and the way it is run. Motives are behind many developments in society. Individuals as social actors, interpret issues giving new meanings and motives to initiate changes; To Weber, society enriches from individual contributions. Social actors research to perceive the world in their own way.

Weber is the first sociologist to advocate a social action approach. He tried to combine the social action and structural form in to an integrated theory but failed to do so. So also sociologists like Paul Willis and Anthony Giddens made similar attempts but with no tangible results. Anthony Giddens' structuration thory has curved out a niche in this respect no doubt.

Weber disagreed with Emile Durkheim's view that the society is the master of the individuals but not other way round. To discover what meanings the individuals can bring to their social world, Weber used the method of 'Verstehen' which means 'empathetic understanding', in other words, understanding the world from the actors' points of view. All actors will have different meanings according to their own perceptions which will be put together to build a better society. Using Verstehen method, Weber has identified four different types of social action; characteristically, they are all pure and ideal types.

The first one is the 'instrumental rational action': In this type, the actor assesses both the goal and the means by which the goal can be achieved. For example, if one has a goal to achieve distinction in athletics in International competition, he or she has to follow a strict regime of professional training including adequate rest, relaxation and dieting. This could give maximum physical fitness essential for the goal. So, not only the goal but also the means to achieve that goal are important. With out the means, goal can not be achieved. This is called 'instrumental rational action'. Nevertheless, it would still be an 'instrumental rational actions' if after considering the painful training regime to go through, one decides not to pursue and gives up the scheme, thinking that it would not be worth the sacrifice to make for, for missing all the mundane pleasures and enjoyment in life.

The second type is the 'value-related rational action': What value would be gained by sacrificing a specific purpose. This action is rational based on the equation between the goal and the satisfaction of the sacrifice being made for. For example, non-violence strategy adopted in the Indian Independence Movement to achieve the goal was successful, so the strategy was justified. The sacrifice made such as penance, fasting, fortune and imprisonment undertaken were well worth the sacrifice made. According to Weber, if the action proves to be too difficult to undertake and as a result given up, this could be justified as an 'instrumental rational action' too.

The third action is the traditional action: The traditional action is something that is observed like decorating the house during Christmas or to lit the house in Diwali festival. Its value is immense which builds up a harmonious atmosphere around. The value of traditional action moves up and down along with the change of life styles as well as other changes in society. Nevertheless, Max Weber still believed that this kind of action at least brings some happiness in the life of people even though it may be for a short period. Some traditional actions never die away as they continue to hold good for society.

Lastly, the 'affective action' is some thing done in the form of venting anger or rage to release frustration or emotion which may be a temporary relief but not a solution to dealing with the problem. For example, in a family row if the husband or the wife smashes up some utensils or glasses or overturns dinner plates making a mayhem and frightening children what good that could be. This sort of action can relieve emotions for the time being no doubt, but the after effects would become very painful and regrettable to everybody in the house. Weber believed that this kind of action is less affective and important in to day's society. They are the direct results of the unusual emotional outbursts but the consequence of the outrage would not be worth the deed.

In his book, 'Economy and society' Weber wrote that sociology is a science which is concerned with social action and its course and consequences. The social action is something to which an individual defines and gives meaning to his or her actions and also attaches a meaning on account of behaviour of others. They simply do not react to stimuli, they act. The individual is conscious of the fact that his/her action is something that only concerns the society; nothing else. To Weber, motives of the individuals are important as well which generate forces of action.

Weber believed that explanations of human action should be adequately grasped on the level of meaning. He discovered that ascetic nature of the Calvinists helped them accumulate wealth through motives of morality, parsimony and strict religious order. Inadvertently, these strict moral codes gave rise to capitalism. Weber asked the question why capitalism developed in the west and no where else even when other countries like the Ottoman Empire, China and India possessed great deal of wealth and power. Weber argued that these and other countries which made wealth but did not save enough to reinvest for the purpose of more. They spent their wealth in splendour and luxuries whereas the Calvinist Protestants saved and practised frugality. Their austerity and accumulation habit led to the growth of capitalism.

In his book, 'the Protestant Ethic and th spirit of capitalism' Weber argued that religious zeal was at the core of the growth of capitalism. Further, the Calvinists also believed that by being parsimonious they were able to herald social changes and bring a new era in which to thrive and prosper. The Protestants puritans believed luxury to be an evil; so their motive was to accumulate and not squander. Besides, this way of life would bring them salvation. This would also bring their journey closer to heaven. Protestant Calvinists also believed in the theory of predestination which allows certain people to reach heaven in the after life. But who are these certain people? They decided that surely those who succeeded in life such as in their vocation or in their industrial pursuits would be the 'elect' ones destined for heaven. This gave them a tremendous enthusiasm for effort to go to heaven; so they gave up luxury and lived poorly, investing all their savings into wealth in order to earn more. Those who did not save they became associated with 'mundane passions'. We will see the criticisms of this theory in the conclusion.

The Protestant Ethic which became the doctrine of John Calvin after the Reformation movement of the 15th and 16th centuries was ascetic, encouraging abstinence from life's pleasures and following strict discipline. This group of Protestants detested laziness, luxury and sexual pleasures as moral degradation. Marriage was only meant for procreation of children and nothing else. Weber argued that religious factor could cause social change unlike Marx who advocated the economic system shaped ideas.

Max Weber and His Theory of Stratification

Weber is also well known for his stratification theory in which he made a distinction between the economic class and the social class. According to Haralambos, "The work of the German sociologist, Max Weber represents one of the most important developments in stratification theory since Marx". Sociology – Themes and perspectives 4th edn p. 36. Weber's views on stratification grew from human inequalities caused by both ethnic and or biological and social circumstances in which the human beings were rooted and branched in to the division of society.

The ethnic and biological differences are very strong causes of social inequalities. For example, racial discrimination of black people in the united States in jobs, housing, education and social gatherings and the caste system in India which segregate people into different vocations restricting their mobility upwards and else where combined with other factors like the qualities of mind and soul or human abilities, bodily strength and health – all these have generated inequalities in society. These have accumulated and formed barriers over centuries; that is why they are so difficult to eradicate. People with fair skin colour and higher status have enjoyed more opportunities and privileges than groups without, for example, white people have enjoyed more power and control over other groups than dark skinned and black people who had less power and control in society.

Discrimination based on colour, caste and classes had been in practice throughout centuries. The practice got worse with the industrial revolution when exploitation of workers in an industrial economy specially in a capitalist society started in full flair. A diversified society, according to Weber, splits into classes. Stratification process has grown in different forms in different periods of history – during the process of social evolution. To him, inequalities also occur economically when people suffer from lack of skills, training, proper educational background and poverty, lack of opportunities, motivation and interests. They accept their condition as a fact of life and assume that it could never be altered. In modern days, diversification of work system has further stratified society into new groups like the blue collar workers, white collar workers, skilled and unskilled workers, affluent workers and so on. Side by side, also exists the traditional division of society in the form of royalties, upper classes, aristocrats, such as the bourgeoisie, bureaucrats besides, the growing number of retired pensioners and the under class.

Max Weber, Karl Marx and Stratification

Marx and Weber perceived social classes in economic terms. But the difference is that Marx saw classes as a twin model – the exploited and powerless working class – known as the 'proletariat' on the one hand, and the ruling class such as the Bourgeoisie and the capitalist on the other; they are bound up in a relations of productions; so a field of conflict is created there with out any chance of escape. In Marx's words, this would inevitably inaugurate a Proletariat Revolution which would break down the power base of the bourgeoisie and the capitalists. Weber did not view classes in that context and could not agree with Marx that revolution would be inevitable.

To Weber social classes are four fold, namely, the propertied upper class, propertyless white collar workers, the petty bourgeoisie and the manual working class as a four part stratification in which there is no room for a revolution. Whereas, Marx found that polarisation between these two dominant groups was inevitable which would lead to a political revolution but Weber found no evidence to support this view that polarisation would lead to a conflict. Rather the middle class would be further diversified to support the expanding bureaucratic system. This would be manned by the skilled and competent workers. They would rather negotiate for better emolument and service conditions than going out for a revolution. Weber also disagreed with Marx that political power necessarily derives from the economic power.

According to Weber power is the ability to get one's way; in other words, one actor with in the social relationshi will be in a position to carry out his will despite resistance. His rational legal authority thus becomes more powerful and dominant which supersedes others in a bid to power.

In Weber's terminology, a person's class situations is essentially his market value. People in similar class situation also have similar employment and economic opportunities which lead to higher statuses. Weber disagreed with Marx's conflict theory as mentioned above which is linked to a proletariat Revolution. Weber could not see how different classes polarise into a two-pronged attack. He criticised Marx for exaggerating the importance of class conflict which will gradually fizzle out under pressure from the society. Besides, the four class system as devised by Weber, two additional dimensions of stratification are also found – political party exercising power and social status which occurs from the professional background.

Max Weber's Concept of Democracy

Weber's concept of democracy is unique which also corresponds to his theory of bureaucracy. He believed that direct democracy would not work in a macro society with large population. Moreover, it would require a lot of expertise to run large-scale societies which the direct or participatory system would not be able to cope with. With racial and religious diversity in a society, it would even be more difficult to run such a system. In ancient Greece, direct democracy worked well because the country had a small size of population or similar sort of country where people would be able to take decisions in small groups on the spot similar to the Swiss Cantons which took decisions in meetings publicly in the Cantons without going into the lengthy process of vote counting.

Direct democracy is also known as participatory democracy. Some large countries nevertheless, practice a limited amount of direct democracy in the form of referendum, for example, in the United states and Western Europe referendum is held to assess public opinion on particular issues of national importance which otherwise could not have been taken on party lines. Direct democracy has been used recently in the European Union where 'referendum' method as one of the means of direct democracy was tried to ratify the E.U. constitution. The result shocked the members of the Union when the majority voted against the ratification (non). This has amazed the ruling power in France and Belgium who had assumed the result would be positive.

Weber also believed that democracy would work well with in a multiparty system, because people would have a choice who they would vote for and who they would not. In this system, each party would present its programme to choose from but this would be virtually impossible in a direct or participatory government. Even though democracy is a rule by the people at large, but in actual fact, it becomes a rule by the elite – when power is assumed and run by a few. The perception is that a few knowledgeable persons are competent enough to making good decisions instead of involving the millions in to the process, which presumably would end up in a political chaos.

While Marxists believe that socialism would lead to a participatory democracy; Weber was doubtful, if direct or participatory democracy would ever work in a socialist country. In his view, the multi-party representative democratic system could work in large scale industrial societies if each political party besides representing their party interest would also represent the interest of the nation. To him, representative democratic system could also work for a multi-racial and multi-cultural communities comprising different classes a. d cultural backgrounds, provided that the bureaucratic interference is kept down to the minimum.

Weber believed in a plural democratic system in which he had a proponent, Robert Dahl who was also in favour of a multi party system provided that the system would be able to represent the interests of all sections of people. But his findings showed that possibility was a rarity because one party always come being too powerful and in control of everything and smaller or weaker parties remain insignificant. However, Robert Dahl believed that legitimate parties willing to join in the government should submit their ideas of how to run a good government. All ideas and proposals of different parties should be submitted for consideration. After a thorough examination of all the proposals, a selection of the most credible proposals would be accepted. In this process, the unsuccessful proposals would be rejected and successful ones given a chance that their parties are allowed to form a government. It is pertinent to bear in mind that those who gain power are to share power rather than one group taking control and dominating over others. This is the essence of the multi-party system. According to Weber, multi-party representative democratic system is the best way to represent a range of interests.

But there is tendency that in a pluralist democratic set up, one party or group becomes too ambitious to carry their agenda and passed over others ignoring them. Weber did not believe that one party can be truly democratic. As it happens, powerful groups push ahead their issues for consideration than those who could not lobby hard to get their matters moved forward. If one party virtually becomes powerful and executes its policies unilaterally by virtue of majority, the consequence would be disastrous for democracy. The minority parties would eventually, lose their interest in politics. Weber argues that, in order for the democratic systems to be successful in a meaningful way, the parties joining the government must represent different interests and have different outlooks. Secondly, there must be vibrant political leaders who would be able to cut down bureaucratic bungling. Weber values multi-party democracy because it generates quality of leadership.

Weber argued that unless there is a strong leader who could lead the country successfully, the government would be virtually a prisoner under a strong bureaucratic control. It is also the case that decisions are imposed upon those who disagree with them. They had no choice but to accept these unpleasant decisions even though these stood against their interests; for example, in a capitalist system, most decisions are made to serve the interests of the investors who are the capitalists. There are many issues which never get a chance of being talked to in the meeting in a one party system because these are seen not as worth as others. For example, matters like the child abuse, violence on women, sexual harassment of women at work place etc. are seen not as important as national or public matters but as local issues – not considered for public discussion and left alone.

Bureaucracy is one of Weber's widely accepted and gossiped aspects of sociology. To him, bureaucracy is ingrained in his theory of administration. Bureaucracy has spread from the manufacturing industries to all public institutions, to include a few, such as the civil service, the education service, the defence, the police services and so on. Weber's model is a functionalist one which aims to develop the system of administration. Talcot Parsons was impressed by Weber's perception of public administration to the extent that he adapted it to his mechanism of organising the Social system.

Bureaucracy was first conceived as an important area of public administration during the period of agricultural revolution in Europe. This system required management and maintenance of products of agriculture, such as to keep accounts of profit and loss of the business, supervision of workers including payment of emoluments and regulating service conditions etc. The structure grew very large when the industrial revolution expanded industries up and down the country producing massive volumes of work both in terms of products, sale, exports, imports and staff management. An office was therefore necessary for every industry to keep records of statistics, finance, ledgers, staff attendance registers, wage and salary payments in tact etc. Division of labour further specialised the system of bureaucracy. Max Weber saw bureaucracy as the dominant form of organisation in industrial society.

In modern industry, the complex work system is needed to be organised structurally in order to maintain efficiency. There is a need for a hierarchy of officials and a system of rules to maintain the structure. Weber saw an emerging bureaucracy as a characteristic feature of the modern industrial society. To him, bureaucracy is also a rational action in an institutional form.

Bureaucratic organisations are becoming huge and complex in post world war period as new institutions are being set up every now and then in order to cope with the development of industries vis-a-vis needs of life in the changing society. Their number is numerous and their functions are multifarious.

According to Weber, modern bureaucracy is a highly effective method of organising the staff, because there is a clear-cut hierarchy of authority from bottom to the top with a chain of command making coordinated decisions possible. Every member of staff is allocated to a task as official duties and each higher officer controls and supervises the work of every one below him or her in the hierarchy. In this way, there grows a hierarchy in the structural frame in which everyone is accountable for their role, functions and power to their nearest superiors. The staff rise from the bottom to the top based on their skills, education, efficiency and seniority except the top echelon who are recruited direct to the executive ranks through the competitive examinations. Weber argues that modern organisations should aim to have an 'ideal type' of bureaucracy because of its effectiveness.

In Weber's view 'rational legal authority', the cornerstone of the bureaucratic system emerged only after the Second World War. Then, the legal rules have been formulated to protect the power and positions of both the ruler and the ruled. The objectives were simple and clear-to have an effective and efficient administrative structure above to deliver goal directed services. Weber says that this is an organisation designed rationally to coordinate the work of many individuals. There is always a reward for imaginative work and solving difficult issues. There is also reward as promotion to high profile departments such as department for Exchequer, Home office and Foreign office. They are governed by the carefully crafted rules and regulations to be strictly followed by all and the public are contacted by circulars and media announcement. To day, the Trade Unions object to the government against bureaucratic bungling, Red Tape and excessive repressive measures. Weber also believes that some bureaucratic officials at the top exercise more power than others but at the bottom people are kept powerless.

Weber's bureaucracy is an ideal type if it is pure or the purest form. He realised and conceded that the purest form was impossible to achieve in the true sense of the term but insisted that the aim has to be there and efforts should be made to reach the best. There are always doubts if the 'purest form' is achievable at all. But he argued that the ideal type was a model of a bureaucratic system that should remain so as a goal for all administration.

Bureaucracy is also based on good record keeping – if the records are not kept in order, in case of urgency, there would be delays retrieving them causing chaos and discontent amongst clients – leaving no doubt the utter incompetence of the staff. Progress of work would be effected, costing a lot to the industry. Records should be stored in file and folders classified according to the official or civil service rules. To day, with the development of technology, this system is transferred to the computer system which is run electronically and more efficiently. The service is easily accessible by the keyboard operation than the ordinary filing system.

The office is also run by fully trained staff. Again, the objective is to achieve maximum efficiency in delivering the services on target. Officials are mostly full-time and salaried. Each job has a fixed salary which enables staff to make a career with in the structural frame. Promotion is possible on the basis of quality ad quantity of work. Good attendance and punctuality is an absolute necessity. From the office no one is allowed to take resources home for personal use. One of the norms that has developed in the service is known as the 'Parkinson's Law' which shows that you are busy doing a lot of work more than others even when there is little work to do. You create a lot of work unnecessarily for your sake trying to get early promotion which may not come at all. Also, you would not be able to finish it on time. So why bother.

Peter Blau, the American sociologist has made extensive research to find how realistic was Weber's ideal type bureaucratic concept. According to him, Weber's system of ideal type could be counter-productive. It would be difficult to maintain strict vigilance over bureaucratic rules for long; some flexibility in management would be required to maintain the productive level. Work environment must be made more congenial to the staff. In small industries like mining, flexibility and informality are a good necessity to ensure the flow of production level. Without a normal atmosphere, a tension and stress are bound to occur to the detriment of the production.

Blau also found that the 'Bending the rules' has become the norm in many industries. Secondly, he found that there existed 'informal structure' which operated side by side the formal structure. This has not effected either the bureaucratic system or the production level. The dual system has been tolerated in many industries as it was found harmless. Many industries would not mind if workers' unions were formed. Weber himself was aware of the bureaucratic system having some disadvantages. First of all, it limits individual freedom. Second, it prevents spontaneity, creativity and individual initiative in the performance of the functions. There is a serious lack of work spirit which is sacrificed for the sake of efficiency; also relationship amongst staff is too formal and procedural rather than informal, relaxed and less procedural. Weber was also worried that bureaucrats might become accountable to no one but bureaucrats.

Weber himself deplored, "It is horrible to think that the world would one day be filled with little cogs, little men clinging to little jobs and striving towards the bigger one". Despite the forebodings, Weber still believed that bureaucracy was essential to the operation of large scale industrial societies.

Arguing within the functionalist framework, Robert K Merton points out several dysfunctions of the bureaucratic system which can easily lead to inefficiency and beat the main purpose of the system. For example,

In the event of an emergency or an urgent situation, bureaucracy can malfunction because strict adherence to rules and procedures would prevent officials taking urgent actions.

Secondly, ritualistic methods may delay the targets being achieved. The system also develops communication problem between the office and the public which could jeopardise the goodwill and reputation of the institution, effecting the prospect of development. Excessive discipline and efficiency drive kill personal initiative and obsess the staff. Bureaucracy also encourages a particular type of personality to develop amongst officials which can undermine the goals of the organisation.

A Critique of Max Weber

Weber has been criticised for not taking a firm stand on either the structural or the individual pattern of society, nor has he succeeded in establishing a unified social theory based on the amalgamation of both. His wavering between the two has created confusion which never disappeared. He was at once a Marxist and an individualist relying on structural and action strategies – all at the same time. His aim to blend the self with the structure in order to combine a working relationship was not achieved. His oscillation between the two remained distinct all the time. His individualism is not free from social control either, so they are dependent on the society's common programme which of course is based on the active support and participation of the individuals. The society can develop and improve only with contributions from the individuals. They are thus inter-dependent as they are in the representative and participatory democracy. The individuals take active part in promoting the democratic system. Weber's action theory actually converges into his pluralistic perspective of democracy.

Secondly, his emphasis on austerity of the Calvinists' life, a fundamental puritan sect of Protestant religion was no different from those of the Catholics who also followed strict rules in life including practising penance and frugality. So capitalism was not developed by a deliberate policy of the Calvinists as presumed by Weber but possibly grew as a by product of their adherence to God's will to lead the life of austerity. Their accumulated wealth was reinvested rather than consumed in luxury which according to Weber was also at the root of the growth Capitalism. That is also true to many other religious faiths like Hinduism and Buddhism but capitalism did not develop there; possibly reinvestment for more capital did not take place there. The possibility is that between their religious beliefs there could be some thing else more important than just creating wealth which thus could be either seeking for power or to popularise Calvinism over other Christian varieties.

Weber argued why capitalism which had developed in some Western countries had not also emerged in the East. He argued that some teachings of Hinduism and Buddhism actively discouraged the development of capitalism but in the West some puritan beliefs and Calvinist doctrines otherwise portrayed the necessity of developing capitalism for the sake of god. Salvation in eternal life was the hope behind the dedicated belief. In replying to Weber's claim of Calvinism being the precursor of capitalism, Eisenstadt, argued that the claim could not be justified because first upsurge capitalism occurred in catholic Europe – Italy, Belgium and Germany even before the Protestant Reformation.

Historian Tawney also disagreed with Weber's interpretation of Calvinism as the progenitor of capitalism. According to him, capitalism had already emerged before the 17th century when Join Calvin preached his gospel. The society had already changed due to technology introduced in many countries. The capitalist class had already come into being when some protestant bourgeoisie traders were converted to Calvin's doctrine and gave it a colour. It is also confusing to accept when Weber stressed that frugality and austerity was the key to growth of capitalism; if we look at the capitalist society we find that capitalists are big consumers too. Those who earn money they can still save a lot after living in luxury and spending lavishly. May be some puritans took life too seriously and did not want to miss the chance of going to heave. Therefore, all his arguments can not be fully defended. Some facts appear to be historically anachronistic.

Thirdly, Weber was also criticised for excessively using the 'Verstehen' method without giving sufficient evidence to justify the action and at the same time putting greater emphasis on actors' motives as indicators of social development than other factors such as social forces which have constraining effects on human behaviour. Fourthly, he was also criticised for his theory of bureaucratic system which has lost its dominance in the modern world. To day, bureaucratic organisations are flexible in the competitive world.

Questions

1. Explain briefly the concept of modern bureaucracy.
2. What are the main features of Bureaucracy as developed by Weber.
3. Critically estimate the stratification theory of Max Weber.
4. Make an assessment of Weber's theory of Religion with special reference to "The Protestant Ethic and the spirit of Capitalism".
5. Explain Weber's Concept of 'Democracy'.

References

Albrow, Martin. Bureaucracy, 1970. (Pall Mall Press).
Blau, P.M. and Meyer, M.V. Bureaucracy in Modern Society, 1971.
Dahl, Robert. Who Governs 1961.
Weber, Max The Protestant Ethics and the Spirit of Capitalism 1958.
Max Weber's Political Writings, Cambridge, 1994, page 24.

10

Symbolic Interaction Theory

Introduction, Character, Erving Goffman, George Mead, Herbert Blumer, Criticism of Blumer's Methodology.

Introduction

The symbolic interaction theory is about communication and interaction of people expressed either verbally or by body language. The symbolic interaction sociology is formed from many diverse influences left by people like John Millar, Adam Smith, Charles Darwin, and pragmatist philosopher, John Dewey and others. The main concern with the symbolic interaction is not its intrinsic 'meaning', but meanings perceived by people in day to day communications which vary from one person to another. People look at things from various angles of vision and convey them to people portraying meanings different from the situations they have encountered. They form meanings and particular attitudes about them; they make sense on the pattern of behaviour and shape up meanings to follow in course of time.

All these put together constitute the symbolic meaning of certain objects, things and even of human beings. For example, people's impression of some body is formed once one is seen and soon can be read from the facial expression. We approve or disapprove of these expressions; also of the manner of behaviour, from which source to form an image or meaning of the person's act. Also, people establish relationships based on negotiated meanings; for example, a newly married couple, learn how to behave, act and react from each other's norms of behaviour, attitudes, standards and values they had already developed through out their life prior to marriage; they learn and relearn how to lead life forward rather than dictated by the elders or the society.

Thus, symbolic interaction is a process of developing one's conception and perception of objects, issues, situation and other matters and with their meanings to shape their environment in the way they like. It is an active, creative and conscious characteristics of the individuals. The concept is fundamentally based on the meanings people make of things around them and express through their language. Mead argues that language allows us to see ourselves more clearly and consciously and to form images of ourselves as well as of others, objects and environment in the society. Mead argued that once we have formed an image of something say an elephant we need not to see the elephant again what it is was like because the image of the elephant was in our mind.

Erving Goffman has described in his, 'The presentation of self in Everyday Life', the techniques we use in order to influence people how they would see us. This is 'impression management'. We create our personality in order for others to appreciate and to socially accept us. Goffman calls it 'continuous performances' like the actors, teachers, professional doctors or hard working students. Our body language, speech, facial expression – all are part of the impression of ourselves, we are constantly trying to make.

The idea of performance is very important to Goffman's work. In his view first impression is the best impression. For example, a teacher plays tough as a starter to give the best impression to the pupils about what is to follow, so that they would know who is the boss. It would be hard for the teacher if he or she had not created a tough professional impression before the beginning of teaching. If the kids had formed a different idea about the teacher that they could play about and chat in lesson which would be ignored by the teacher then you had a trouble being made.

This idea is given a wholesome meaning by George Mead (1893 to 1931), an American interaction theorist who taught philosophy and psychology at the University of Chicago during 1893 and 1931. According to Charles Morris, "Philosophically, Mead was a pragmatist; scientifically, he was a social psychologist". He belonged to the generation of old traditionalists like Aristotle, Decartes, Leibniz, Russel, Whitehead, John Dewey and others. Most of them were either philosophers or scientists or both. He was a prolific lecturer and his lectures were attended by students even coming from other fields. He delivered lectures without written notes. Even though he was not a prolific writer still he wrote over eighty articles in his life time. Most of his work was about immigrants, women's suffrage, labour issues, educational and democratic matters. When he died, his students gathered all his lecture notes and published a book named, 'Mind, Self and society' in 1934. This book is the chief source of Mead's sociological theory. Because of his lifelong association with the University and the contribution he made to it, the university is known as the Chicago school of 'symbolic Interaction'.

Mead has explained what is symbolic interaction by giving an analogy of the difference of behaviour between a man and an animal. If you kick a dog what will it do to you?; there could be some possible answers. It will bark at you but if the dog is a ferocious one it might bite you as a quick response, or if it is a pet one it might run away for fear of life. But if you hurt or kick a student how would he react to you?; it is difficult to predict. He might be crying depending on his age, or be apologetic thinking it is his fault or if he is a delinquent student he might try to hit back or ask the teacher to apologise at least to compensate for the loss of his social respect or other reprisals might take place including involving the parents. Now what is the difference between an animal's reaction and that of the student?

For Mead, how the student would react would depend on his ability to put himself in place of others and to see himself from the point of view of others. This he calls 'role taking' and thus introduces the concept of self. For mead, the self is viewed as having two elements such as 'I' and 'Me'. This is his classic example of 'Symbolic interaction' in which 'I' is constrained by 'Me'. When something happens to somebody, the self in the form of 'I' takes immediate charge; for example, in a class room lecture, if a student finds it dreary, he might off to go out for a breath of fresh air, or for a cup of tea; this is his 'I' which took the decision. But on second thought, he changed his mind thinking it might be considered an unsocial act or that he might be considered failing to concentrate on the lecture whilst others were paying attention. Mead argued that this is his 'Me' which has taken charge of and restrained his 'I'.

Mead has understood the crucial importance of language which is a key to creative social interaction because language is a major vehicle of social communication. Even though there are thousands of words, terms, phrases etc invented through the ages in so many languages in order to convey our meanings to the society, still the scientists, poets, philosophers and intellectuals are working at their maximum level to create new words and linguistic forms. The purpose is to provide 'linguistic symbolism', also to discover the meaning of the language to improve interaction process through meaningful communication.

Herbert Blumer, a professor of the Chicago school has first used the term 'symbolic Interaction' in his chapter, he wrote for the journal 'Man and society'. In the chapter, Blumer has identified the cornerstone of the symbolic interaction perspective as a 'common set of symbols and understanding possessed by people in a group' (Herbert Blumer's article in the Man and Society, 1937, p. 159) Symbolic interaction theorists assume that the common set of symbols and understandings can make a child's social environment 'symbolic'. Symbolic interaction perspective essentially is a sociological perspective which focuses on the individual 'with a self' and interaction between internal thoughts and emotions of the person and his or her social behaviour. In the words of Anthony Giddens, "Individuals are viewed as active constructors of their own conduct who interpret, evaluate, define and map out their own action rather than as passive beings who are impinged upon by outside forces" (Anthony Giddens-Central problems in social theory. 1979. p. 50).

Symbolic Interaction is a micro sociology based upon the interaction between members of society. Unlike functionalism and Marxism which are best known as consensus or macro sociology and are run by the society's rules and regulations, whereas, the symbolic interaction is a product of the individuals' wishes and aspirations which have any chances to shape their destiny through the consensus perspectives. The symbolic interaction allows individuals to act independently without hindrance to shape the society's destiny in their own choice. As the society is consicously and actively shaped by the actions of the members it is also regarded as the social action theory. Symbolic interaction is not strictly a structural form like Marxism and functionalism but often conform to the general structural pattern.

Herbert Blumer, was one of professor Mead's students who upheld his influence. The core idea of 'symbolic' is the language which we use to communicate with others on a day to day basis interactively and exchanging meanings. 'Symbolic' means images of things as represented by language. Herbert Blumer has indicated some important ways how sociologists should study society.

To this he disagreed with Emile Durkheim's concept of 'suicide' in which Durkheim had shown certain social features to be responsible for the suicide rates such as the degree of integration or regulation occurred at the time of the suicide taking place.

According to Blumer, individual consciousness was deliberately ignored in such cases. Blumer was also sceptical about the variable aspect of the suicide rates which he thought was the creation of sociologists who could use the variations according to what they wished to prove. Blumer has also raised questions about the methodological approaches of the sociologists. So he has developed a methodology of his own for the study of social interaction. The first step in a methodological process is for researchers to be a part of the interaction process, in which to observe and interpret the actions of others and to try the world through their eyes. This is necessary, according to Blumer, 'having a feeling inside the experience of the actor'. Blumer argued that the research process must be as systematic, rigorous and objective as possible.

Criticism of Blumer's Methodology

Symbolic interaction according to Mead, springs from the concern of 'language and meaning'. Mead claims that language allows us to become self conscious of ourselves. It also means that we look at ourselves from the meaning people have assigned to us. In the eyes of people we may be considered as good people because we have behaved ourselves conforming to the norms and values of society. So, that carries a lot of value in public estimation of ourselves. Nevertheless, in interaction perspectives, self awareness, self act and self evaluation are more important than public estimation. Symbolic interaction tends to ignore the influence of social structures. Of course, Blumer has produced a plausible case for variable analysis but the economic factor in the social class situation which affects behaviour could not be ignored.

Secondly, Despite the perspective of interaction between self and society, it does not adequately deal with macro issues of power and structure. It is true that interaction provides great insights into issues of power and control at the group level or small organisation but the question remains how the interaction process can be extended to the macro level. Third, there is some criticism about 'freedom to interact" as a mode of enriching social communication, self and societal achievement; sometimes that process ends up in the democratic decision making which can ignore minority views undermining the spirit of the individuals. Democracy is generally considered as a 'cult of incompetence'.

Reference

1. Charles Morris' Introduction to Mead's 'Mind, Self and Society' 1934 p. ix.
2. Herbert Blumer. (Man and Society, 1937, p. 159).
3. Anthony Giddens–Central Problems in Social Theory, 1979, p. 50.

11 Phenomenology

Introduction, Edmund Husserl, Cicourel and Phenomenological Methods, Alfred Schutz, Dorothy Smith – Phenomenology and Women's Role, Verstehen and Typification.

Introduction

Phenomenological sociology is an offshoot of the phenomenological philosophy which had its lineage in the general European philosophical tradition dominantly influenced by the German thinker Edmund Husserl (1859-1938).

Phenomena is a Greek word which means 'appearance'; in other words what it looks like what you see near you. The definition of phenomenology as endorsed by the Encyclopedia of sociology states, "phenomenology is a method of philosophy that begins with the individual and his own conscious experience than any assumptions, prejudices and philosophical dogmas". This illustrates the fact that phenomenology is concerned with its immediate phenomena or environment related to the individual's understanding of the reality in the world than any thing that lies outside its periphery.

Social Phenomenology is concerned with interactions amongst process of human actions and their aims to construct situations. Phenomenology explains 'reflexivity' as an interactive consequence of all human projects. It projects human consciousness as 'intentional' which constitutes thinking, perceiving, feeling, remembering, imagining and anticipating. The objects of these intentional acts are the sources of all realities of common sense.

Edmund Husserl was a German mathematician who realised that objective science was inadequate to locate the reality in the human consciousness. He also realised that there has to be some understanding relating to individual consciousness of the social life. At that time German political situation was not conducive to sociological thinking and fearing a backlash from the German right wing government, Alfred Schutz, a student of Edmund husserl and other sociologists emigrated to the U.S.A., where they transmitted their ideas to the American academic circles. There, Phenomenology gradually built up as a branch of the Interpretive Perspectives. It also became instrumental in forging relationships with the Ethnomethodology which in its turn tried to integrate Parsonian social order in to the domain of phenomenology. Your social world concerns you; it matters the fact that you construct one for yourself by the method of enquiry and one for the society. So, phenomenology expects people and sociologists to define their social world and situations from a personal point of view.

Edmund Husserl stresses that making sense of everything that we come across every day is a job of a sociologist; his/her idea is to experience everything being a part of it through his or her senses; without being there you would not gather knowledge. Our knowledge actually grows from our sensory experience we accumulate from the phenomena. Other than these Husserl maintains that every thing else is a pure speculation or fantasy which has to be avoided. According to him and also other sociologists, the individuals can come into contact with the outside world through their senses such as touch, smell, hearing, sight and taste but in order to make these sensory experiences more meaningful and realistic, the human beings have to organise their experiences in to phenomena according to their common characteristics. For example, animate/living species have common characteristics but they can be both mammals and non-mammals who can again be sub-divided into different species. According to Husserl, this sort of action can give knowledge but not necessarily the truth of the phenomena which can only way be obtained through sense experiences of the objects such as smell, touch, sight, taste as said above. This then would enable phenomenological understanding of the world from the social point of view.

According to Cicourel (1964 and 1973) Phenomenology enhances theorising of sociological problems and improving sociological research methods by using the method of "bracketing" and the "Verstechen" method. Verstehen requires an empathic effort to move into the mind of the other. Phenomenology does not use 'deductive' methodology from propositions that would require empirical tests. Phenomenology also uses Introspective method. Our society is a human construction so why not its theories and methods. They are also constructed for research purposes. Thus, phenomenology provides theoretical techniques and qualitative methods to improve human meanings of social life. Phenomenological researches prefer researching on small groups, social situations and organisations using 'face to face method' of participant observation.

Alfred Schutz

Alfred Schutz's main contribution to methodology is his concept of 'typifications' meaning classes of things that are experienced by people. Instead of individual experience only, these are shared experience of the members of society. Schutz stresses that knowledge is shared but he does not think it is fixed and unchanging. Commonsense knowledge is constantly modified in the course of human interaction. Accumulated knowledge shared by all enables people to understand each other at least partly. This way one can be reassured that there is an ordered pattern of norms in the society but it may or may not be lasting for long. Human beings experience the world in terms of typifications.

Phenomenology also expects people to ask questions about the prevailing notions, values and rationale of a social system and not to accept social issues and matters taken for granted. This perspective takes a critical look at the social order and those challenges which are culturally learned ideas. It raises questions about women's role in the family and in the world. One component of phenomenology is the feminist perspective highlighted by the American sociologist Dorothy Smith. Her extensive research on the women's issues has enriched phenomenological perspective of making feminism. Women's experience combined with materialistic methods of Marx and Engles are integral parts of feminism. The women's issues have raised the question such as, "Are women bound to be at home as a matter of innate 'need' while men's needs are in the public sphere of wage work?. What is the women's role besides rearing up children? More child minding functions like nursing, nurturing and training them to become social being or have they some role to play in the society?

Contemporary women challenge the age old practice taken for granted that their role is to rear up children only and not able to take full part in public life like men. Why? The new generation of women want to alternate their position with men. They have alternative ideas about female identity and other realities of women. Phenomenology indicates that subdued position of many culturally and socially deprived people-people racially victimised, ethnic and religious minorities, neglected groups like lesbians and gays can benefit from the perspective of phenomenology which provide answers to many of their issues. With phenomenological sociology they could be able to challenge their stereotyped position and put forth alternative realities.

Edmund Husserl has incorporated Max Weber's concept of Verstehen and stresses that an individual should define personal situations in every day life.

Verstehen and Typification

According to Weber, understanding motives of people why they are acting and behaving in a particular manner can be done by 'Verstehen' method meaning you imagine yourself in the position of the person you are seeking to explain like the empathic way: be in the shoes of the other person you are seeking to feel his/her feeling and experience.

Typification

Alfred Schutz undertook the task left by his teacher Edmund Husserl to develop further the concept of 'reality'. Reality according to Husserl, occurs when individuals gather experiences about some social issues – favourably with others' experiences. Together, that could become a shared definition of knowledge and reality. This may be developed to coordinate with the common culture.

Also that social actors have to categories their experience of situations and to interpret the work of others in order to find relevance to theirs. Typification happens when particular meanings are produced by actors, coordinated with contributions from others so as to build a consensus called typification. In other words, it is a conceptual category of the group which describes a phenomena. So according to Schutz, the ways the human beings classify objects in the world is not an individual process but rather a collective process. The categories of objects thus used are not personal but are shared with others as indicated above. Typification builds up a stock of 'commonsense knowledge'. Different typifications are developed in different cultures because there is no guarantee that any two individuals or cultures will perceive the world in the same way. So there is a possibility that differences may occur in the typifications caused by different experiences. Nevertheless, Schutz insists that communications and conciliation must continue with individuals and different cultures to share our values and perceptions so that we share our typification with others and share understanding. Schutz emphasises the importance of the qualitative method of enquiry for work rather then the quantitative method. Giddens was influenced by Schutz's work. He has praised Schutz's work saying that his work has "vast bulk of the stock of knowledge"—to use Schutz's phrase".

Phenomenological thought has inspired the construction of theories of post Modernism, post structuralism, neo-functionalism and Reflexivity (Ritzer 1996). Phenomenology also has inspired the premise of language being socially constituted.

Phenomenology thus advances the notions that humans are creative agents in the construction of social worlds (Ainlay 1986) and all realities are the creations of phenomenology. In the absence of human consciousness producing positive social realities, what would be found in the world is the meaningless, inconsistent, disconnected, formless, chaotic and a nightmare scenario in the field of phenomenology.

Further Reading

Aho James. A The Things of the World: A Social Phenomenology 1998 Westport.

Peter Berger L. Invitation to Sociology 1963 A Humanistic Perspective Anchor New York.

Edmund Husserl General Introduction to Pure Phenomenology, 1931, New York, Humanities Press.

Thomas Luckman (ed) Phenomenology and Sociology: Selected Readings, 1978ik, New York, Penguin.

Part 5

12
Conflict Theory

Introduction, Source of the Conflict Theory, Ideology, Marxism, Contradictions, Rolf Dahrendorf, Criticism of the Conflict Theory.

Introduction

In sociology, Conflict theory is about conflicts in society; sometimes, there are intractable problems which can not be easily resolved but other times there are agreeable conflicts which can be resolved but need more time to reach a solution. Conflicts which drag on for a long time can be very disturbing to peace which could even break into open hostilities. The conflict theories are a major alternative to the functionalist approaches which analyse general structure and functions of a society. In a consensus situation such as functionalism, shared norms and values are essential to the survival of a system which seeks a stable and peaceful society. And only a peaceful and stable society is able to undergo changes when demand arises.

In contrast, the conflict theory emphasises the dominance of some groups over others and social order is based upon persuasion and control. Social change can not take place under dissipation and suppression. Despite the repressive situation, attitude to the ruling authority is hardened to break into formidable opposition; if that is not possible, then some form of discreet movement continues to grow. Student movement in the Tiananmen Square in china for bringing democracy broke into chaos and the authority suppressed it in 1989; even though it was a sporadic movement, it suddenly broke out against the oppressed communist regime. But the movement just got crushed by the mighty Chinese military machine, nevertheless, the movement had sent a shock wave to the authority that time has come for a change which should not be ignored.

Sources of the Conflict

There are basic conflicts of interests in societal level primarily associated with wealth, power, status and control. Conflict also arises from accepting or rejecting particular norms, values and ideas developed by political parties, social, religious and cultural groups who try to impose their particular brand of norms and values on others in order to gain control of the society.

Whereas, in the consensus perspectives regardless of who the groups are, an understanding is achieved through mutual agreement amongst them about what social programme, aims and objectives should be undertaken. Concern about some groups being too powerful and influential personalities also who try to dominate over smaller and weaker groups cause the real problems. What action can be taken to combat those able to exploit? May be that it is a mild form of exploitation, not too extortionate, yet, some form of action or deterrent becomes absolutely necessary.

In the West, with liberal democratic form of governments, the societies are being divided between the rich and the poor and the gulf between them is ever so widening converging in to two major classes – the ruling and the subject class. The Ruling class owns 'the means of production' and the profit earned from the industrial production is also owned by them. The subject class by producing goods earn wages which keep them more or less happy. Profit produced by them goes to the owners in which they have no share. So conflict is rooted in there which some times grow to the extent of open rebellion, but to mature it to that extent takes a long time.

Unfortunately, many of the workers are not even aware of that they are being exploited; so they are being exploited for decades. In the western societies, with industrial expansion and monopoly capitalism resulting in the vast accumulation of profit and farther re-investment, side by side the growth of the working force which the industry need, imagine the profit which multiplies but not shared with the workers. The growing power of the capitalist control of the economy and its capacity to patronise political groups which ensure their security and safety is one of the chief sources of conflict. As inequality grows between the capitalists and the exploited poor working class the conflict grows momentum, eventually to lead to strikes and trade union movement for better service conditions.

Ideologies

Conflict theories produce different ideologies. An ideology is a set of values and beliefs each party is identified with which prepare for a government. A party portrays their values as if they are better than others and that people must accept them. Ideology can disguise and distort truth. Ideology propounded by the rich is designed to protect their interests more than the interest of the poor. The poor in their turn aim to implement their ideology representing their interests which the rich deny. In this way, conflict grows in society.

The conflict perspectives also include social groups like ethnic groups, racial groups, gender groups, religious groups and even professional groups who try to publicise their ideologies as better than others and that their cause should be given adherence too. This causes further tension and confrontation already ripening to a solidarity and action. Tolerance is the key to avert a conflict, but when resilience runs out there grows more open hostilities. Ethnic minority groups suffer from inequality of opportunities, racial harassment and discrimination much more than others. There have been many urban riots in America, Great Britain, France, Germany and other cities of the West which are reflections of frustration and disadvantages suffered by all minority groups.

Conflict is ever present in an unequal society because of disparity in earnings and those who also suffer from unequal treatment and exploitation and discontented who are ready to go against the government. Resources are limited as well.

So people are chasing to grab the scarce resources. Those who have more already are better placed to have even more. The result is, clashes of interests intensify causing social conflict. Some times social order breaks down, when it does it is restored by the use of force; even then discontent simmers underneath only to explode later on.

The theory has grown from the Marxist thought which explains the evolution of society through the class conflict. Karl Marx has explained the conflict by his dialectics of historical materialism. The theory interpreting the historical process which shapes society is directly effected by the material conditions prevalent in the country. The economic condition itself is run by the capitalists who own all the 'means of production' resulting in a society divided between those who have a lot and those who have not got enough.

Contradictions

The conflict perspectives are an amalgam of a variety of radical ideologies – the authoritative one is the dominant Marxism. Factors which constitute Marxism are the following.

Contradiction and conflict are a basic nature of human society. There are two structures in which the society is based, namely the infrastructure and the super-structure. The infra-structure is an economic base of structure which enables other perspectives to grow from it such as education, religion, law, art, culture, political institutions etc. – these are all developed by the super structure, which is the second part.

Social classes, according to Marx are divided into two main classes – a small but wealthy ruling class and relatively poor subject class. The ruling class exercises authority and power engineered by the power of the economic sources such as 'the means of production' which include land, raw materials, machinery, tools, capital, buildings except the labour. All the means of production are owned by the capitalists who support the ruling class. Some of the members in the ruling class also come from the capitalist class. The subjects class – the proletariat is made up of workers who sell their labour in return for wages.

The relations between the capitalists and the workers remain at a permanent base of contradictions.

Marx saw fundamental contradictions which have prevailed in all class societies. In a capitalist society, contradiction in production and class system is inevitable. The production line for example, is a site of conflict between the workforce who sell their labour and skills in lieu of wages and the ownership of the company who are individual investors and capitalists – they want the workers to work hard to produce more economy The prime purpose according to the conflict theorists behind investment and management of industries is to earn more profit accrued from the hard labour of the workers. Between them the causes of conflict centre round wage claims, working conditions, treatment of workers, their fringe benefits including sick leave, retirement pensions, promotions, attendance regulations, absenteeism etc. The owners on their part may deal with grievances bit by bit instead of out right rejection but make promises for consideration in the future which usually they don't honour. Meanwhile, they keep on pressuring workers to put in more for better deal. This is a kind of repressive exploitation that never ends. This leads to a confrontation. Sometimes, persistent efforts to reach a compromise can settle the pay issue but the real issue is never resolved.

According to Karl Marx, stalemate could lead to a workers' revolution and if possible to overthrow the capitalist regime. A Communist society emerges as a result, which monopolises the means of production as it would be communally owned, classes disappear and workers are freed from exploitation.

This situation however, will not happen over night because of the structural pattern which delays understanding of exploitation of the workers. The situation of confrontation and ultimate revolution is comouflaged by what Marx called 'the ruling class ideology'. This ideology is formed of the beliefs and values created by the ruling power in which the capitalists have a significant stake. So the super-structure grows to protect the interests of the capitalists. Legal rules and regulations are put in place to save their interests. Marx calls it 'a false consciousness' which in his view would collapse and revolution inevitably breaks out.

This view is disputed by another prominent conflict theorist, Max Weber in whose opinion polarisation would not take place between the ruling party and the proletariat, but compromise and mutual agreement between the discordant parties would bring the issues to an acceptable solution and a revolutionary situation is thus neutralised.

Functionalism also has occasional difficult situation to face in which to reach a rational solution but time and patience are needed to resolve very conflicting issues. The difference is that functionalists believe in consensus and agreement as ultimate motto where as the conflict theories which have many variations though hang on to division and conflict some times they take on a soft ground aiming to resolve difficulties through dialogues rather than by extreme means as suggested by Marxism.

Functionalism puts emphasis on social stability and equilibrium in which to work in harmony so difficult issues are dealt with as humanely as possible.

Even though the conflict theories grew as a reaction to structural functional ideology, in fact, it has not been able to uproot itself completely from the functional roots. According to the conflict theorists, society is divided in to groups having unequal amount of resources and power by a few and no resources and power for others. The root of conflict lies fundamentally in material possession and those who have not got that are those who are subservient to those who have, but this causes inherently an antagonistic situation. According to them, conflict enables people to reinvent life in society; there fore, it is dynamic and ever changing and conflict remains a driving force. Characteristically, the conflict perspectives are oriented towards social structures and institutions. Nevertheless, the theory discovers dissentions and societal disagreements that emphasise change through upheaval. It can also attain peace and stability like functionalism but that can be done only through coercion and repression, which is not the ideal way to run a society.

Ralf Dahrendorf

According to Dahrendorf, consensus and conflict in society will go on together even though sometimes conciliation could be achieved but that may be for short period.

Dahrendorf has been a distinguished member of the contemporary group of the Critical theorists who besides being influenced by Karl Marx was also a follower of Max Weber. Max Weber himself unlike Karl Marx, was a moderate Marxist believing in social compromise rather than social conflict. In ideological difference, Max Weber stood as an amalgam of interaction, functionalism and Marxism which is quite different from what Marx's extreme ideology was about. In his view, Dahrendorf explains that the first and second world wars were perfect examples of conflict between the super powers who aimed at acquiring and controlling the territories of others. These and other reasons emanating from the war gave rise to several conflict ideologies, values and economic interests amongst nations. Societies became effected by the divergent ideologies. What Dahrendorf has thought was due to the conflicts in the world, a balance of power was established which was a good sign. This helped bringing peace and stability which was lost during the war.

Dahrendorf has found that all organisations are in positions of dominance which they can use against subject races-those who are powerless. Some have power and authority who can issue commands but some do not have. This Dahrendorf found as the main cause of the conflict in the post capitalist societies. Furthermore, Dahrendorf has examined the dominant groups which could issue commands and also interested in keeping the social structure in tact because these could protect them, their power and authority. Those who are in subordinate position are keen to change the social structure because the structure deprives them of the power they need to bring change. This is an important cause of social conflict no less important than that of Marx's economic cause of social conflict.

Ralf Dahrendorf has identified many dissimilar groups with in the conflict perspectives. They are called Quassi groups which are in conflict with each other. The Quassi groups whose job is to find likeable characters to join their groups for obvious political purposes. The recruited individuals will thus form the interest groups from which to form the conflict groups – whose main aim sociologically would be to develop the groups' ideology and structure. These are most essential features of their organisations. Their goals are to be decided and the activities and actions formulated.

Dahrendorf has also identified ingredients of conflict lying between the capitalists and the managers of fund. The latter control the capital of the capitalists, but not the capitalists and while doing so see their interests have to be taken care of. They spread the companies' business field where there is scope for development as well as opportunities for more commissions and benefits like bonus and share rights in the stake. They see that the companies don't get all the benefit than their fair share and at the same time themselves collect fat salaries for themselves plus fringe benefits. Dahrendorf argues that the capitalist class has become 'decomposed' because the owners of the capital have lost control of their capital which is now under management of the controllers. So between the capital class and the controllers exists the potential for conflicts between them.

Theorists of post industrial society find that separation of control from ownership has rather made a positive effect on the society to the detriment of the wholesale profit motif of the capitalists. The capitalist class has to cooperate with the development schemes arranged by the managers rather than facing further 'decomposition'. Professor J.K. Galbraith argues that the increasing power in society is exercised not by capitalists but by the industrial bureaucrats. So the owners of the capital has lost their power to manipulate capital for their interest which is now curbed by the technical expertise because they know how to handle money gainfully than their capital owners. John Kenneth Galbraith – The new Industrial State 1967, Hamish Hamilton, London.

Criticisms of the Conflict Theory

The conflict theory is subjected to several criticisms.

The first and foremost one is that it primarily relied on the social conflict rather than the social stability and order. The theory is remotely concerned with reconciliation and agreement which is the cornerstone of the functionalist perspectives. The conflict theory is also alleged to remain committed to radicalism. Dahrendorf, one of the leading conflict theorists, even being fundamentally Marxist has deviated from the ideas of Marx while developing his macro model minus Marxist ideas. The conflict theory as propounded by Ralf Dahrendorf finds affinity more with structural functionalism than with structural Marxism. Another structural problem with the conflict theory is its lack of conceptual integrity. As the number of the theory increases, they develop logical problems, incoherence and inconsistencies. The conflict theory as indicated above is basically a macro theory like functionalism and Marxism but it fails to develop a proper structural form to replicate the macro characteristics.

A society to be a true reflection of sociological ideas must reflect both order and conflict which more or less exist even in the most ideal society – one with out the other is not possible. You can not have a society with no social conflict and a society full of conflicts without order at all is virtually impossible. Dahrendorf has not demonstrated fully that society is made up of both conflict and order. Consensus and dissension in the society are its inevitable parts like opposite sides of the same coin.

Further Reading

1. Dahrendorf, Ralf – Class and Class Conflict in Industrial Society, 1959.
2. Maciver, R.M. and Page – Society, 1964. Galbraith, John Kenneth – The New Industrial State, 1967, London.

13
Karl Marx, 1818-1883 (1)

Introduction, Philosophy of Marx, The Communist Manifesto, Dialectical Materialism of History, Theory of Alienation and Class Struggle, Place of Marx in History, Why there is a Renewed Interest in Marxism.

Introduction

Karl Marx's sociological ideas constitute a distinct flair of his own – different from other classical thinkers who is also credited to have established the discipline of scientific sociology on a firm footing. Marx did not consider himself a sociologist per se but having taken all his works into account, one can not but help accepting him as one of the greatest sociologists of all time. Moreover, his contribution to sociology opened up new avenues of knowledge, creating opportunities for serious research work by the academics. In some respects, he is comparable to the French sociologist – Emile Durkheim who is also renowned as a founder of sociology based on scientific level. Duncan Mitchell has remarked that most of the modern social sciences owe their existence in greater or lesser degree to Marx.

Marx introduced a new concept of society in which people would not have to identify themselves as class people but only as belonging to a society where classes are eliminated, and a fully classless society established; this will be a society in which people would be liberated from the capitalist control and exploitation. As a matter of fact, it would take place after a Proletariat Revolution, caused by inexorable circumstances of class conflict and capitalist hegemonic rule. This would hasten the establishment of a socialist society. In his early life, Marx was influenced by the German classical philosopher Hegel whose dialectical idealism of history inspired him to read society also from the point of historical processes. However, Marx rendered his interpretation of the historical processes from the material point of view which shapes history whereas Hegel searched for the idea of 'the spirit of the nation', Marx searched for the evolution of scientific socialism; perceived in the perennial class struggle that would change society from one phase to another in the process of social evolution. Also occurs the dialectical processes ensuring eventual resolution to the social change. Furthermore, he discovered that the economic condition was the most important factor of all to cause class conflict and ultimate revolution. Class characteristics also continued to change with every phase of development of society. T.B. Bottomore accepts that Marx has provided a comprehensive theory of social change.

Marx perceived Hegel's philosophy as idealistic exploring expression in the rise of nations under great masters in successive periods of history through the dialectical processes. According to Hegel, these nations have manifested their values, ideas and virtues in their nationhood to demonstrate their superiority and greatness over weaker nations. His great emphasis, 'March of the nation', however did not impress Karl Marx who saw the so called great march was rather built on the exploitation and ruthless violence over weaker nations, enslaving their people and tying them up with severe tax system.

Born in Germany in 1818, Marx had a Jewish descent and studied Law and Philosophy at the Bonn and Berlin universities and in 1841, he received a Doctor's Degree from the University of Jena. His liberal views on politics led him to consider Journalism as a career and in 1842 became an editor of the economic and philosophical manuscripts. Marx married his boyhood girlfriend who happened to be a daughter of a Government official. This helped him survive financially when he fell in dire circumstances. He became editor-in-chief of several political journals in Germany; but later, being chased by the authority for his radical view on the state's political and economic conditions, he moved to Paris and later to Brussels where he carried on his journalistic career for some time.

Marx was deeply involved in student politics and he even spoke of violence if that should be necessary to pave the way for a better society. His newspaper was suppressed in Germany. In France, he became acquainted with some socialist writers, and fortunately met Frederick Engels with whom he established a life long friendship. In 1847, he was in Brussels where he started writing his great economic interpretation of history. In 1848, produced his second historic document–this time together with Frederick Engels, known as the 'Communist Manifesto'. This caused sensation amongst contemporary political thinkers who allowed him to read the document in the Communist International. He made a firm declaration that the Proletariat revolution would take place inevitably as a historical fact in the future.

This document was published in February 1848 at a time when Europe was facing an all round Revolution in almost every cities.

Philosophy of Karl Marx – The Communist Manifesto

The communist manifesto contains all the ingredients of an impending revolution and the means to achieve a new socialist world – free from exploitation and class rule. Development like that angered the German ruling authority and Marx was found guilty of causing serious social unrest. Realising the danger ahead and the prospect of being taken away by the authority for internment once and for all, he packed up and then left Germany for every sacrificing every thing he did for the country. His university career was in ruins. He settled in London and lived miserably in poverty with his family until fame and fortune came much later. His lifelong friend Frederick Engels who he met in France whilst he was there was the saviour of his life as he rescued him from extreme poverty. Engels was a business man and was well off. Marx painstakingly worked day and night to produce one of the most memorable political documents in history; The Das Capital' in three volumes. He remained greatly indebted to Frederick Engels for help and advice.

Marx's contribution to explain the concept of evolution of human society is unique because he found that our society was the product of economic transformation. Marx held that human society passed through various stages – each with its own well defined organisational system. Change from one system to the next is due to changes in the economic factors, namely the methods of production and distribution. The material forces of production are subject to change due to market forces which try to cope with domestic demand as well as external trade. A rift occurs between the underlying factors including each stage of social development and the relationships built upon them. A change in the material conditions of life brings changes in all social institutions, such as the state, the family, religion, employment etc. Socio-economic scenario gets changed along with the development of each stage. According to Marx, "Legal Relations as well as forms of state could neither be understood by themselves, nor explained by the so-called general progress of the human mind, but they are rooted in the material conditions of life... The mode of production in material life determines the general character of the social, political and spiritual process of life. According to Marx, the social order has passed through five phases called the Oriental, the ancient, the Feudal, the capitalistic and the communistic phase which I have discussed in the later part of this essay.

Marx changed the way people perceived society as a product of the 'divine Providence' which could not be interpreted in any other way.

He taught people that they were being exploited by those who owned "the 'means of production". They were no other than landlords, business magnates, entrepreneurs, capitalists, rulers, hoarders, black marketeers, middlemen and many other profiteering agents. They are called the capitalists and rulers who enjoy enormous power and privileges at the cost of working class labour. They earn huge profit from their investment accumulated from excess profit earned from hard labor of the workers. Marx argued that the poor workers remained ever so poor – this state could only change through a radical way – the Proletariat Revolution.

Marx was trying to make people understand that they must be aware of the circumstances in which they had been trapped and subjected to for hundreds of years; it is a vicious circle in which people are struggling for generations. Marx mentioned about the 'surplus profit' earned by the workers in the factories, mills, lands, and other kinds of industries but is expropriated by their owners. He warned people not to blame their fate for their sufferings but the social conditions they were in.

Marx crystallised the social thinking of the time; bringing politics and power under the scrutiny of his economic theory. He maintained that only labour produces wealth. But much of the wealth is transformed into profit which the workers are deprived of. The workers are paid wages which do not reflect the wealth they generate. There is a gap between the wealth produced and the cost paid to different items including the wages. This gap is the profit. This is a contradiction between the forces of production and the labour power of the workers which produce the wealth. There is a relation of production in the industry which facilitates the appropriation of much of the wealth by the capitalists.

How far was Marx's prediction right in terms of the Revolution in Russia?

With specific reference to Russia, the 1st World War exposed the deteriorating economic situation under the incompetent autocratic Romanov Czarist rule. The Bolsheviks in Russia took the cue from Marx's revolutionary ideas which thrilled them to revolt and a prospect of a socialist state free from exploitation and oppression. So, the Bolsheviks prepared for a revolution against the Czarist rule in Russia which was in power for three hundred years. The then emperor, Nicholas 2nd announced emphatically that he would carry on governing Russia as long as he lived. He was defiant and not prepared to change the mode of his government nor accept any compromise with the communists or even leave the Empire for ever no matter how threatening it was for him. He was cautioned that he would be overthrown and the monarchy abolished but he could not careless.

Having had seen the Czar defiant and even unwilling to introduce reforms long overdue, the workers rose in revolt in the city of Petrograd in February, 1917. Their demand was for peace, food and wages at first, because people were starving in the country and then the political reforms afterwards. This is the first revolution in Russia which took over the Duma – the Russian parliament, and the popular leader Alexander Kerensky formed a provisional government but that was short lived. Kerensky was a moderate leader representing the Menshevik part, who preferred to go slow in terms of introducing reforms. But the extreme wing of the socialists known as the Bolsheviks wanted a radical change of the country as fast as possible. They were joined by two returne exiles, Lenin and Trotsky who also supported the movement for over – throwing the existing regime. As Germany threatened to attack Petrograd, the Bolsheviks under Lenin and Trotsky took over by a sweep of a coup d'etat and overthrew the provisional government of kerensky and accomplished the second Bolshevik revolution in November 1917. Kerensky fled from the country leaving the affairs with the Bolsheviks.

Realising the gravity of the situation and the impending threat of German aggression, Lenin opened negotiations with the central powers and concluded a separate peace agreement with Germany and her allies by the treaty of Brest Litovsk in 1918. It was a humiliating treaty beyond belief as it forced Russia to surrender all the territories acquired by her since the time of Peter the Great. For Lenin and his Bolshevik party, there was no other way than this because Germany was too powerful to fight. In return for peace accord, Russia was then in a position to concentrate on her country's problems – to implement reform programme including the abolition of all private properties and distribution of lands to the peasants. The Bolshevik party unleashed a series of reforms involving social, political and economic systems.

How far was Marx's Prediction right in terms of the revolution in Russia?

The romanov Dynasty which rules Russia for such a long time was now finished for ever. The Czar Nicholas 11 and the members of his family were all shot dead in July 1918.

As mentioned early, Karl Marx was a different breed of sociologist than many others. He was not sure if he was a sociologist but his sociological ideas were amongst the foremost. His style was different, he interpreted history dialectically to prove that the Proletariat Revolution would take place with out fail. This would end the capitalist control of the economy and the exploitation of the workers once and for all. The process would continue until a classless society was fully established. Marxist theory offered a radical alternative to functionalism; nevertheless, there are similarities too. Sociologically, Marxism is structural like functionalism. The functionalists advocate predominance of the society over individuals who are to be subservient to the needs of society. Marx also had close link with the system theorists that society predominates over individuals and emphasised that human consciousness is largely shaped by the social relationships involved in the process of production. Further, he maintains that 'It is not the consciousness of men that determines their being, but on the contrary, their social being determines their consciousness'.

Karl Marx disagreed with the consensual type of sociology which is based on agreement by the majority. To him, sociological ideas indicate only one thing and one thing only i.e. the inevitability of the socialist revolution in which there could be no room for compromise. Marx also disagreed with Charles Darwin's the evolutionary process of social development who spoke of change through 'adaptation' with the natural environment. To Marx, human beings control and master the nature for their selfish ends, not compromise or adapt to it. If the humans would have to compromise with the nature then the society could not have been developed the way people wanted. People decide their destiny. It could not be any other way.

Marx's main concern has been to change the society and the way it was ruled. He discovered that people's life was dominated by the economic conditions such as the 'mode of production' through out history which in his terms was the 'economic relations of production'. This economic relations led to excessive profit making by the capitalists at the expense of the workers' hard labour. Also, people were tied up with very severe tax system. As a result, this created a divided society between 'those who have a lot and those who have not' at all; which was a recipe for class conflict, which to lead to a violent revolution.

There have been many types of revolutions in the world. Fundamentally, according to Karl Marx, the economic factor was at the root of all. The Greeks, the Romans, the French and the Germans became great nations no doubt, but collapsed not long after their rise to fame; because of the subject races being economically exploited, enslaved and oppressed who eventually revolted against their rulers. Also, the French revolution of 1789 for example, was caused by the exploitation, oppression and over taxation of the poor people including the third Estate by the corrupt bureaucracy and an incompetent Bourban monarchy. The people got inspired by the intellectual movement of the time which exposed the ancient regime for its incompetence and provided the incentive and moral courage to the oppressed people.

Marx put more emphasis on the economic factor more than others because the infrastructure of society was economically based through out history except the phase of primitive communism when the 'mode of production' was still not put in shape. In this phase, no body owned property and without ownership of property there could be no mode of production. Only the mode of production, according to him can produce contradictions and conflicts in the economic relations of production which can generate social classes. The economic factor is pivotal to move the society to a tangible change than Hegel's 'spirit of the nation'.

Hegel used history to demonstrate the development of self-awareness of a nation whereas Marx's concern had been to explain the evolution of human society caused by the economic circumstances of people. According to Marx, Dialectics are opposing forces which can cause transformations in society. They are known as thesis, antithesis and synthesis. The conflict between the first two opposing forces results in a solution known as synthesis. The synthesis then becomes a social force and continues to uphold itself as a social phenomenon which then prevails over other social forces. It becomes a thesis when it faces an emerging force to challenge the thesis. This is known as anti-thesis. They conflict with each other as a part of the dialectical processes and continue until a synthesis develops. The dialectical processes continue unabated until the Proletariat Revolution wipes out the relics of the bourgeoisie aristocracy including their system of Government. The old reactionary forces of the capitalist power and their privileges are also removed and the erstwhile objective of a classless society is brought into existence. This brings to an end of the Dialectical processes of history because the very class conflict which enabled different classes to exist has come to an end leading to the elimination of the class structure.

Marx's Theory of Dialectical Materialism

Marx's dialectic of history is also referred to as the dialectical materialism. History begins with the means of producing the subsistence of life which according to Marx is material basis of society such as food and shelter. People's ideas about the social and economic conditions with in a country can be a good material for a revolution no doubt, but according to Marx this is not enough for a radical change which can only take place from the contradictions and conflicts in the economic system. The system of production in the economy is the major dynamic factor for a revolution which would necessarily bring fundamental social change.

To Marx, the economic factor motivates the course of history. The modes of production according to Marx determine the character of social, political, legal and spiritual spheres which constitute the super – structure of society. The infra-structure consists essentially of the economic condition represented by the means of production including its operation system. According to Marx it is not the consciousness of men which determines the material conditions of life but it is the material condition of life which determines their consciousness. The element of determinism is dominant in historical materialism which determines all other aspects of life. The conflict in the economic system is the materialism of society which causes the socialist revolution.

There is some criticism concerning Marx's dialectical process to lead to a political revolution and to bring about radical social change. There have been many political and social changes without a revolution. Military conquest and also great reformers have done so without having to resort to a bloody revolution.

Marx and his Class Theory

What Marx has said is that a class is bound up with a particular historic Phase; change of a historic phase also brings in a change in the class system, which links itself to the nature and development of production. Class struggle is continuous and different with every phase of historical progress; so also in the ultimate phase which occurs between the proletariat and the capitalists in which not only the oppressive economic policies of the rulers but also the ideological conflicts between the rulers and the ruled lead up to a revolution. This continues in the final phase till the proletariat succeed in establishing a Communist system. Power is distributed amongst all people who set up a classless society by removing the vestiges of all capitalist power and their economic structure it takes a tong time to clear up all residues of class control. Class struggle necessarily leads to the dictatorship of the proletariat which lasts until a complete transition to a classless communist society takes place. Social equality for all is granted in a free communist society. At this phase the state will itself gradually wither away. Correspondence of Marx and Engels, 1846-1895, p. 67.

According to Marx the class system is the product of the economic relations of productions. There has been no social class or classes in the primitive period of history when people lived more or less in some sort of communes. This period according to Karl Marx is when the primitive communism had been the way of life; when also there was no class strife as discussed above. There could be cases of internal strife amongst the communities or tribes for tribal leadership, or personal relationships or control of internal law and order situations on a daily basis than anything like ownership dispute or profit making business. People did not want to own land and property at all. Land was in abundance, but no body liked to posses it for future. These communities or tribes never lived in one place for long; they were nomads, they kept moving until they found something where life would be more comfortable, they settled down there. Survival was the prime motive that drove them along; any acquisition of land would be rather a hazard on their migratory life.

The Fundamental Contradictions

With the emergence of private property and in particular 'ownership of the means of production', the fundamental conflict in society was laid down. This has led to social transformations; to Marx, this is the dynamics for social change. According to him, the material needs of life are at the very root of human existence which cause social conflict between those who have the most and those who have the least or none at all. The 'means of production' are known as the forces of production which include the land, machineries, technology and resources–better known as the capital but the know how requiste to producing industrial goods and services belonged to the workers.

The forces of production correspond to the 'social relationships' or labour relationships of production. Marx called them 'the economic base of 'infrastructure' of society'. To the functionalists social conflict between the two or more opposing forces may exist but only temporarily. Differences get resolved by the society and stability restored because this becomes necessary for the interests of all. To functionalists, the economic factor is important no doubt, but not absolute; other factors like religion, education, culture, legal and political institutions are also as important as the economy to bring changes in society which Marx considers as 'super-structure of society' created by the infra structure. To him, other factors are secondary even though they are important to life and helpful in enhancing 'social consciousness' of people. As a materialist philosopher, Marx considers this as nothing but 'false consciousness'. The real and true consciousness of people is the awareness of the economic disparity that exists with in the contradictions – inherent in such situation.

Class Consciousness

Marx explained class consciousness as understanding of one's own class position in relation to the political reality of the situation. That the social group has full grasp of the economic situation and aware of the nature of exploitation of the workers in the Production. Class consciousness also develops class solidarity when the workers, the peasants and deprived people find common identity, shared interest and purpose, then they unite into solidarity to take collective action. Marx has also found that the workforce realise that they are trapped in between the social production and individual ownership in the production system. The capitalists are individuals who own the production system of the country different from the social production of the workers. So a sort of polarisation of relationship develops between the capitalist class and the workforce.

Class consciousness was virtually non – existent in the phase of primitive communism. It began to grow slowly in each subsequent phases. Those who had no land, investment and profession were considered as working class people, probably they were working some where as slaves, serfs or menial workers for earning their living. Their consciousness was their awareness that they were working class people, different from other classes. The working class people themselves try to identify with others in the same position to build class solidarity.

Karl Marx has identified four main modes of productions in history which have succeeded one after another. Already discussed above the Primitive Communism which was free from economic relations and without class conflict. These things developed in subsequent modes of production. In each successive stage of historical development, economic relations began to take precedence over other considerations. Mode of production began to dominate and determine the inter-class relationships. In the 'ancient society' which was the second phase of change, mode of production was based on the relations between the masters and the slave labour. The masters exploited them for their benefit. The slaves had no choice but to deliver services at their maximum physical and mental capacity in the hope that one day they would be freed from their drudgery.

The masters were a class of their own because they had enough land, power and position and also the possession of the slave workers. The slaves or servants had to fall into a class of their own along with the exploited poor workers. In the 'pre industrial feudal society' which was the third stage of the mode of production, many landlords acquired more land besides their inherited property only to become wealthier and more powerful. In this period, exploitation of the workers was the established norm of the economic system. The feudal lords exploited their serfs and entailed them with strict conditions that they would earn their living only by working in the land of their landlords. Sometimes the conditions were tied up to include their successors. Their earning was not enough to buy land for themselves, so they had to depend on their hard labour which was sold to the landlord for their living. In this way, Marx saw the society emerged as two broad-based classes – the landlords as bourgeoisie and rulers in control, where as the landless workers as serfs and slaves.

In the 'industrial society', which had the last mode of production, things began to change fast. Marx had explained this phase of society more elaborately than previous phases. Many landlords besides farming took to other ventures as well such as trading and merchandising goods and commodities. Demand for manufacturing goods soared high after the Industrial Revolution which required a large work force which also changed the labour relations with the capitalists. They became capitalists and free-entrepreneurs. Many of the landlords in order to have a bigger stake in the industry sold some of their land and invested the capital in the production line. The Industrial revolution has changed the nature of production that is, production on a mass scale for making more and more profit. More and more workers work needed to man the industry. The consumers no doubt enjoyed more choice as production diversified and the products were readily made available.

According to Marx, production on a massive scale creates a class of wealthy Capitalists on the one hand, and landless workers on the other. The aim of the huge investment in the production meant more profit to lead to more capital. Furthermore, more capital gives more power to control besides economy, other aspects of life like social and political spheres. Lenin enhanced Marx's theory of capitalism to constitute domination beyond the borders which gradually takes the shape of imperialism.

According to Lenin, rise of capitalist power expands businesses globally allowing them to build imperialistic governments abroad. In the capitalist mode of production workers got more streamlined and marginalized on the factory floor and more exploited. In Marx's view class relations as a result, reaches a stage of no return to compromise but to one thing only – the inevitability of the proletariat revolution against the capitalist system. To Marx, the ruling class is composed of big business magnates and capitalists. Marx had written, "All human history thus far is the history of class struggle". Marx and Engles-1968, page-35. Marx also predicted that "the fall of the bourgeoisie and the victory of the proletariat are equally inevitable." Karl Marx -- collected works, volume 6 page 482 + 496.

Marx denied that he was the first one to have discovered the class system in history and its struggle. To him, the bourgeoisie historians have done that job before him. He wrote in 1852, "My own contribution to the existence of classes is to show that it is bound up with certain historical phases in the development of production; that the class struggle necessarily leads to the dictatorship of the proletariat; and that this dictatorship itself constitutes no more than a transition to the abolition of all classes to building a classless society". Karl Marx's letter to Weydemeyer 5 March, 1852, Collected Works, vol – xxiv, pp. 62,. 65. Marx has also cleared that, "That history of all hitherto existing society is the history of class struggle". The Communist Manifesto, 1948.

Concept of Alienation

Concept of alienation was first tracked in the work of the young Hegelian Ludwig Andreas Feuerbach's book 'The essence of Christianity'. According to him, cultural values and ideas created by man in the society are unwittingly dedicated to gods or divine forces. They had a faint idea about the existence of god but began to develop a perception that these cultures are alien cultures – so they are depository to gods. By giving away their cultural values to the accord of gods they became alienated from themselves. Feurbach was however hopeful that situation would improve once the human beings are made aware that these values and norms are their own and their heritage, no body else's. These can be practised in society for their good and for their faith.

Marx has developed his own interpretation about the concept of alienation at first agreeing though with Feuerbach that religion represents human self – alienation. According to Marx man has created God and by dedicating all their ancestral values to the alter of God, they had made a mistake. In his view, positive values of religion can not be ignored as they are useful guidance to the members of the society and should therefore be allowed to remain with them and function.

Marx explained that modern bourgeoisie society is the very acne of alienation, since it rests on the workers' loss of control over their labour and their subordination to the capitalism. To Marx, the private property is the product, result, and the necessary consequence of alienated labour and for ending the alienation of labour requires a social or more precisely a socialist revolution. K. Marx-Collected works vol. III pp. 279, 280.

Marx believed that the origin of alienation could be traced in the economic system of a country at a time when exchange of goods and services was conducted by the system of barter. Barter is a medium of exchange of a trade such as a knife whose utility or value can be bartered for the utility of a bucket or a stool or it can also be bartered for a vest or a pair or shoes or similar things. Barter is simple but caused problems when the value exchanged could not be correctly measured. So dispute arose whenever some dealings took place. This problem was averted by the invention of money which could correctly measure the value or usefulness of goods and services against the value of money which thus took over the barter system. The workers in the market are paid for their labour but the products are taken away by their employers. This made workers feel alienated from the products they had produced.

He further argued that since the workers had no control over the work processes, the intrinsic satisfaction to be gained from labour disappeared. Work is no longer a source of pride and offers no real pleasure in producing the commodity. It is only a job to be done. They are mentally withdrawn or alienated from the work they were doing. According to Marx, alienation reaches its height in the capitalist system of production when the workers are made a victim of the market forces – the 'boom and bust' over which they has no control. The workers felt that they were mentally debased and physically exhausted because of their mental detachment from the work they were doing. The bourgeoisie realise as much 'surplus profit' as possible from their labour which causes a polarisation of relationship with the employers.

Not only that they are alienated from the products they produce but also they are alienated from their fellow workers because of the division of labour which is so diversified. Each worker works on his own with least contact with fellow workers. Gradually, this situation leads to a sense of selfishness as they are given the feeling that they are working for themselves and their families only, but not for the society. So they are alienated from the society too. Marx has also said that the economic system develops the infrastructure which also shapes other aspects of life. He also points out that in a capitalist infrastructure there develops a high level of alienation, because, alienation is the consequence of wage labour. According to him, alienation worsens along with the mechanisation and further division of labour under the capitalist economic system.

Over the years, sheer desperation and a working class consciousness build up to a point when a revolution against the bourgeoisie authority becomes inevitable.

Marx has been criticised for his concept of 'alienation' which can not be scientifically measured as the workers would not be able to measure it. Louis Althusser, a new Marxist, also agreed with it.

Many sociologists got confused with Marxism and its hard core communist ideology since his death. They got more confused when in reality, many of his predictions fell far short of their goals. Socialism, he predicted would succeed in the industrially developed countries, at first, in the West and then in other countries. In the middle of the 19th century when revolutions broke out in France, Germany, Austria, Spain and Italy, it was generally believed that Marx's forecast was coming to be true, But the reality was different. The autocratic rule of these countries crushed the revolutionary forces and the dream of a socialist take over was lost forever.

Other predictions such as the inevitability of a Proletariat revolution and the coming of a classless society – all seemed to be a far cry.

This is because of a large scale social reforms introduced in these countries including Britain which smothered the instincts of the revolution. Educational development and expansion of higher education enabled many revolutionaries to change their philosophy of life. They took to practical thinking of developing their careers through education and training rather than through the bloody revolutionary method which may not come ever. Therefore, they took advantage of the educational opportunities offered realising that those would meet their needs much more than other ways. Many people also moved up to the middle class status as a result of promotions in their professional careers. Revolutionary activities would rather destroy their chances of moving up to the careers. The word 'proletariat' itself got melted into the working class' ideology which transferred its trust and allegiance to the trade union movement rather than to revolutionary leaders, believing that it would resolve their grievances through democratic means, such as demonstration, strikes and negotiations than revolutionary method. The latter could bring unforeseen problems like imprisonment, torture, detention and so forth.

Moreover, socialism failed because of the inherent contradictions within the system. What appeared was that socialism was tried on an experimental basis; bourgeoisie ingredients were still alive and kicking well. Socialism could not be forced upon people who got to be convinced about its rationale and practicality before it would be accepted by the people. Its social justice was fundamentally right but whether it was achievable in the true sense of the term was another matter. Socialism established in the Soviet Union and other East European countries since 1917 did not deliver clearcut results. For example, the goal of a classless society in the strict sense of the term, was not achieved because of the sustaining bureaucracy which remained camouflaged under the administrative system. It lingered in a lesser form though but its latent corruption could not be eradicated either. Secondly, social equality, an important goal of socialism was only partially achieved when land was being declared as state property and commonly owned; but everything else was discriminatory even when the socialist government was in power for so many years.

But Marx was optimistic that the socialist mode of production would allow workers to initiate products they were interested in but in fact that was not allowed to happen on grounds that it would interfere with the official specifications. Self initiative is an important element in capitalist industry; it could also make a difference in the production of output in the socialist mode of production but was not there in the socialist system. So, alienation remained as a fact in soviet industry.

The workers were deprived of making their special contributions in the production of goods and services to prove their products as competitive in the market. But that was not allowed to take place. They had to produce what was forced upon them – to do piece goods without uniqueness and without any sense of their marketability. The workers remained as 'alienated' as ever and gradually lost interest in the stereotyped productions. The consequence of this was a stark reality in the soviet economy that faced near collapse against Western competition. In the Soviet Union the economic growth was the lowest in Europe and the standard of living was the poorest.

Despite all the great ideas he stood for, Marx was still being criticised for not being able to be more precise and scientific. His idea of a revolution was seen to be too radical and not achievable. Marx realised that people were yet to appreciate the full value of his scientific theories explaining history through 'Dialectical materialism' and also the 'Scientific Socialism'. Unfortunately, some of his earlier predictions failed to deliver the objectives which raised doubts about his scientific explanation. This let people down because they had believed his thought was right. All the conditions of a revolution were rife in Germany though, but it came in a far off country like Russia in 1917. From then on the influence of Marx began to wane. Marx also failed, "to anticipate capitalism's capacity to renew itself" – Alex Callinicos, Social theory, A historical Introduction, Polity press, 1999, p. 99.

Place of Marx in History

Despite all criticisms against Marxism, Abraham and Morgan point out, "Even the worst critics argue that Marxian theory provides an excellent framework for the analysis of conflict and change in modern society" (Social though p. 50). This is true because the value of Marxism has sipped into people's thinking in so many ways that it is difficult to measure how much. It is alive in the hearts and minds of people all over the world and it has resurfaced in some modified form in the name of Neo-Marxism. Marxism has developed many varieties which indicate that Marxism is capable of renewing itself in the wake of needs and social changes.

Secondly, Karl Marx's position in history as a revolutionary thinker and a man of rich sociological insights have been firmly established once and for all. It is because of him and his close associates namely Frederick Engels and V.I. Lenin that socialism and communism have become one of the most dominant political thoughts of the world to day. The world has changed a lot since the Bolshevik revolution of 1917 in Russia and subsequently socialism took over in countries like Peoples' Republic of China, North Korea, North Vietnam, Cuba and most of the East European countries. Many countries have also started to see socialism as a future ideological order of the world but when that would be real only time can tell.

Karl Marx – Why Now there is a Renewed Interest in Marxism?

Marxism is coming back but in a different way. Sociologists in general, agree that it is impossible to ignore or dismiss Marxism completely because it is rooted in to the social philosophy in so many ways that not only it has enriched the whole spectrum of ideological and theoretical fields but also generated new avenues of thinking. Anthony Elliot and Bryan Turner have confessed, "It is impossible to understand twentieth century philosophy, economics, politics and sociology without a through grounding in Marxist theory". Profiles in contemporary social theory, edited by

Anthony Elliot & Bryan Turner, page 7, SAGE publication, 2001. They new Marxists have raised its profile by enticing it with theories of structuralism, feminism, post modernism and so on. Marxism is identified with issues of equality and equal opportunities, justice, ideology, anti-nuclear and anti-imperial policies. Although, as a central social philosophy and a scientific sociology it has lost its pre eminence but otherwise it has remained an effective deterrent to where capitalism and exploitation still thrive at their worst.

Gregor Mclennan maintains that on a substantive level, "Marx's account of the basic logic and volatility of capitalist society looks as powerful as ever". Handbook of Social Theory, edited by George Ritzer & Barry Smart. Sage publication, 200, p. 43. Professor Giddens also maintains that Marx's writings had a far reaching effect on the Twentieth century world. Until recently, more than a third of the world's population lived in societies whose governments claimed to derive their inspiration from Marx's ideas. Professor argues, 'Marx's ideas, used in a critical and selective way are likely to remain an important intellectual resource in the Social Sciences'. Anthony Giddens – Sociology, Polity press, 1993, p. 708.

It is also believed that Marxism has brought resistance to excessive exploitation of workers, oppression and unfair treatment of people generally and strengthened the hands of Trade union movement in their bid to eradicate inequalities from the work places and to improve workers' service conditions. The benefits of Marxism thus can never be exaggerated.

Questions

1. Explain the concept of society in conflict theory.
2. What is materialist interpretation of history?
3. What according to Marx are the basic contradictions of Capitalism?
4. What is alienation? What according to Marx are its different forms?
5. Critically examine Marx's theory of revolution.
6. Discuss Marx's concept of class fully.
7. Explain Marx's dialectical method for the study of society.
8. Assess the relevance of Marxism in to day's society.

References

Bottomore. T. and Rubel. Karl Marx: Selected Writings, Penguin, Harmondsworth 1961.

Berger, P. Invitation to Sociology, Penguin, Harmondworth, 1966.

Giddens Anthony. Sociology, Polity Press, 1993, p. 708.

Gregor Mclennan Handbook of Social Theory, edt by George Ritzer and Barry Smart Sage Publication, 2000, p. 43.

Anthony Elliot and Bryan Turner Profiles in Contemporary Social Theory, Sage Publication 2001, p. 7.

14

Neo Marxism

Introduction, Humanist Marxism, Gramsci, Structuralist Marxism, Louis Althuser, Evaluation, Paul Willis, Counter School Culture.

Introduction

Neo Marxism draws its origin from the – old classical Marxism of the 19th century. The new Marxism has variations which are also parts of the conflict theories. In many respects, these new perspectives look similar to the mainstream thought of Karl Marx and Frederick Engels but in reality they are not and in so many respects they are different. New Marxism drops some of the old precepts of the Marxist thought, such as, the inevitability of the 'Proletariat Revolution, a classless and a stateless society and equality for all people these would inevitably follow in a socialist system after the capitalist rule was completely replaced by the socialist system.

None of the predictions proposed by Karl Marx and V.I. Lenin materialised in the real sense of the term except in the case of Soviet Union and some East European countries which tried to implement marxist concepts to herald a socialist regime at least in a fundamental way. But their success was only short lived in the wake of the rise of capitalist power beyond control. Nevertheless, there still exists some vestiges of the Marxist system in parts of the far East, South America, part of Africa and Asia compared to what Marxist and Leninism had envisaged on a global basis. What exists now is in many respects a reformed Marxism – self regulated and adjusted in the name of New –

Marxism which is somewhat different from the old Marxist and Leninist thought.

Under the aegis of a lot of social changes, Marxism has been changed. The new ideology of Marxism et al includes amongst other things, ideas proposed by contemporary Marxist sociologists. These represent moderate, liberal and democratically attainable objectives rather than orthodox ideology which can only operate in extreme circumstances. Karl Marx still remains as popular as ever but his ideology has gone through a massive reform which produced a new kind of Marxism. It is now reformulated. The new approach is about the application of Marxism in to day's social and political environment which are certainly different from earlier situations.

The new approach otherwise known as the New Marxism reflects the concerns of the changing society. it has a few variations including some are with theoretical implications.

One thing the Marxists would not like to do is to undergo a thorough revision of the whole tenor of Marxism because that would seriously damage the image of the Marxist thought and would be unacceptable by a majority of the followers.

The neo Marxist ideology so far has made some impact on the sociological thinking. The collapse of the communist system in the East European countries, has highlighted the need for reforming Marxist thought so that people can see its relevance to the needs of present day society. The theories of Marx concerning, the 'means of production', surplus value, class conflict, proletariat revolution, dialectical materialism of History, the ideology of communism and the classless society are being reformulated to a great deal during the last fifty years or so. The communist thinkers are having a fresh look at their stock of ideas to see what more could be done to make it acceptable by the people.

First of all, let us see what the neo – Marxists have changed so far. They have reformed Marx's theory of economic determinism into the 'economic pragmatism' – a more realistic economic mode suitable for the current changing society in the capitalist world. In a Welfare or a socialist society, the Marxist creed has replaced the Right Wing principle of 'according to the ability of people which becomes now the needs of people'.

The infrastructure of society, according to Karl Marx is the result of two forces – the forces of production and the social relationships of production. The debate about the relationships between the infrastructure and the superstructure has been the key factor in Marx's economic relationships explaining how do the infrastructure cause the building up of the superstructure such as institutions like religious, cultural, political, educational and economic units and the values that go with it.

Humanist Marxism

Gramsci

One of the leading neo-Marxists is the Italian sociologist, Anthonio Gramsci, who was also the leader of the communist party there. Gramsci, argues that 'reciprocity' exists between the infrastructure and superstructure indicating that superstructure also aids the forming of the infrastructure and vice versa. This is however, contrary to what Marx had said.

Gramsci further added that Marx has put too much emphasis on the power of the 'owners of the means of production' ignoring the values of other factoers such as culture, religion, education, political institutions, pressure groups and so on, which produce major influences on various aspects of society. Ignoring these factors as unimportant was a major drawback on the Marxist thought. He agreed with Marx to the extent that owners of the means of production would hold power no doubt, but for how long; that was the question.

Contrary to Marx, Gramsci argued that unless the ruling authority was able to confide with the people convincing them about the benefit of their ideological rule, they would not be able to hold on to their power for long. Public consensus was a must to the continuance of power over people. To have a monopoly of power would require justifying their rule; it might need meeting peoples' demands and settling their grievances. Just 'owning the means of production' would not be enough to guarantee their long term existence in power.

Gramsci argues that the bourgeoisie would use every ways and means to try to stay in power; even by forging alliances with the civil society such as groups and individuals in a search of forming a 'power block'. Gramsci calls it the 'hegemonic' rule – a rule which aims to win over people on their side making them believe in their values and functions. People would benefit from the values and functions if they would follow and trust the ruling authority. At the same time, the authority would not hesitate to use coercive power if that should be necessary for the sake of maintaining the law and order. Any uprising against the government would be dealt with severely.

Stephen Luke calls Gramsci's hegemony as the 'third face of power' – the power which influences people to adapt to the dominant ideology of the society. Gramsci argues that the 'false consciousness' of the people would not last for long; soon people would know what was going wrong and what the realities of the situation were in which they were trapped and exploited by the power.

The rulers constantly use false pretences to justify their capability as rulers. To end the 'hegemonic rule' people would have to coalesce with like minded groups; together, they would be able to fight back against the oppressive rule. Alliance with the proletariat would also strengthen their case in their bid to fight even to start up a revolution. That is a way effectively to root out the capitalist system. If they would succeed in their effort to overthrow the ruling power then they would be able to set up a new system such as a socialist government.

Gramsci: Dual Consciousness

Gramsci talks about the 'Dual consciousness' of the people which is in part a consciousness of the values of the hegemonic rule ingrained in to the minds of people and the other part is their experience of day to day life under the bourgeoisie rule. This experience helps people forming an image about their rulers – their nature of treating people and the manner of exploitation etc.

Gramsci argues that eventually the hegemonic rule would collapse once failed to convince people about the efficacy of their rule. Once the working class is satisfied that the hegemonic rule was against their interest, they would fight to the end to decompose the system.

Contrary to Marx, Gramsci argues that the Proletarian Revolution will not inevitably result from the economic crisis. It will result from the experiences of the people including their own ideology of socialist rule which according to Gramsci is the humanist Marxism. Gramsci also stresses on the necessity of the popular culture and youth involvement in the resistance against the authority's rule. Gramsci's ideas had a major influence on the neo-Marxists theory of power.

Gramsci also differs from Marx when the latter has put emphasis on the divisions with in the working classes saying that they could be exploited by the ruling authority using the 'divide and rule' strategy. also they would keep the rich and the poor apart in order to stay in power. According to Gramsci, the ruling class also was divided in to such as, the financiers, the small and large industrialists and land owners and so on, on the other hand, the industrial workers and agricultural peasants were also divided. This is a major division with in the subject class but workers of different industries would fraternise and join in solidarity when such situation would be needed to foil the capitalist ploy, specially when the fight was against the employers.

Gramsci explains that when workers of different industries could fraternise for a common cause, they are not at loggerheads with one another and the authority would not dare to exploit the workers. For example, the workers of the agriculture and industry would not have such conflicts between them to enable the rulers to exploit the situation. Gramsci attaches equal importance to all the factors such as the culture, ideas, education, religion and also the economy being responsible for causing the social division and creating classes and sub–classes. Karl Marx's economic determinism as a sole cause for social division was found simplistic and unacceptable by Gramsci.

Ralf Dahendorf, an influential member of the Frankfurt school also criticised Marxism saying that the concept of capitalism explained by Marx related to the 19 century situation when it was a right thing to do so. The 20 century presents a different panorama of economic and social scenario far advanced of Marx's thought. Marx's ideas are not appropriate to explain fully the social conflict in the current circumstances.

Ralf Dahrendorf

Important changes had taken place since Marx wrote his thesis. Western countries have now reached a stage of 'post industrial societies. Marx's 'two class theory' that 'those who have and those who have not' is practically insignificant in to day's circumstances. Classes have now been radically transformed to represent diversified workers and different professional groups.

The working class is much more educated and trained to do professional jobs and the middle class is even more diversified. Inequalities have been reduced to the extent that it is difficult to know who belongs to which class.

Because of the fast growing social mobility and social reforms including reduction of poverty, spread of education, and the enhancement of union powers, the owners of industries have less control over the industry than ever. Managers rather than owners have become more significant and powerful than the owners. So Marx' assertion that the conflict between the owners and non-owners of wealth to cause a revolution is no longer acceptable as a valid ground.

Meanwhile, the failure of the Communist regime in the East European countries at the end of the 20th century testifies the weakness of Marxist and Leninists systems which under the circumstances required a through revision. In was found that the Soviet communist system was slow and regressive and unable to compete with the growth of the Western countries which produced more jobs, more wealth and more welfare benefit for the working class people. So, a silent revolution spread throughout the Eastern European countries to repudiate the socialist ideology and to bring back the Western style democratic system with rights and responsibilities for all people irrespective of colour, religion and race. People would be rewarded according to their abilities, effort and commitment rather than according to their needs.

Thus, a new democratic system has been established in the East Europe in which multi party electoral system was given the right to compete in the general election. The tenor of political culture began to take shape in the fast changing scenario.

Before the silent revolution, Soviet regime under communism was not immune from bureaucratic elitism. Large scale monopoly of political and bureaucratic power was exercised by the rulers before the downfall of the regime, quite contrary to the spirit of Marxism. And significant social inequalities existed in the communist societies even after half a century of communist rule there. Social classes existed more or less in disguise rather than disappear according to the ideology of communism.

Post Industrial Society

New Marxism has recognised the changing atmosphere in the social scenario. Social classes, for example have changed their characteristics as they widened their base. The middle class have been diversified in to at least four sub-classes caused by economic regeneration which offered more jobs with better emoluments and job security.

The proletariat also have moved from their impoverished condition to earnings and some even have reached the level of lower middle class due to increased skills. The neo-Marxists have improved Marx's views and ideas. They have shown that Marxism could be applied to a wider field on a broad based philosophy and can deliver more benefit to people than otherwise. They can minimise social evils of exploitation, inequalities, corruption, poverty and misuse of power. The major conflicts in the society between those who have a lot and those who have a little can be compromised and redeemed.

Another version of Marxism which also comes under the boundary of Neo-Marxism is the structuralist Marxism which states that we are the products of structures rather than authors of our own actions; Structuralist version of Marxism decries Marx's theory of economic determinism as the sole factor of social division. Althusser, a celebrated French sociologist has developed the Structural version of Marxism which was started by a philosopher called Levi Strauss, the founder of a school of thought of Structuralism.

According to Althusser our society is based on three levels or formations rather than one – the economic formation of Karl Marx. The other two are the political and the ideological formations. Essentially, they are dependent on one another. Each of these social formations is autonomous according to Althusser they have their independent statuses and functions even though they are a part of the whole. Economy of course, effects the political and ideological structures no doubt, but economy can be regulated by the political system. Ideology can also effect the pattern of the other two. So why economy should be a sole determinant of the social system?

Althusser argues that in order to achieve the Marxian 'reproduction of the relations of productions' necessary preconditions must be fulfilled; such as, workers must be trained in their particular areas of work to produce better quality goods. Skills are therefore necessary to be a successful factor in the industry.

Also, Althusser puts emphasis on two other factors such as education and mass media which he designates as 'ideological state apparatuses'. Education and mass media teach people the benefit of being social and responsible to the society. The 'ISA' ensures that people are put in their allotted places to fulfil their specific functions. The relations of productions could then function if these preconditions are fulfilled. There is another aspect of the state apparatus which is the 'repressive state apparatus'. According to Louis Althusser the success of the ISA depends on the 'repressive state apparatus' which use effective coercive action by the army and the police on people to ensure that they deliver their responsibility seriously by performing their role. It can be said that the 'Ideological State Apparatuses'. monopolise power to help the rich and those in authority. The structural system becomes deterministic and static as it does not allow flexibility. The Ideological state apparatuses represent the interests of the capitalist class. It uses apparatuses to help to maintain and to justify the capitalist system and also to disguise the reality of exploitation and oppression which the power of capitalism exercises.

Some neo-Marxists have tried to develop Marxism by borrowing ideas from other sociological perspectives. Paul Willis, a British sociologist whilst studying 'transition from school to work' combined some ideas from Marxism with ideas from interaction perspectives. He developed a distinctive neo-Marxist approach to education. Earlier, Bowles and Gintis had studied schooling in the U.S.A. which was producing mainly docile workers who had to remain obedient and hard working manual workers for the industry. Paul Willis contradicted some of Bowles and Gintis findings with his own research findings. Paul Willis observed and studied a group of boys of 12+ yrs old in a suburban U.K. school and discovered that the school could not teach them skills required to use in the work place even when they spent years in schools and moved up to the next year and on. They did not seem to be docile and obedient. They spent all their time developing counter – school culture which included having a laff and ignored everything teacher taught in the school. They ridiculed those who paid attention to the teacher. The whole findings contradict Bowels and Gintis assertions.

To continue more with Paul Willis' findings which was in England, included experiences from the children's points of view. Majority of the children he studied came from the working class background during their period of schooling when they developed counter school culture quite opposed to the values and the ethos of the school.

Educational facilities offered had also little effect on their learning. Academic studies and qualifications were disliked by many students. Some came to school to meet friends and to have a nice time laughing and chatting with one another. Willis argued that education could have unintended consequences as a result – not beneficial to capitalism. School does not necessarily produce children as docile workers of the future as claimed by Bowles and Gintis. Some may become docile as a result of teaching but there are others who will make their own rules inside the class room evidenced from Paul Willis' findings.

It is true that Willis' study of a small group of twelve boys could not be counted as representative of the whole scenario but the report still presents some important facts worthy of serious consideration. Why some kids do not like to know what the teachers are teaching or that they are not getting the information they liked to know. There are evidence to show that kids who leave school without necessary skills later regret why they missed education when offered to them.

Further Reading

1. Antonio Gramsci Selection from the Prison Note Book, 1971.
2. Ralf Dahendorf Class and Class Conflict in an Industrial Society.
3. Louis Althusser Lenin and Philosophy and Other Essays, New Left Books, 1959.
4. Paul Willis Learning to Labour, 1977.

Part 6

Part 6

15
The Critical Theory and the Frankfurt School

Introduction, A Brief History, Aspects of Critical Thought, Theodore Adomo's Authoritarian Personality, Cultural Theory, Aims of the Critical Theory, Functions of the Critical Theory, Jurgan Habermus, Legitimacy Crisis, Conclusion.

Introduction

The critical theory is originated in the Frankfurt school of Germany in the 1920s and 30s but its heyday was in the 70s and 80s. This school has been a very powerful social science research organisation based predominantly on the Marxian thought. Over the years, a number of prominent Marxist scholars got associated with the development of this school who brought to light some new sociological concepts which matured in to a powerful social theory, called the critical theory. Fundamentally, in its origin it is shaped by the classical German philosophy of idealism but later was indoctrinated by the Marxian thought. Because of its communist lineage, it was driven underground during Hitler's regime and some of the scholars migrated to the united states to escape Hitler's wrath where they recreated the Frankfurt institution. From there, they published their journals as a mouthpiece of the critical philosophy.

The critical school of thought flourished abroad despite hardship, with active support and contributions from philosophers, scientists, Psychologists and educationalists – some of them were also non-Marxist scholars. It became a multi disciplinary institution similar to their old school in Germany and developed theories comprising many fields of knowledge including social science. People like Max Weber, Max Horkheimer, Jurgen Habermas, Lukaks, theodore Adorno, Herbert Marcuse and non Marxist like Edmund Freuid made enduring contributions to the growth of this school with their unique historical, philosophical, classical musical and psycho-analytical scholastic knowledge. As already mentioned, they also drew ideas from the German philosophers like Kant and Hegel-comprising values like reason, truth, beauty etc but again these were updated by historical and philosophical wisdom as an inspiration to the nation. Eventually, Marxian ideas of economic determinism and socialism dominated their thought more than other ideas which aimed to transform the society differently, from what it was before.

Aspects of Critical Thought

In the early stage it was felt by the scholars that the critical theory had a role to play developing sociology firmly based on rational argument. Unlike, other perspectives, developed by individual sociologists with a single or unitary objectives in view, the critical theory's objective was multi-dimensional. Its orthodox view of Marxism has been reformulated in order for it to be accepted by a wider audience.

The concept of the critical theory was non-objectivist and non-materialistic. It meant that it would not align with positivistic sociology. And their ideology should remain non-authoritative and non-bureaucratic too. The critical theory is neither structural not Action theory but its unique position lies in between the two signifying a third way or an attempt to develop a synthesis. Habermas, however, holds a different view. The critical theory, according to him, can be located in between Philosophy and science. Patrick Baert (1998, p. 139). According to Raymond Guess, 'A critical theory is structurally different from a scientific theory in that it is reflective and not objectifying' R. Guess (1981, p. 79). The critical theorists in order to improve their empirical research methodology followed a rigorous social and scientific techniques perfected in America. Furthermore, a psycho-analyst from the Frankfurt school named Eric Fromm (1900-80) contributed by combining Marxist and Freudian ideas in to the critical theory which explained how social class influenced peoples' psychic structure and political views. Max Weber increased the calibre of the critical domain by adding his brand of Marxism better known as 'Weberian Marxism' in which he excluded the revolutionary element from the perceived Marxist thought.

Theodore Adorno's Authoritarian Personality

According to Adorno, the authoritarian personality is a product of anti-democratic and prejudicial environment with in a family where relationships between parents and children are characterised by dominance and submission and where family members are intolerant of lack of conformity. Prejudice is a psychological issue. The prejudiced personality imbibes psychologically oriented Fascist cultural patterns who gradually work in to the social structure and influence the system.

The Frankfurt school and its counterpart: the critical theory confers about what makes its ideology different from other perspectives. The fact is that the human ability which can transform the environment has been systematically suppressed specially of the working class people by the capitalist society and their right to make rational decision about their lives also have been denied. The capitalist system does not allow the workers develop their potential fully and play their creative part in the production line. This causes boredom and working life depressing. The consequences of the working conditions under the capitalist system produce nothing but a mass of mindless alienated workers. The workers do not feel proud of what they produce because their creative mind has not been allowed to function fully.

Frankfurt school also confers with Gramsci, a neo-Marxist from France in which the later argues that the ideology of the capitalist society has been succeeding integrating people into the capitalist system. And two other developments have taken place the rise of instrumental reason and the development of the mass culture. The instrumental reason is a strategy devised to succeed in a capitalist world. It is a way to discover the efficient way to do things successfully. But in reality, it becomes an instrument as a means to an end. Culpable people use it to hoodwink and exploit the vulnerable in the society. According to the enlightenment theory, 'reason' does not liberate people in he capitalist society but becomes a mechanism of oppression. The instrument of reason has also penetrated in to the cultural world by popularising music through eye catching publicity.

Cultural Theory

During the 30s, the Culture theory was further augmented by the cultural input, as the capitalist system was in full swing, many got interested in to the cultural pursuits like art, music, literature, journalism, media communication and so on. Rich people invested heavily in art and culture industry over the years. Gradually, the nature and character of culture industry have got changed to make it a subject of commercial exploitation specially, the media has been used to focus and publicise the art and to make it cheap for people to buy. This became a hot ideological issue at the end of the 20th century. The critical theorists looked at the perspective from the Marxist point of view. The traditional Marxist concept considered 'art and culture' as a part of the superstructure and therefore different from the infra-structure. Marcuse has criticised the culture industry as the 'instrument' of capitalism creating 'false needs' for the interest of profit. Mass culture is now turned into an industrial exploitation. The system is geared to ensure that it is being reproduced for more profit. According to Horkheimr, "culture to day is not the product of genuine demands; rather it is the result of demands which are evoked and manipulated" Horkheimer, "Art and mass culture' (1941), pp. 302-3. Adorno in his 'Dialectic of enlightenment' deplores the fact that music of Mozard, Bethoven, Schoenberg producing pacifying effects on society have been sidelined and replaced by the popular culture including pop music by the capitalist society in order to make more profit. The traditional culture is trivialised and its independence destroyed.

But Adorno disagreed with the Marxist view. He produced masses of cultural documents arguing that art and culture-without them being a part of society could not be meaningful. He added that, as long as the culture is a reflection of society it could not be above society or alienated; so it is unequivocally an integral part of it. Music, art and culture can integrate an individual into a cohesive society so also it can develop more understanding amongst nations. In the 'Dialectic of Enlightenment' produced by T.W. Adorno and M. Horkheimer (1972), in which the culture industry is thoroughly discussed to show its pacifying effects on nations. For exsample, Bethovens's ninth symphony is selected as an anthem for the European Economic community. (Ian Craib-Modern social theory, 1992, p. 216.)

Aims of the Critical Theory

The critical theory aims to establish a rational society with rational institutions to promote truth, freedom and justice (David Held-Introduction to critical theory, 1980, p. 15). Despite differences amongst the theorists around many issues, they all agree to one thing – they all want to focus on contemporary social and political issues. In their view, individuals are being exploited and their rights, skills and values are being used for the benefit of those in powers. The economic system is exploitative of workers who give their labour to sustain the system. The critical theorists adopt a more rational and passive method of fighting oppression, injustice and exploitation through systematic criticism of the agents who perpetrate repression of people. The oppressors of all kinds who resist social change and continue to degrade people morally and ethically should be thoroughly criticised publicly so that on the one hand, they get morally thwarted, on the other, the public get conscious about the situation and would bring pressure upon them. This would break their obstinacy and make them understand the changing mood of the nation. They may be morally inclined to participate in the talk for change in society. The path of critical theorists is not extremism but radical pacifism. Through education and public pressure things might go changed for the better.

The Functions of the Critical Theory

The critical theorists believe in social transformation which can be achieved through changes in the education system, the economy, employment, health, public relations and so many other social issues. Changes would being fairness and justice to people in the society which they were denied by the capitalist and the socialist systems. The critical theorists are convinced that the capitalist and socialist ideologies would ever promote human rights fully and help disadvantaged people realise their full potential. They point out that there is a third way-an alternative way to capitalism and Marxism-because both of which are limited by their inherent deficiencies and the third way is a radical pacifism as indicated above. In radical pacifism changes would be brought through peaceful way through dialogues, meetings, discussions, interactions and the processes would continue till the objectives are achieved. Nevertheless, they would not quit Marxism but would reformulate it to suit the needs of the time.

Jurgen Habermas

Habermas is regarded "as the most important contemporary member of the Frankfurt school tradition of critical theory." (Craig Calhoun et al., Contemporary sociological theory, 2002, p. 356). Born in Germany and educated in three universities there, Habermus completed a PhD degree on Frederick Shelling in 1954. He was a student of Theodore Adorno, a critical psycho-analyst under whom he worked as an assistant researcher in the Frankfurt school of social research. Later, he became a professor of sociology at the university of Frankfurt after having had written several important books. His contribution so sociology includes many fields of knowledge, covering philosophical and theoretical areas, communication, media, Sociology of law and political sociology. In the words of Patrick Baert "His work vastly transcends the German speaking world". (1998), p. 134. In his view, knowledge can not be fully scientific. To quote Habermas, "purely scientific knowledge is impossible" (Craig Calhourn et al. 2002, p. 352). Amongst many critical theorists, Habermas is reckoned to have given a clearer view of the critical theory than most. He has identified three distinct approaches which converse in to the critical theory. They are the metaphysical and abstract approach -- in other words known as the empirical analytical, the second is known as hermeneutics and the last one is the critical approach. The Emperical-Analytical is a positive approach whereas the hermeneutics identify inter-subjective meanings based on interactive procedures. Lastly, the critical theory is a mixture of or a synthesis of the two approaches mentioned above.

Habermas was seriously interested in politics and in the relevance of sociology and social thought in political affairs. He denounced views of Fascism, defended the importance of democratic institutions and the rule of law and was against the rule of violence. He was a rationalist, even though heavily influenced by Marx. As a critical sociologist he tried to link between culture, social structure and personality. He was also impressed by the ideas of phenomenological sociology.

His belief in social change could be achieved through his theory of communicative action. Like Carl Popper, Habermus believed in open discussion and criticism in social matters for which what is required is effective communicative skills. Progress in ideas acceptable to all can be realised if equal opportunities are allowed to all participants in the discussion process. In his view, for the human ability to perform effectively, verbal communicative skills are crucial. To be effective in communication, one has to be intelligible, clear, truthful, justified and sincere in expression. For rational communication, speakers should be put under no constrains in assessing evidence and arguments, so every body should have a fair chance in the discussion. This is what Habermas calls the 'ideal speech situation'.

What Habermas deplores most is that politics is run by instrumental rationality rather than by 'communicative rationality'. Instrumental rationality enables a few with most money and power to make decisions leaving the vase majority outside the discussion process. Thus peoples' lives are run by a few generally known as capitalists. Habermas believes that such a system can not sustain their predominance for long. A change from capitalism to any other form of system acceptable to all would be brought into existence by mass movement.

Habermas, like many other neo-Marxists is a Marxist who coheres with most of Marxist ideas. Nevertheless, he criticises Marxism on the ground that it is a closed door ideology which rarely can change. That is why Marxism is known as dogmatic and conservative because it is not amenable to change easily. Capitalist society is to collapse as a result of the conflicts in the class and divisive economic system which in his view, is not going to happen soon because the state there will intervene and try to prevent anything like that to happening.

He also disagrees with Marx's view that the state is a part of the superstructure not infrastructure and according to Habermas, that position has changed since the state has penetrated in to the infrastructure over the years and it is now a part of the economic system. Also he disagrees with marx on the subject of rich becoming richer and poor poorer – making the gulf between the two wider, saying that the class differences have been rather narrowed down on many counts and the result now is less confrontational between the rich and the poor. The trade Union movement has helped to resolve many of the outstanding and difficult issues and grievances with the employers and therefore neutralised their sting power. He further comments that the class consciousness of the masses is now less acute than ever and chances of a social revolution is now a far cry.

Legitimacy Crisis

In his book 'Legitimation crisis', Habermas criticises Marx's view of the economic crisis inevitable to bring the capitalist system to an end. Habermas argues that state intervention in the capitalist countries would delay the collapse of the economic system for an indefinite period and other measures undertaken with effect to stave off the crisis and compromising class consciousness as indicated above. The increased state involvement in the economy changes the situation all around. The state also faces its self created problem of inability to sustain the delivery of services at peak level and if that happens, and most probably it would because of shortage of resources, then the state would face serious 'legitimation crisis'. Naturally, the population would expect the state do more for them in terms of social justice etc or face boycott and confrontation. In such a situation, the state would strategically take the side of the bourgeoisie and preserve their interests at first rather than surrender to the demands of the people. The situation can develop to the extent that it can threaten social stability. Whilst solving the economic crisis it could create for itself a serious 'legitimation crisis'.

Further Reading

Adorno, Theodor The Authoritarian Personality.

Habermas, Jurgen The Legitimation Crisis, London, 1976.

The Frankfurt Institute for Social Research – Aspects of Sociology, London, 1973.

Craib, Ian – Modern Social Theory, Wheatsheaf Books, 1984.

The Frankfurt Institute for Social Research – Aspects of Sociology, 1973, London.

Horkheimer, M – Art and Mass Culture 1941.

Adorno, T.W. and Horkheimer, M Dialectic of Enlightenment, 1972.

Held, David Introduction to Critical Theory, 1980.

Craig, Calhoun et al. Contemporary Sociological Theory, 2002.

Part 7

16
Stratification

Introduction, Definition of Inequalities – Man Made and Natural, Caste and Class, Theories of Stratification, Functionalist Perspective of Stratification, New Right Perspective of Stratification – Critical View, Marxist Perspective of Stratification – Two Class Model Theory, Weberian Perspective of Stratification – Four Class Model Theory, Concept of Caste and Class, Class Structure is Capitalist Societies, Embourgeoisement Thesis, Contemporary Theories of Stratification, Neo-Marxist View, Neo-Weberian View, Proletarianisation Thesis, Underclass Concept.

Introduction

Definiton of Inequality: Man Made or Natural.

The concept of stratification represents social differentiation – a kind of social inequality. Social inequality has a history of its own showing where it had originated in the beginning. Biologically, every human being is different from the other: they vary in their personal qualities – some are more intelligent and some are not, some are tall and some are short; some have white skin and some have black skin. Their abilities too are different from one another. Some have more hunting skills, some have in painting; some have authority and leadership unequal to others who follow them even without being compelled to do so and some have it in athleticism; but there are many who are not equal to them, they are less gifted and capable. There are physically very strong and weak people all the time. These differences are mostly caused by genetic variations predominantly, but sometimes influenced by cultural effects taken together they became known as natural or biological differences. Still, there are many more biological differences amongst human beings which are not countable. Sociologists argue that biological differences probably, cause biological inequalities.

According to the French Philosopher, Jean Jacques Rousseau, biological inequalities are natural and physical because they are produced by nature and consist of differences in age, health, bodily strength, and the qualities of mind and soul etc., where as social inequalities are caused by the society such as who are rich, who are poor, who have more privileges and power and who have less and who should be rulers and who should be subjects etc. According to Rousseau, biological differences are not that serious as the socially created inequalities which are at the basis os social stratification.

According to Andre Beteille, search for a biological basis for social stratification is bound to end in failure, because, identification and gradation of qualities in stratification can be done only by society not by nature. It is often argued that biological differences become biological inequalities as such, as they are defined in cultural variations. Some societies have used biological differences in their stratification system. For example, in Hindu society, Varna or colour has been used as a criteria to define the caste system. Also, in the United States, Black middle class is not deemed equal to the white middle class because of their colour. Some societies consider old age a symbol of wisdom who deserve respect from the society but many societies thin old age is nothing but a social burden and therefore not worth a Status. But the controversy that biological differences to cause social inequalities would not die away.

Stratification can be simply defined as "structured inequalities between different groupings of people" Anthony Giddens (1993) Sociology, p. 212.

Stratification sometimes is compared with geological layers. Critics argue that to compare stratification with rigid rock layers-one on top of other is an analogy not just appropriate in a social structure. Stratification in the West is not same as the stratification in India or China and some other countries in the world. In India, the whole concept is perceived in one and only one with the 'Caste system' whereas in the West, caste is one of the four discriminatory groups such as slavery, estates or feudalism, caste and class.

In the West, the social class as a concept did not emerge until the industrial revolution which started in the 18th and 19th centuries to cause industrial expansion. Work was done based on the 'Division of labour'. Each person had to work on a particular job in which he had specific skills to result in mass production. Industrial production also rose along with improved mechanisation of machineries. The revolution had created a very large working class group divided into skilled, semi-skilled an unskilled people. Just workers would not be enough to do all the functions. So there was a need for people to work as managers, foreman, executives, engineers, clerks, accountants, technicians, typists and so on. These people have become the middle class. Furthermore, industries needed investment. Money can come only from the rich who could provide land, labour, capital and organisation. Those who were able to provide all these resources became known as the 'owners of the means of production'. They also came to be known as capitalists – the class of wealthy entrepreneurs.

In India, most people are stratified into different castes instead of classes based on their role in society. The Brahmins, for example are placed at the top of the system because the jobs they did involved teaching, scripting, preaching, interpreting legal matters, pleading cases, advising the kings and other officials and so on. All the academic and intellectual works were done by the Brahmins. They were also the authority in the scriptural works were done by the Brahmins. They were also the authority of he scriptural matters and were entitled to perform the religious services only in the realm. No other persons were allowed to do these functions. There was a time, when the Brahmins were regarded as visible deities. Shastras and scriptures have ample references to The Brahmins' holding spiritual powers.

Down the caste system are the Khatriyas, the warrior caste. The members of the Royal families came from this caste who were also the rulers and defenders of freedom of the realm. Then came the Vishyas, the trading and the business caste and class. The last caste was the Sudras who were at the bottom of the pile doing services to the people. They were the peasants, domestic and factory workers and so on. But there was a large number of people who were not considered fit for the caste line. They were below the Sudra caste in other words, known as Nama Sudras. They did all the menial jobs including cleaning streets, toilets and removing the dead animals from the streets and carried them to the open field for feasting the vultures. They were known as 'untouchables'. Mahatma Gandhi felt very unhappy having had seen their plight and therefore gave them a status the 'Harijan' the children of god. This gave them at least some respect in the society.

Varna Concept of the Caste System

The exact origin of the concept of 'Varna' is not clear but the literal meaning is the 'colour of skin'. The caste system developed after the arrival of the Aryans in India from different parts of central Asia and Europe. The Indo-Aryans were fair skinned, but the Dravidians the original inhabitants of India were dark skinned. These people were known as Dasa varna mentioned in the Vedic literature. So there was a racial separation of Indian people into fair skinned and black skinned people since the arrival of Aryans thousand of years back.

The main castes were broken down into many sub-castes or (Jatis) – their number could be as many as hundreds. They could be identified by their surname, kinship relations, village or locality in which they were born.

Generally speaking, to day, when we look at societies all over the world, we find that it is composed of different castes, classes, races and ethnic groups. Classes are determined by how much wealth one holds and what kind of work one does and the responsibility one holds in his position. Other criteria are also used such as education, training, parentage, place of living, and kind of people they meet.

The caste in India is a different thing. It is fundamentally a vocation that one is born to do and the caste he or she is born in is not to be changed. This emphasis however, is questionable, because, when the doctrine of Karma is taken into account which allows people to move up and down the caste system depending on the quality of work they had rendered in their past life.

Race and ethnic groups of people are decided by their birth into racial, cultural and religious backgrounds. A class can constitute members from any social groups if they are certain specific type of profession. They are all parts of our social structure. But the caste system is fixed by its own structure which is immobile until the last day of life when as said above the doctrine of karma may change one's position.

The term 'caste, according to professor Giddens comes from the Portuguese word, Casta, meaning race or pure stock. (Anthony Giddens – '93, p. 213). But in India, Caste had a different origin. There are different theories explaining the origin of the caste system in India. Some have identified divine origin, some have found sociological, some racial and some have found historical and political as roots of the caste.

But the emphasis was put on the role play of each caste – what job each caste holder did. Colour and birth as mentioned above also played their parts in determining their strata in the caste system.

The India constitution has outlawed the caste system. To day, officially there is no caste in India; but unofficially there is. These things die hard. The Brahmin caste had been at the top of the ladder from the time the caste system was devised. Traditionally, they had been the custodian of law and the legal system of the country. They were wealthy too by owning large tract of land – bestowed by the king for their meritorious service to the realm. To day, things are different. With change of time and society, the Brahmins have got merged into the larger society and have lost their special position. Theoretically, they are still the priestly caste rendering all the religious duties including marriages. Anna Prasanas, prayers, Pujas, consecrations etc. But their legal profession is now thrown open to talents. The Brahmins, are now much poorer compared to the people of other castes.

It is argued that stratification was effected by the notion of biologically based inequality. For example, colour of skin of the white people presumed to have given them superiority over those who are non – white. Apart from the colour, Nazis also claimed racial superiority based on purity of their blood. Andre Beteille has investigated if racial superiority and purity of blood of the white and the Nazi Germans had a case to be defended genetically. He found no trace of biological truth in such claims. The claim of intellectual superiority of the Brahmins based on superior genes also could not be defended because there is no genetic evidence to prove this. According to the French philosopher, Jean Jacques Rousseau, 'biologically based inequality' is limited by their number, but 'socially created inequalities' constitute a major part of social stratification.

A stratified society had always existed in all ages, but in different forms. Stratification as a concept has been changing ever since the dawn of the agricultural revolution of the 17th century. To day, people talk more about social classes than about a stratified society. Even in India, caste as an important factor of stratification is slowly losing grip; in the urban areas specially people in professional and skilled jobs are categorised as social classes rather than as castes. In the West, it is just one of the factors amongst many. Inter-caste marriages in India are taking place fairly regularly without much opposition. In the rural areas, of course, it is still causing some concerns but the law protects inter-caste marriages. Therefore, any serious attempt to oppose such marriages is considered punishable by law.

Functional Theory of Stratification

Functional theory of stratification in seen in the perspective of the functionalist theory of society which proposes that stratification should form in the best interest of the people. The sole purpose of a stratified society is to try to integrate different parts of a society in to a stable frame. In essence, stratification should be functional. It is made from individuals' or groups' performance on whatever vocation of life and career they are engaged in; their work would be assessed and the values judged to see their importance to the society; their status would be determined and rewarded accordingly.

Those who work hard and perform better would surely be rewarded more than those who perform less. In functional perspectives, Prize posts will be left open to all talents and people who would prove their abilities would deserve them. They would earn their place in the hierarchy and rewarded accordingly. Those who fail to live up to expectation will be left with ordinary posts and their status would be much lower down the ladder. Value related status and reward are the cream of the functionalist theory.

In America, where Talcot Parsons comes from, reward is the key word that motivates people to work hard and earn their place in society. People who have achieved distinction in education and training, competition, athleticism, music, drama, fine art, science, commerce, battles, inventions and so on would be rewarded with more benefit than others. This is also true to many other countries. But the difference is, chances of recognition of talents and success are more real in America than other countries. In America, people who contribute particularly to the growth of the economy, science and technology are highly rewarded with lucrative posts.

Talcot Parsons argues that in a stratification system there is bound to be some winners and some losers. Naturally, the latter would remain at the bottom of the ladder. Of course, that would not mean that they would be a waste product. They could be used also to build the social system. With necessary training and education, they could be turned in to real productive human beings. Dignity of labour would induce every body to fit in where they would fit in the society. According to Parsons, stratification is an inevitable part of human society.

Despite social integration, for which Parsons had been endeavouring, there could be cases of disgruntled people unable to integrate in to society, which according to some critics could lead to social conflict and unrest and eventual break down of the system, as Karl Marx had predicted. But Parsons disagreed with that kind of notion believing in that the 'common value system would keep the discord under control. Secondly, Parsons also believed that 'inequality' in people's status, power and position are facts of life and are unavoidable too. Everybody can contribute to the good of the society including those who are in authority and those who are working in the bottom strata of social system. People with power would be able to prevent people cheating, stealing, conspiring to kill and doing criminal damage to the social system by punishing them. Their responsibility involves securing 'collective goals' of the society for which they are being well paid.

Davis and Moore, the two functionalists further added to the ideas of functionalism indicating that top jobs with power and prestige are few and far between. Naturally, filling those jobs would mean that there would be intense competition and only the best and talented persons would be selected and others would be rejected. For example, the job of a brain surgeon or an astronaut is a highly skilled one which can not be found every day. The right people will be those who have the specific skills, aptitude, intelligence, education, personality, patience, self confidence etc. and only they would be selected for particular arduous training. When successful, they would fill those jobs and rewarded accordingly.

Does this mean that the society would be run only by the few experts? Davis and Moore emphasised that there should be role allocation for people of all categories so that every body will find a place to serve the society in their best way. Even less able people can be trained to become useful to fill jobs normally left vacant. This is a fair deal for all. They argued that there is a functional implication of stratification in the interest of the society.

According to Davis and Moore stratification is a 'device by which societies ensure that the most important positions are conscientiously filled in by appropriately qualified people. Like Talcot Parsons, they believes that inequality based on differential rewards is an inevitable feature of an organised human society.

Another American sociologist Tumin, criticised Davis and Moore saying that stratification inevitably keeps some people at the bottom of the social ladder for ever-denying them the opportunities they would desperately need to develop their career; lack of which would be the social justice denied to them.

The new right advocates 'free market' economy for a liberal society based on the capitalist model. The free market offers choice, innovation and efficiency. Competition exists in this condition which boosts producers and investors to improve products but should be cost effective. That will guarantee survival in stiff competition. State intervention will not help rather it will hamper investment, innovation and initiative consequently effecting the economy.

British sociologists, Peter Saunders and David Marshland have been advocating the ideology of new right thinking. Peter Saunders has developed the theory of stratification for the functionalist perspectives. He argued that if all positions in the society are rewarded equally what will happen to the society and how long will it survive as a credible nation. Not for long. First thing – it will fail to function competently. For example, some people would surely be incompetent in doing their jobs perfectly, because those jobs are beyond their capability.

Some would not even prefer to take those difficult jobs assigned to them. There would be a problem of under performance by some workers with in a short time. Peter Saunders stressed that right job for the right person should be the key in order to maintain productivity at a good level in a stratified society. He pointed out that in the capitalist system, naturally there would be more inequalities than in the socialist societies. But true 'equality' in the real sense of the term could not be achieved because it would not work. New right strategies stimulate free enterprise and boost the principle of 'survival of the fittest' in a competitive world.

New right perspectives have been criticised for undermining the effects of stratification in the name of social stability and equilibrium. According to some sociologists, free market economy produces a society more divided than ever. The gulf between the rich and the poor under a free market economy widens and unemployment and poverty get worse. In the stratification system people in the upper strata are favoured more than those down the line. As a matter of fact 'social justice' is denied to those who belong to the lower strata than those in the upper strata. That is obvious; sociologists who advocate stratification as a system, acknowledge that fact and say that stratification produces inequalities.

Marxist Theory of Stratification

Karl Marx and Max Weber have developed social theories which have a lot of conceptual perceptions on the subject of stratification and class. These ideas can be put together to construct a proper stratification theory. The early history of Karl Marx has been fully discussed in the topic on Marx. Even though Marx has not systematically developed the stratification theory, yet most of his work is concerned with social classes, division of society, division of labour, slavery, serfs, bourgeoisie, capitalists, ruling class and so on. He mentioned about the aristocrats, gentry or slave holders, serfs, free peasantry, capitalists many times over in his great treatise the 'Das Capital' which he finished before his death.

Even though the concept of stratification of society rolls round again and again in his work, the central theme of his discussion of society is between two classes – those who produce as workers and those who exploit them and reap the benefit of their work as employers or the 'owners of the means of production', in other words, known as the capitalists. In the early stage of history, land was a primary source of wealth and those who owned it called the land owners and those who worked in the land was known as the peasants. In the later age, this situation had changed with the coming of the Industrial Revolution, when the industries were founded, the nature of work changed from the domestic to the industrial production. The names of workers and owners changed as well; those who owned the industries such as factories, machineries, tools etc came to be known as the industrialists and capitalists as well, because they used to invest quite a lot of money in industry to produce more and those who worked in those industries by selling their skills and labour came to be known as the workers or the working class. Marx also called them as 'proletariat' meaning 'those who have nothing much to loose'.

Marxist perspective of social stratification reflects conflicts with in society which generate a divisive structure – they do not integrate like the functionalist perspectives. The functionalist stratification is a prerequisite to social stability whereas Marxist concept polarises the society into the ruling class and quite opposite to this is the subject class who would have to work as laid down.

Weberian Perspective

Max Weber, was a German sociologist who contributed greatly to the concept of stratification different from Marxist two class model. In is view, stratification is caused by the economic factor as said by Marx; but political power was also important as a factor. He located four groupings which constituted the stratification system.

In his view the property less white collar workers have become important part of the system because of their job security, professionalism, education and training.

The four class model of stratification system of Max Weber:

1. The propertied upper class.
2. The property less white collar workers.
3. The petty Bourgeoisie.
4. The manual working class.

Weber argues that white collar middle class is expanding under capitalism and becoming very vibrant and domineering. Weber has also found that a successful bureaucratic administration manned by large number of competent civil servants and clerical staff have become a key to modern government. Diversification of social classes instead of polarisation in to two hostile groups as Marx had predicted has taken place. Petty bourgeoisie (small land owners) also, in his terms are merging with either trading class like small manufacturers on even farmers and those who are educated and trained joining the white collar jobs. Lastly, Weber disagreed with Marx about his view that political power comes from the economic power. Power comes from intellectual and class power as much as economic power. Working class power is derived from unity and solidarity.

Similar to Marx, Weber equates class in economic terms like 'forces of production' which divide society between those who have and those who have not. But the fundamental difference with Marx is that the property less people have expanded in numbers which Marx could not visualise; nor could he see that this group would become an economic force in the future. Marx said that the 'petit bourgeoisie' would one day melt into the proletariat rather than develop into a middle class. The salaries of the middle class would be high and demanded highly. Their newly acquired status as managers, administrators, top civil servants, scientists, supervisors etc. would dominate the market and affect the stratification system.

Class and Status in Weberian Stratification Structure

Besides social classes, there can be status groups with in the classes as well. With in the Tory party, privilege exists for those educated in well known public schools to get top civil service posts than those in the party educated else where. Some times, there are unwritten rules which operate stronger than the written rules. Status is nothing but an honourable position acquired by privilege of birth or education or class position. Some times, award of titles can enhance one's status. Some times, membership of exclusive clubs like golf, cricket or even prestigious football club like 'Real Madrid' can raise one's status in society but these are regarded as social status not political status which can only be acquired by becoming member of a dominant party.

Status groups can also create divisions with in the classes. Even with in the working class there can be divisions based on status similar to the middle class. The manual working class can be grouped into affluent or respectable working class, ordinary working class and rough working class. Status in the working class is determined by skills, security of jobs, number of years in the service and the income packets. Many workers have been promoted to supervisory posts in the factory or foreman but it is doubtful whether their status would qualify them to get membership in the middle class club.

Status and Parties in Weberian Stratification Concept

Parties are a political phenomenon essentially, but there can be parties with less political character. For example, pressure groups do a lot of non political work like CND, Human rights group, RSPCA, Enviorn protection group and so many like them. Their membership comes from different political and non political organisations. But their activities is to put pressure on the government to change their course of action by making them aware of the consequences that would follow if they continued with their action. For hunting is an old but cruel sport of the old bourgeoisie class but some of the members just can not give up this age old habit and carry on protesting against the government ban. This is a group of different character trying to represent class interest rather than anything political. In the words of Weber, "parties may represent interests determined through "class situation" or "status situation". In the U.S.A. Black power represents both the class and status group interests even though they campaign crucially to improve the economic and social conditions of the black people.

Class Structure in Capitalist Societies

Class structure in the capitalist societies is the product of the stratification system. To day, in advanced industrial societies this concept is used instead of stratification. A person's class is determined by wealth one owns and the kind of work one does. In fact, the class structure is caused by the division between capital and labour. Wealth is an important factor because rich people own more wealth than others and some of them are very rich and are called the capitalists and according to Karl marx, they own 'the means of production'. A small number of people own most of the wealth of world and this number is steadily rising because of the expansion of industries in the 20th century.

Generally speaking, classes are divided into three groups, namely the upper, the middle and the working classes. Max Weber divided the classes into four groups, such as the upper, petit bourgeoisie, middle and working classes. Weber gave great importance to the expanding 'property – less white – collar workers' because they are educated and skilled and their number has been rising. But the manual workers are not. Marx put more emphasis on the manual workers who was also called the industrial proletariat. Marx, however, found two major classes in the industrial societies; they are the Bourgeoisie who with some reservations could be called the capitalists and the proletariat who are the manual workers including peasants, labourers, Lumpen proletariat (who are seasonal workers) etc. Marx emphasised that broadly, there are two classes: the dominant ruling class who owns 'the means of production' and the subordinate class who sells labour.

The Case of the Upper Class

The upper class constitutes various categories of people who can be land lords, owners of industries, investors, shipping magnates and anybody who is a multi-millionaire or a billionaire who invest their wealth in production line for earning more profit. Also upper class includes people who are not very rich but are from well known families with status down the ages who once belonged to the ruling class or as leaders of society. This kind of people usually had great influence on the government. Upper class is sometimes equated with aristocrats who more or less has similar backgrounds but in to day's terms, includes also, according to Westergaard and Resler, company directors, top managers, senior civil servants, higher professionals etc. Many upper class people even rose from lower middle class background. Exceptionally, there may be a few who rose to the top of any establishment from the working class background.

In Britain, before the Industrial revolution, the landed gentry or for that matter the aristocrats were the dominant group of the society. Family contacts, business links, marriage with rich families of similar background etc made the aristocrats and upper classes a 'closed' social group. John Scott in his book 'who rules Britain, (Polity press, 1991) argues that three main groups such as land owners, manufacturers and financiers gradually got together to form a 'tightly integrated group with overlapping business activities'. They operated in the London arena – hub of business centre with very close inter – communication with in the group and they are a part of the Upper class as well.

The Rise of the Middle Class

In the 20th century, there arose another class which was developing in between the upper class and the working class. Always there existed a middle class but it was small in size. Situation changed in this century after the expansion of education, civil service, National health service, public administration, trade and industry and so on. The middle class became larger and larger as the Industrial revolution had spread up and down the country. In simple terms, the middle class is a group of people who are non – manual workers. Karl Marx of course recognised the existence of 'office staff' which he called commercial wage earners but he could not fit them into the stratification system; some times, he called them 'petit bourgeoisie'. According to him, this group had no future, so it would gradually melt into the proletariat; but it did not happen in that way. The middle class began to grow larger, but a significant number grew powerful and rich by being senior professionals such as managers, administrators, successful business people and so on.

Again the professionals are divided into higher and lower professionals. The higher professionals include judges, barristers, solicitors, architects, doctors, dentists, lecturers and professors, scientists, accountants, engineers and so on.

The lower professionals include school teachers, nurses, librarians, social workers, higher grade clerical officers, junior executives, secretaries, steno typist and many more.

Embourgeoisiement Thesis

Embourgeoisiement means "becoming more bourgeoisie; a Marxian style term for becoming more middle class" Anthony Giddens, sociology 4th edn., 2001, p. 295.

The thesis published by a group of sociologists became very popular because of a large number of skilled, semiskilled and experienced working class people otherwise known as the blue collar workers made their way into the middle class category since the 70s, specially in the Western societies. The reasons for such a transition are not far to seek. They are well off and able to buy properties in the expensive areas where professional people live. They are also able to buy foreign cars, washing machines, television sets, telephones and even computers and also afford to go on a summer holiday. They are now able to send their children to private schools and themselves be members of the mainstream Trade Unions, football clubs and so on. They also feel that their attitude to work and career has changed considerably. Their earnings fare better than the comparable groups.

Goldthorpe et al welcomes the trend but still could not give a clearance to their acquiring a middle class status. There are several reasons for that. First, blue collar or affluent workers still lack the middle class characteristics in the true sense of the term. They are still socially segregated and are aware of their status difference with the established middle classes. Goldthorpe et al carried out extensive researches in the Luton area in the south of London where there has grown up a prosperous working class segment mainly worked in the car plants and chemical factories and earned high wages because these were growth industries. Nevertheless, they did not earn as much as the middle classes but they earned certainly more than the clerical workers and lower middle class people. Another difference is the job security and fringe benefits enjoyed by the middle class workers which were denied to them. Other differences included attitudes, values and outlook which remained there same as before but some noticeable change occurred in terms of children's education. The affluent workers still spent their life privately at home and at pubs. Goldthorpe et al noticed that these workers preferred to a non-militant trade union movement – a change towards the middle class attitude.

Two new Marxists who have developed concepts of Marx and Weber are the American Marxist Theorist Eric Olin Wright and the British neo – Weberian sociologist John Goldthorpe.

Proletarianisation Theory

The Theory of Proletarianization suggests that the routine white collar workers such as lower middle class workers have become part of the Proletarianisation process which means that they are now considered more akin to the Proletariat group than less to their lower middle class status. This view is associated with Marxist sociologists like Westerguard and Resler who see that routine non-manual workers are as little different from manual workers. In their views, the earnings of non-manual workers and manual workers have become almost same since the 70s. The American Marxist Harry Braverman supports the Proletarianisation thesis because he has discovered that many routine non manual jobs have become distilled even though the number of white collar jobs has increased; but at the same time the skills required to do their jobs have been reduced. He further argued that since the 70s, similarities between the clerical workers and manual craft workers have become very close to the extent that difference have become minimal. Now a days, the clerical workers are trained to do only particular tasks because tasks are broken down into different roles for the purpose of mass production. Earlier, each clerk had to do many tasks and considered an important staff of the office but to day they only do their specified jobs. Moreover, computer has simplified jobs which only require specific skills. Braverman argues that skills required for routine white collar workers are now minimal. As a result, they have now become Proletarianised.

This claim is denied by David Lockwood who disagrees that clerks are Proletarianised despite the fact that earnings of clerical workers have not risen above the skilled manual workers. He judged things from the market, work and status situations. According to him, the clerks have a distinct market advantage over manual workers-such as job security, shorter working hours and chance of promotion and also fringe benefits like pension rights etc. If the manual workers got more pay that is because they did overtime. Secondly, office workers work in small offices, whereas manual workers work in factory floor different from the office environment. May be their responsibilities are shared but the clerks' qualifications and skills are not standardised which are important for their status. Lockwood however agrees that there has been a phenomenal rise in the number of office clerks including women workers because of the increased requirement in modern offices but that should not be used as a case for Proletarianisation of the clerical workers. Lockwood feels that there has occurred a slight deterioration in the position of the clerical workforce but not to the extent to move down to the working class status. He thinks that they might have occupied a middle ground in between the middle and working classes. This is called 'status ambiguity'. This means that the clerical workers are now placed in the 'intermediate strata', according to J.H. Goldthorpe et al.

The Underclass Concept in the Western Societies

The term underclass issue is now current in many industrial societies. The term indicates that a large number of people have not found a place in the social class structure of Western societies. Many sociologists think that they are a pile at the bottom of the working class. So who are these people? They could be any body who do not go to work because they can not be fitted into the work patterns or they do not have the necessary work culture at all. Some ethnic minorities may fall into this category because of their lack of training and of language skills. Without proper language skills, requisite training could not be passed on; without these two essentials, jobs can not be offered to them. School drop outs without any apprenticeship places fall into this category. But some still make an effort to pick up their work habits doing casual or fractional work. In course of time, they may be offered some durable work as a test case, which could help them as a start to build up their careers.

But without a regular job, one can not be classified into the structural functional system; also one can not be a member of a particular union. The underclass is a disadvantaged and marginalised group in the society. In the eighties, the sociologists recognised this as a serious sociological issue not only because they are unclassified in the broad spectrum of society, but also that they are deprived, dejected and locked down as hopeless cases. Many stigmatise them as victims of their own failure.

But the underclass concept is more complex than it is portrayed in the society. It is true that sociologists are not unanimous about their identity because of their no experience to have a working class status or that they are not form any recognised group to qualify to be included into the structure. If the underclass is kept within the concept of the working class then they could be treated as unskilled and deserving to be employed and trained; or at least, offered terminal jobs with a minimum pay. Of course, most of these works would be on a daily basis conditional on to good behaviour and hard work. Some working class labourers are also unskilled but they have proven record of good behaviour and hard work backed by a lot of work experience. The underclass labourers don't have that; so they do not equate with the working class labourers.

The underclass in the United States, constitutes largely racial and ethnic minorities. In Britain, according to Ralf Dahendorf (1987) the underclass comprised of about 5% of the population but he warned that their number was growing rapidly.

Karl Marx referred to this group as 'Lumpen-proletariat' who consist of people like misfits, vagrants, thieves and dregs. Marx continued saying that they were the scum of the depraved elements of all classes such as vagabonds, escaped galley slaves, swindlers, discharged jailbirds, lazzaroni, pickpockets, tricksters, gamblers, beggars etc. Marx and Engles 1950, p. 267.

Professor A.H. Halsey wrote in the Guardian (13.7.87) @ Britain's class society' "The class structure of industrial societies including Britain is developing an underclass of those who can not be placed in the stable workforce... They suffer accumulation of social pathologies-educational failure, illiteracy, broken families, high crime rates, poor housing and spatial concentration in the inner city. They are disproportionately recruited from the young and the ethnic minorities". Professor Halsey has also argued that this underclass have no stake in the official society and not accountable to any mainstream. But they survive on welfare benefits.

Causes of Underclass

Sociologists have found some common causes for generating underclass problem. Economic and social causes are predominant. Oppenheim has identified several reasons for the rise of the underclass population in British society. In his words, the people in this class are economically impoverished and materially deprived. In essence it is the by product of poverty which was rampant in British society during the 70s and 80s. Unemployment has been another main reason which let down many aspirants getting on with their life. The unemployment figure rose to 3 million in the 80s. During the Labour rule of the late 70s, economic recession reached its epic proportion; there was no work for majority workers more than three days a week instead of five or six days; people lived on causal work, many were laid off because there was no work to go to. Rise of single parent families rapidly rose to 1,300,000 by the end of 1991. Single parent families were a shock to the British society because most of these families had no fathers to take responsibilities of their families; only mothers had to bring up their children with of course help of state benefit but all by themselves. Children need fathers but that was a far cry for these families.

Amongst social causes, many belonging to this group do not develop positive values of life necessary to develop personality and career. Such values also constitute the need for education, aspiration, self respect and respect for society. It is not the case that they never tasted the value of labour; many of them worked as reserve force during the time of economic boom but laid off during the time of bust. With no social recognition it is difficult for them to develop self respect; they took life as it came and that it was made for them.

Underclass in Britain is described by the American political scientist Charles Murray in 1989, as follows. That they are defined by their behaviour. Their homes were littered and unkept; the men in the family were unable to hold a job for more than a few weeks at a time. Drunkenness was common. The children grew up ill-schooled and ill behaved and contributed a disproportionate share to the local juvenile delinquents. Murray, 1989, p. 26.

Earlier in 1984, Murray blamed misguided government in Britain, which provided too many benefits to the underclass creating dependency culture which allowed them to continue with their unattractive and unproductive lifestyles. Murry suggested that to remedy the situation benefits offered by the government to the underclass people should be drastically cut in order to force these people to take responsibility for their own lives.

Charles Murray, must have taken the employment situation in England into account which unfortunately reached 3 million mark in the 80s and cutting benefits whilst jobs were not there, the situation would have been disastrous. No money and no jobs; life would not be worth living. It would rather increase beggary, theft and increased anti-social activities. So the Government continued their policy of helping them rather than letting them go further down in their life.

Questions

1. Define a social class. What criteria do you use in measuring social classes?
2. What are the main characteristics of Marxism. Discuss.
3. Write a critique of Marxism.
4. Explain stratification as a structured inequality between social groups.
5. What are the main differences between the caste system and social classes.
6. Explain Weber's theory of class. In what way, it is different from Marxism?
7. Explain the theory of Embourgeoisement.
8. Explain the theory of Proletarianisation.
9. What are the characteristics of the Underclass.

Bibliography

1. Beteille, Andrei, Caste, Class and Power, Berkeley, 1965.
2. Ghurye, G.S. Caste and Race in India, Bombay, Popular Book Depot 1950.
3. Crompton, R. Class and Stratification, Polity Press, 1993.
4. Ketkar S.V. The History of Caste in India.
5. Giddens, Anthony. The Class Structure of the Advanced Societies. Hutchinson, London, 1979.
6. Oppenheim, C. Poverty, The Facts Child Poverty Action Group, London, 1993.
7. Murry, Charles. Losing Ground, Basic Books, New York, 1984,
8. 'Underclass' Sunday Times Magazine, 26 November, 1989.

17
Caste and Class

Introduction, Caste and Class Distinction, Theories of Caste, Justification of Caste, Changing Caste System, Transformation of Caste into Class.

Introduction, Caste and Class Distinction

The concepts of caste and class are dichotomous – they are intermixed and complex in meaning; to separate one from the other can not be done distinctly. They are understood as a twin subject and read in relation to each other. The caste in India, however existed before the class was conceived of, actually, the class concept grew out of the caste system. They are linked to each other in more than one ways. According to Lundberg, 'a caste is merely a rigid social class into which members are born and from which they can withdraw or escape only with extreme difficulty' (Lundberg, Sociology, p. 315).

In the early days, when the caste was heard of in the Rig Vedic period, it was predominantly a product of social and service usage; the racial undertone also existed like the dark skinned Dravidians – majority of them were categorised as the lower castes – meant to do inferior work like menial jobs including cleaning streets, lavatories, removing dead animals from the street which other people would not do. They were illiterate and unsuitable for skilled or intelligent jobs, so they had to do the menial jobs.

Lower castes were divided into jatis – many of them did not do menial jobs but became peasants – tilling the land for growing crops, fishing, building huts and cottages, hair cutting, cobbler's jobs, making tools, weaving and making clothes etc. The caste concept is thus formed from the kind of work each ethnic group did. Those who did the street and toilet cleaning, clearing dead animals from the street were categorised as the untouchables and put at the bottom of the social structure. Some of them even could not qualify to be included in to the lower caste but below the caste structure generally known as the casteless people and suffered more ignominy than others. They are easily discriminated from the rest of the social groups because of the colour of their skin and the kind of work they did.

'Varna' or the colour of skin played a dominant part in the caste system as much as the kind and nature of work they did. The lower caste known as Sudras was in a better social position than their counterpart Nama – Sudras which meant untouchables. Caste of the fair skinned Brahmins was kept as a 'closed' system as against other castes which were 'open'.' The caste as a closed system that is moving from one caste to another and inter marriage for whatever reasons were completely forbidden. The caste system was also based on purity and pollution, superiority and inferiority factors. The Varna played a particular role in society. The four Varnas are Brahmans, Khatriyas, Vaishyas and Shudras.

The ideology of Varna – Dharma was later developed to include innumerable 'Jatis' or sub-castes based on the doctrine of 'Karma' which teaches a Hindu that he is born in a particular Jati because he deserved to be there on account of his actions in the past life. The code of duties of life for every one had been stipulated by the Dharma. If he performed well and behaved best without harming anybody, then he would earn a better place in the hierarchy of caste or Jati in his next birth. Mrs I Karve has argued that Varna and Jatis have coexisted as two different and related systems for at least one thousand years. Opinion varies in terms of dates and conceptual implications.

The system remained rigid for over a long period. Even though the caste and class existed side by side for centuries, no one dared to interfere with the system knowing quite well that the society would not condone any breach of caste rules whoever broke it; it would be considered an act of defiance to the long established social system. It would also be considered an act of sacrilege against the religious system. According to Max Weber, the caste system is an extreme example of social closure which prevented people from reaching out for status outside the system.

But the class is entirely a different matter which was strictly based on occupation, birth, education and social status one enjoyed. Unless where class and caste got mixed up to the extent to cause a social furore, there was no problem; the class is a mobile and flexible matter, not subjected to scrutiny and social approval; a person from one class can move up to a higher class if he or she has the right credentials like placed in a high status job or married to an upper class family. A working class girl can improve her class status by marrying a middle class boy even if she came from a lower caste family. In the early stage, even social status and wealth were not considered important for moving up to a higher caste. For example, if a Khatriya or a Vaishya moved up to a higher class with a promotion from his vocation he would still remain in his original caste which does not change.

The caste people had to accept what has been provided by the caste rules; any violation would be deemed as disrespect even when they were upgraded to their class status. Marriage in the caste system was endogamous which meant, regardless of classes marriage remained caste based. If any body married from a different caste they would be made outcastes.

In the class system everybody has a chance of moving upwards in the hierarchy of social classes. Sociologists argue that traditional social class system is being eroded and being replaced by a moving hierarchy of unequal positions. This is so specially in the U.S.A. Else where, the situation warrants clarification because social mobility is so persistent in to day's changing society. For example, in the case of upper class persons or for that matter aristocrats, they try to link their status to their birth and the place of their living. Also, they can claim that their education is from prestigious schools, colleges and universities, which automatically put them at a better position than students from other institutions. Some of the institutions worth the name select their students from parents of professional and higher income groups who normally come from upper middle and aristocratic classes. People belonging to these classes also have aesthetic interest in art, architecture, sculptures, paintings and fineries which other don't concern. Instead of these factors, social class is a moving phenomenon whereas the caste system is not. The rate of social mobility in class system is very high.

In the U.S.A. particularly, there has grown a large number of people from no class position to climb hierarchy in various professional occupations. Whereas, it is not the case in the U.K. Ethnic minorities are discriminated against indigenous groups except for a few who have exceptional abilities and are allowed to move up to a higher level. By comparison with the caste system, social class, has an 'open door' because, class does not bar people from the mainstream group to reach higher class but that has to be achieved through hard work, performance and by developing personal qualities and language abilities.

Theories of Caste

(a) Traditional or Divine Theory

The caste system is the oldest social system in the world. According to the Hindu traditions, it had a Divine origin rooted in the Rig-Vedic period. Hindu scriptures present ample reference to the existence of the caste system. With the arrival of the Aryans in India around three thousand B.C. the caste system began to take full shape. The Legend goes to portray that in the tenth and the final scripture of the 'Rig Veda' the caste was conceived of in the power of the cosmic man 'the Purusha' the original supreme being who saw danger if the society was not structured. To function fully it should have a frame in which they would have jobs to do. This was necessary in order to have a stable and long lasting society. Hence, He created an immobile hierarchical system: He looked at his own anatomical stature and created a society out of it making each part functional to do a specific job. Each part was made into a particular caste according to its distinct capability which to deliver the society's manifold functions. In this way, the caste system was constructed to become an integral part of the Indian society.

The Brahmins, for example, were endowed with the legal, spiritual, intellectual and educational capabilities; so they were made a superior caste. They were also responsible for conducting ceremonial functions of the state and also to advising the royalty in case it was needed in difficult circumstances. Blessing the society generally was one of their religious prerogatives. It is believed that they emerged from the brain and mouth of the 'Purusha', the Supreme Being. The second caste was the Khatriyas who emerged from his powerful arms to become warriors and rulers. Most of the royals were members from the Khatriya caste.

The third caste emerged from the thighs of the 'Purusha' meaning that they would be traders, business men, money lenders and cultivators. They would have to be industrious, hard working and travelling a lot for the sake of business and commerce. The last was to be born from His feet as Sudras who would have to serve the three superior castes above them.

In Rig Vedic term the caste as Verna which means colour or complexion of the body which according to some interpretation, has also been at the root of division of society as castes. The superior Brahmins are white complexioned and the bottom Sudras are black complexioned who did the menial jobs. In between, the mixed complexioned did a variety of jobs as mentioned above. There grew up another group of people over the years who failed to reach the status of a caste and therefore were known as the out caste or untouchables who had to work as cleaners and disposers of dead animals. They would remain segregated from the rest of the society because of the impure type of work they did. This showed that the inequalities prevailed in every segment of the Rig-Vedic society based on abilities, colour and status. The scriptures of Manu also confirmed the status of the Brahmins as superior to the Khatriyas and others.

(b) Occupational Theory

According to this theory, some sociologists, specially Nesfield discovered that strict 'Division of Labour' based on skills, aptitudes, interests, mental and physical capabilities were at the root of instituting the caste system. In his view, function and function alone created the class and the caste systems. Skills and functional differentiation led to the occupational division into such as teachers, priests, officials, carpenter, brick layer, fisherman, black smiths, cleaners and sweepers and also other categories. The caste system has been a hereditary institution – generally, son stepping into father' occupation; may be there were a few exceptions when some refused to follow fathers' occupational role.

(c) Evolutionary Theory

The caste system grew up as a result of slow social process. Amongst other factors, the hereditary occupational reason was also behind this process. Like all other institutions such as the education, economic, legal systems etc, which grew up slowly over the years, so also the caste system. The choice of people in society was very limited in the early annals of history; so the need to move towards a social system which could guarantee the basic necessities of life became important; the system became almost permanent, it was difficult to change. Several other factors are also to contribute to the process of evolution. For example, beliefs in the reincarnation and the doctrine of karma. As the system became rigid i.e. no mobility towards the upper strata of society, the only hope remained was to improve the lot by strictly following the 'doctrine of karma' which offered a chance to lift oneself into a higher caste in the next life only through hard work, strict adherence to the rules of society, honest and pious living etc.

Besides, a multiplicity of other factors occurred over the years which fostered a rigid caste consciousness and to the formation of a structural functional caste system; which are as follows:

Effect of external pressures on Indian society occurred as a result of foreign invasions and its influence on the life and activities of people, forces like racial attack and negative propaganda against Hindu society etc.
Need to unify and to maintain the fabric of Indian society against other cultural Impacts,
Predominance of the Brahmins,
Rural underdevelopment and the feudal system of social control; etc
Hereditary occupations,
Static nature of Hindu society,
Ideas of exclusive family, ancestor worship and the use of sacramental meal,
Cultural diversity, clash of patriarchal and matriarchal system, religious bigotry, superstition, racial superiority and so on.

Rationale of Caste

The caste system like many other social systems is hierarchically organised to reflect the various social stratums of the country. It is a kind of 'division of society'; instead of using social class, one can comfortably use the division of society by social caste. Each strata has a specific role to play for the benefit of society based on their particular skills and hereditary occupational rights. So, the son of a warrior, for example, would be a soldier and the son of an untouchable would work as a cleaner like his father and so on and so forth. The gradation starts from the top and runs through to the bottom known as four castes as mentioned above. Below the four caste frame, comes the 'untouchables', also mentioned above, who were not assigned a place in the frame because of their low birth and with no particular role, so they remained outside the system but gradually picked up a job which others would not do. This job is cleaning services to include, road, market place, drains, toilets etc, and also to remove dead animals from the street, parks, public places and so on. This became their hereditary vocation which continued unabated for centuries.

In real life situation, castes or jatis are divided into many sub-castes or endogamous groups whose superiority and seniority to one another remained always questionable but practised as people accepted their social status told by priests and headmen. The caste system is both cultural and structural portraying social and religious values on the one hand and control, possession and subjugation on the other.

The justification of the caste system lies in the fact that the system had kept the society in tact for centuries. Despite social inequalities and other malice caused by caste order, the society remained effective in terms of functions, law and order and unity. It is also believed that they system protected the society with its values against hordes of foreign invasions and occupations that took place over thousands of years. There was no need to use force in maintaining the system which was working and delivering services to the country quite well.

The caste system has also created a specified position for every citizen; so no one is in doubt about what his or her social status is and the role to play. According to Hutton, the caste provided every person his choice of marriage, rituals, religious activities and to seek help when necessary including his funeral. As a result of the caste system, various functions of society are guaranteed for ever. No work is left without it being assigned to somebody. It has provided a method of effective division of labour no where else could be found.

Negative Aspects of the Caste System

The negative aspects of the caste system are as many as positive aspects which are as follows.

One of the fundamental flaws of the system has been the inability of the people to move upwards in to the social ladder. It has remained rigid, inflexible and immobile for centuries until after the industrial revolution in the 19th century, when the rigidity began to breakdown slowly. The caste system was outlawed and abolished as a practice by the constitution of India in 1947.

Untouchability is another social malice which in the words of Mahatma Gandhi, "is the hateful expression of caste". It denied the vast majority individual rights to choose and to express one's mind about his or her feeling. A large section of the people in the system was consigned to a servility where from to uplift was virtually impossible.

Talents of people were denied to function or develop because the right of choice was not allowed to exercise. People had no choice, they had to do what was only told to do by the caste rules. So creativity hampered. The divided society was anathema to the development of national consciousness; the freedom movement was slow and disjointed; a fragmented country was a recipe for a longer foreign rule. The fate of India was sealed, so also the future of the people. This state of affairs kept the society backward and retarded in so many ways. So progress was very slow.

Another evil of the caste system was casteism. This ideology is a caste feeling that one's caste is superior to others. It led to a growth of prejudice and disrespect for other castes. Furthermore, it grew a blind allegiance to their own caste ignoring the values of others. Values of decency, good manners and etiquette and a sense of brotherhood of human beings etc were undermined just for selfish feeling of ethnicity and emotion of their own caste which stood against the interest of others. In effect, Casteism was like a curse that befell on the whole society from no where.

Changing Caste System

The effect of the Industrial Revolution in Europe in the 19th century and of the British rule in India was strongly felt by a large number of people. At home, the feeling was one that the system was unjust and inappropriate under the changing circumstances. It appeared that the system was losing its grip on the society in the wake of the western influence and the rigidity was now being shaken to its foundation. The effect has slowly sipped in to the urban culture of India. The opening of English schools and learning of English language have increased the hope of better employment at home and abroad. The prospect of having a democratic government in the near future and rights and freedom of the individuals being granted, the employment opportunity in the army and other services away from home would be brighter. These opportunities would also offer chances of meeting people of diverse cultures, creeds, castes, religions etc which would also loosen their minds and boost morale to fight back caste rules and foreign yolk. Although outwardly nothing changed and people appeared cool but at heart revolting to break the barriers of the caste system. The degrading effect was felt everywhere.

The first movement started by the Indian Missionary in the world stage is Swami Vivekananda who spoke about the degrading effect of the caste system saying that the system is against religion or the philosophy of Vedanta. Reformers like, Raja Ram Mohan Roy and Devendranath Tagore stood for the brotherhood of man and fought against the evils of caste system saying that it should not be allowed to divide the brotherhood of man. Almost all great leaders and reformers of India stood firm to fight the caste system at the root and campaigned for its abolition and to establish the rule of law. Sree Keshab Chandra Sen in Bengal started a movement for the intercaste-marriages and the abolition of the caste system. Mahatma Gandhi fought against untouchability and its abolition made a national priority. He succeeded when the Indian constitution abolished it at a stroke. He gave the untouchable people a new respectable name 'children of God'.

Things began to change fast during the 19th century under pressure from the growing public agitation, the British rule did not hesitate to lend their support to its dissolution. In 1856, under pressure from the Bengal reformer Vidyasagar, the then vice chancellor of Calcutta university, the Widow Remarriage Act was passed in 1856, which removed some abuses practised by the lower castes. This allowed the widows to choose their future husbands as against the wishes of the hereditary priests and village elders to choose for them. Twenty years later in 1876, came the ruling of the Bombay High court which overturned the authority of the caste to declare a marriage null and void and order a widow to marry someone of their choice. In 1872, a special Marriage Act was passed which allowed an Indian of whatever caste or creed to enter into a valid wedlock with a person of another caste or creed if they declared that they did not belong to any religion. This act however was subsequently modified by an amending Act of 1923, to clarify that part of the declaration, 'They did not belong to any religion' applied to only Hindus, Jains, Sikhs and Brahmos and no body else.

Gradually, a host of regulations were passed to remove barriers effecting the untouchables; and others about their rights for education, social, economic and political benefits and free school places for depressed classes etc.

Whatever steps were taken to uplift the condition of the lower castes including the untouchables did not go far enough to his at the roots of the problems. These actions were taken by the administrators, not by the political consensus of the British government, who were keen on safeguarding their interests as a first thing than anything else.

In actual fact, these piecemeal measures were blessings in disguise because these whipped up desire for more and more reforms and not less. More measures came through as the years passed and specially in 1951, the new Indian constitution abolished the caste system fully and made it a law that anybody mistreated and discriminated a person because of his/her caste would be prosecuted.

The class concept in India was ingrained in the caste system since its inception. Often they were treated as one. The class concept became an interesting sociological subject in India only in the 20th century. The social classes developed slowly which rose and fell along with the changing economic and political situations. During the time of economic boom classes were formed based on wealth, business and trade and the high earners became the upper class who actually came from the top three castes namely the Brahmans, Khatrias and Vaisys but during the economic bust they melted into their castes again and remained in top positions. The top classes were landed gentry and business magnates; class or without class they remained at the helm of affairs. The political turmoil also created and recreated the class scenario. According to the Portuguese traveller Magasthanese in India in the early 4th century B.C. there existed seven classes, such as philosophers, peasants, herdsmen, craftsmen, traders, soldiers, government officials and councillors. There was further development of the classes down the years such as Maharathis, Mahasenapatis as top of the classes and the second class were consisted of the government officials as the Amatyas and Mahamatys. The lowest in the classes were gardeners and other menial workers. As indicated above, classes were formed and broken down and reformed again along with fallen towns and organised life due to invasion and militarism.

The middle class in India expanded during the Moghul rule. The Moghul officials both in the capital and provinces included surveyors, revenue collectors, lawyers (vakils and Qaxis), Muftis, who expanded Muslim laws, revenue inspectors, official informers, writers, pundits etc. The administrative officials who helped the Mughal Emperors run the day to day affairs were members of the aristocratic class. Their birth was an added qualification besides everything else to securing the high administrative posts.

The Mughal administration was organised centrally and provincially. The head of the central government apart from the Emperor who was Emperor of the whole country was the Wazir or Diwan. He was the highest person below the Emperor. In to day's terms, he could be compared with a de-facto primeminister under an absolute monarch. Other chief officials like paymaster general, the chief Quzi, the commander-in-chief, the Imperial Household, the head of the judiciary called the chief Quzi. Under them other senior and junior officials were in to day's terms could be upper and middle-middle class people. The lower middle class were office clerks-their number could be high.

The provincial administration was structured and organised along the central pattern. The head of the province was a Diwan who also called a Sadar or Subedar. He was accountable to the Emperor no doubt, but at first must come through the central Diwan. The moghal officials were essentially an urban people divided between the aristocratic and middle classes.

The Fauzdar (supervisor of provincial executive functions) and under him qunungoes and other officials like the civil service in modern terms classwise were all middle and lower middle class people. Caste was less significant in administration. Birth and contact were most important than caste in selection.

Further down the history, under the East India Company's rule, the middle class included surveyors, accountants, tax collectors, judges (hakims), record keepers, and with land reform in Bengal came the Zamindars, tenants, agricultural labourers and Mahajans or money lenders. Later, with urbanisation caused by road building, transport and communication, trade, business and industry developed fast which gave rise to the financial and commercial classes.

The middlemen and interpreters became an important class of people within the middle class during the British rule. The British maintained their functions through the help of these people than direct contact with the people. They communicated with the administrators in English; so they earned good money as middlemen.

Classes kept changing along with change in society and administration. Political transition from one rule to another changed the nature of work, so also their names which caused more confusion than actual type of work.

The class system in Europe changed dramatically with the industrial and technological revolutions. The class structure was further diversified along the line of division of labour. In order to simplify class structure in Europe, sociologists have devised four main classes to include in it all categories of people irrespective of their rank, privileges, wealth, education, responsibilities, positions, birth and type of their work; Some sociologists have divided the classes based on earnings; some have done on the nature of their work. Some are called manual workers and also known as the working class. People like the peasants, domestic servants, fishermen, carpenters, labourers, wood cutters, cleaners, drivers and so on come in to this group. And the rest belongs to the middle classes in broad terms and of course, the upper gentry or aristocrats and land and property owners were above the middle classes.

In India, the working class is made up of different sub-class or castes.

Until the beginning of the 20th century the middle class in India was a small group of professional people comprised of teachers, doctors, accountants, lawyers, engineers, surveyors and local government officials. Since the end of the first world war this changed dramatically with the inclusion of fast growing civil and administrative staff and many newly skilled manual workers. The Brahmins monopolised administrative services because of their mental ability. Karl Marx identified two groups of classes more or less in every society. The criteria used was their economic base, one was a bourgeoisie and the other one, the poor proletariat. In Marx's terms they were 'those who have a lot and those who have nothing'.

Using Western criteria of owning wealth, skills, education, means of production and the total earnings of an individual or the family as a whole, the Indian society can be divided into the following classes. They are as follows:

Super-upper class. People in this group come from the business and industrial houses who own the means of production. They can also be called capitalists. Caste is less important in recognising their position and status. Even though the number of the super upper class are few and far between, they carry enormous power in decision making both in private and public sectors. The government when necessary take their advice and accord them due respect because they contribute a lot to the national economy.

The second one is the affluent upper class. They are high flyers – educated at prestigious colleges and universities both at home and abroad; they occupy top civil service jobs and other lucrative positions like company executives and so on. Caste is not a factor in deciding who they are. Amongst them, there is a rising number of people coming from no privileged back ground but who by dint of their extraordinary abilities in sports, music specially pop music and showbiz including superstars in the movie industry who are significantly rich in to day's society. They can be counted as affluent upper class. So also, in the U.S.A. or in other big cities there is a group who are known as 'Finance capitalists' who don't own any companies but manage stocks and accumulate share-holdings are now core of the upper class today.

The middle class is enlarged to cover a wide range of non-manual workers of semiliterate level and people trained in voluntary education who could do technical work like repairing machines, engines, specialised cooking, hair dressing, computer training, carpentry, glassware, jewellery and pottery making etc. Earlier, these jobs were done by unskilled people without theoretical knowledge of the job but were assisted as apprentices by some body in the work places or inherited skills from their families. Many of them were early school leavers without any qualifications. They were accepted as working class because they had necessary aptitude for the job even though with no qualifications. These unskilled workers having had gained experience after a few years' work were accepted as regular employees in the firm and factories.

But with incrased skill requirement, accredited voluntary training courses in further education colleges have been made available for successful school leavers who prefer to take up technical careers. Also these include all literate people who hold responsible administrative jobs both in industry and in government offices, banks and local governments but with no higher degrees. They are in the lower middle class position. Others in the lower middle class position are included those office secretaries, typists, computer technicians, clerks and cashiers etc.

Accountants, teachers, lectures, professors, doctors, lawyers, scientists, smal businessmen, surveyors and so on are included in to middle and upper middle class positions depending on degrees and level of pay. The word professional is flexible to discriminate between qualified and trained professional and people like plumber, electrician, telephone engineer, carpenter, security personal, etc against people in the professional fields such as lawyers, accountants, nurses, pharmacists, teachers, etc.

Controversy never dies out about the class position of the emerging new skilled people who are manual workers but trained in professional courses. People in this group include qualified plumber, electrician, fitter, engineering workers, train drivers, deluxe coach and bus drivers, taxi drivers, tram drivers, builders and so on. These people have varied pay scales based on years of training, nature of work, experience and responsibilities. These elements distribute them in different middle class positions. For example, a foreman, a supervisor, an inspector even having same qualification and training as others are placed in middle class position or a few may be in a higher middle class position. A motor mechanic for Rolls Royce or Ferrari or Aston Martin is not the same as mechanics for ordinary cars. They have higher pay scales as well as status as their training is a longer and difficult one than other categories of cars to qualify for a higher middle class status. These people are skilled and professional and they earn handsome salaries. These people are now being increasingly recognised as members of the upper working class. For others, lower middle class position is appropriate because of their training, experience and level of pay. Some of them if earning good money may even prefer to be called affluent working class than being called as lower middle class.

Further Reading

1. Beteille, Andrei Caste, Class and Power.
2. Hutton, J.H. Caste in India. 3rd end, Bombay, 1961.
3. Ketkar, S.V. The History of Caste in India.

Part 8

18
Case Study

Introduction, Division of Labour, Durkheim's Methodology, Interpretive View of Suicide, The Realist View of Suicide.

Introduction

The 'Suicide' case study has been adequately discussed in my essay on Emile Durkheim on Part 3. Here, I will write an appraisal of his investigative method which is sometimes known as a combined positivism and realism methods knit together to enquire into the suicide case but it generated some criticism.

Durkheim has won praise for his work on suicide. He is a French sociologist; who liked to establish himself as an original thinker, specially in the realm of sociological science which at his time was acquiring a status of scientific subject. His endeavour was bold, criticism of his method is only a reasonable part of an academic study. He tested different causes of suicide but found wanting in each the clues he was looking for. Then he ventured into other unusual causes unique to the subject. Apart from those causes, which will be mentioned below, suicide is generally seen as the effect of depression and pathological conditions of mind, as explained by sociologists but there could be many other vital causes even Durkheim was reluctant to venture.

Durkheim's aim has been to unravel the causes of suicide from the society than banking on Psychological theories which were very convincing with the academic circle. The society must be responsible in some way or other for a large number of specially the young people who were committing suicide; so Durkheim's venture has been to investigate the sociological side of the issue to uncover the truths from society's point of view than hanging on to the psychological factors. Also, Durkheim's venture had been to target general social phenomena rather than individual issues. He was not reticent to individuals' plight who took their lives either forced by personal reasons or by other social causes beyond their control. But Durkheim was seriously searching for social causes with wider applications. If any body felt useless and needless in society committed suicide just to get out of the pains which Dukheim was not interested in. Durkheim blamed society to let individuals go to the state of no return and commiting suicide. There may be many causes of suicide such as, poverty, deprivation, ill treatment in the family, incest, personal failure in life, oppression and repression both at home and society. The society should have come up to help people out of their misery but failed do that. But Durkheim's enquiry was different.

Division of Labour

According to Durkheim, Suicide also grows from the industrial causes effected by the Division of Labour. Disintegration of society occurs when society moves from Mechanical solidarity to the stage of the Organic solidarity where dissemination of the labour force takes place. This causes distress to people. Individuals who fail to integrate into the urban pattern of life with in the organic stage of development become victims of stress and disorientation of life – a total inability to cope with continuing changes.

Durkheim's Methodology

Durkheim was fascinated by the ample statistical evidence already accumulated by some European countries which he wanted to use in building a theory on suicide; no doubt, it would be unique when completed.

This stock of secondary sources available, could be congenial to comparing as well as to building correlations with in them. Furthermore, these processes, Durkeim believed would improve chances of bringing sociology nearer to the level of natural sciences. Durkheim could then skillfully employ multivariate method to analyze and to isolate disparate factors from his own in order to establish the theory.

Durkheim's study also included which countries had stable suicide rates than others. Some countries had variable rates depending on changing circumstances where as some had stable rates regardless of circumstances. He found that even with in the same society, suicide rates varied with different groups. For example in the Western societies, Roman Catholics and Protestant groups had different suicide rates even though culturally and religiously they came from almost same background. Comparatively, the Jews had a lower rate of suicide even when they had a higher rate of insanity according to the psychological view. But Durkheim could not find any co-relationship between insanity and suicide rates. Durkheim's categories of suicide included Egoistic (insufficiently integrated) people specially with in the domestic society, anomic people most in industrial societies, where individuals were insufficiently regulated, altruistic suicide, where individuals were over regulated and fatalistic suicide, where individuals were strictly integrated in to the social life.

Durkheim passionately believed in the Positivist mode of investigation but could not reach perfection. At times, he tripped to different methods, in fact this practice enriched the quality of his enquires but compromised with the empirical scientific level. It is generally agreed that case study should follow both scientific methods, and use of statistical data. Durkheim used both the recent data and the age old official statistics to make enquires inclusive.

Interpretive view of suicide

Interpretive sociologists are critical about Durkheim's method of defining suicides. Sociologists like J.D. Douglas have raised the question of using official statistics to define suicide cases, because the reliability of official statistics could not be guaranteed. He was skeptical about the coroner's verdict too on death supposed to be suicide, because the coroner has a set theory in which to fit in all suspects of suicide. There is a question of bias also when some one in the family commits suicide but the death is treated as an accident for no fault of their own. This is usually done to cover up for the sake of their honour or family pride. They would not like to be indicted for the suicide. Suicide in the family is a commonplace thing in many third world countries where restrictive practices are imposed on the members. Denial of personal freedom of movement and repression with in the family cause many deaths at home. According to Douglas, all suicide cases must be investigated but mentions that cultural factor has a crucial role to play behind some of these cases. Some cultures encourage suicide as a way to escape from the mundane world in order to reach heaven. So religious meaning of suicide can not be ignored.

Realist View

Realists like Roy Bhaskar, Russel Keat, Andrew Sayer and others argue that despite criticism, Sociology is a part of natural sciences. They argue that some scientists have misunderstood the nature of science. Science can be studied by either a closed system or an open system. In the closed system, all the variables can be controlled and their characteristics identified. With in the Laboratory experiment, closed system is more useful to sort out results than the open system which enables many sciences to enquire and find quantitative study easy. Variables can not be measured as accurately as the Laboratory experiment and make prediction. They are still considered as science because they can use various methods to provide almost accurate results.

Maurice Halbwach has studied Durkheim's methodology and agreed with many of his finds. But one thing which disturbed him much was Durkheim's excessive use of the religious cause for the rise of suicide rates in the protestant societies than those in the. Catholic societies. Gibbs and Martin are disappointed with Durkheim's failure to explain 'social Integration' fully in a sufficiently precise and measurable way.

Part 9

19

The New Right Theory of Education

Introduction, Equal Opportunity Programme, Tory Opposition to the Equal Opportunity Programme, Tory Response to the Solution, Labour's Objectives on Multi-cultural Education, Technical and Vocational Education Initiatives, Criticisms of the Tory Educational Initiatives, Tory Reply to the TVEI Programme, Chub and Moe and the Concept of the Market Forces, James Callaghan Speech at Ruskin College 1976, Mrs Margaret Thatcher's Concept of Market Forces, Criticism of the Tory Government's Educational Reform of 1988-89.

Introduction

The New right theory of education is generally associated with the Tory party's ideology which has revolutionised the educational thinking in Britain during the eighties as it had happened already in the rest of Europe. In England, the current issue of the eighties was the secondary education which also included the Tertiary area. Since the 70s, the Secondary education and its administrative system including the funding mode have drawn criticism from wide ranging interested parties, to include amongst them were the parents, Trade Unions, teachers, educationalists, sociologists, political leaders and so on. So, education as a subject meant everything that concerned with the perfect form of educational delivery to the school children from nursery to the tertiary age group up to the age of 19.

The change became like an organic one; change in one area hastened the change in another area and so on, otherwise, no change would last long. So management of schools, administration of education and the funding methodology became one area which needed an overhaul and which needed to respond to the development of school curriculum. Selection of pupils for schools, internal testing and public exam system-all had to go through a massive change; all the changes taken together meant that a revolution in education has been started since the Tripartite system introduced in 1944. Further education for the age ranges of 16 to 19 plus the adult education also received attention in a separate piece of legislation in the early 90s.

The movement began in the wake of falling standard in schools and declining industrial out put which led to the poor state of education in Britain. The right wing thinkers traditionally link school performance with the economic up or down turn in the country. The irony was that both were underperforming in Britain since the 70s. There has been a steady decline in the British manufacturing industry effecting the rise in unemployment. Decline in educational standard has also caused skills shortage in the Industry. Inequality in education and employment caused by racism, discrimination, prejudice and gender issues already cost the country heavily.

Originally, the right thinking occurred in the United States during the 60s where the standard in education reached its lowest watermark. Awareness of new right thinking also grew in England along with the U.S.A. France and other states of Europe at that time. President Reagan introduced strategies trying to combat falling standard generally known as the Reaganism. Here in England it was the 'Thatcherism' when Mrs Margaret Thatcher introduced a package of new ideas – a product of right wing educational thinking, strengthened by her kingpin education secretary, Sir Keith Joseph.

The new right thinking was largely derived from the economic theories, particularly from those who advocated market systems as a way to distribute resources. It is also based on choice. According to Dunleavy and O'Leary, the core value of new right is 'freedom' from coercion (1979, p. 93). In education, this freedom is reflected in 'choice' which the parents would like choosing their kind of schooling for the education of their children. This is like the consumers choosing what to buy. This is a freedom virtually synonymous with individualism. The producers on their part collect data through market researches – understanding the needs of consumers which they produce in order to attract them. This is the market policy developed as a recourse to survive in a competitive economy. This market system contradicts with the state controlled production system. The state bureaucrats produced their kind of things and imposed them on the market for consumers to buy leaving no room for choice. The argument given is that they are producing what the government allowed them to do under strict resource allocation. Loosing the market was not their responsibility as their jobs were to follow employment regulations regardless of what is produced and its effect on the economy.

In many respects, the new right concept is a product of a radical version of modernism, which advocated opening up of the global economy for the cause of widening the International trade. Side by side, in England, the market forces were required to be given precedence over other matters in order to coincide with the world market, otherwise Britain would remain as an isolated and an underperformed country with consequent effect on her national economy. According to the new right economic thought, the national economy was constrained by a host of internal factors, such as the bureaucratic bungling, excessive government interference in to the private sector, too many controls and worst of all political and ideological battle with in the parties, which diverted attention from the main issues. The result was the national economy grew very slowly. The right wing thinkers argued that innovations, foreign and national investment must surge forth above internal politics. Peter Berger, a right wing sociologist argued that liberalising the economy would help growth of freedom of choice, democratic pluralism and individualism essential for prospering in the capitalist economy.

The Tories came to power after winning a land slide victory in the general election of 1979. Along with it came the Right wing political thought which produced radical ideas for education. Already their was the 'equal opportunities programme" in place introduced by the then Labour party in power in the 70s. This was functioning in full swing along with the greatest change ever made in the secondary education by the introduction of the comprehensive pattern of education. This new pattern eliminated the controversial 'selection' mode used for choosing kids for the grammar school education known as the I.Q. Tests for pupils of 11 years old. This historic Test was earlier introduced by the British Education minister Lord Butler in his Education Act of 1944.

In the early seventies most of these grammar schools were transformed into the comprehensive schools. There were initial protests intitiated by the Tories against transforming the Grammars in to the Comprehensives schools but seeing the general mood of the country which favoured the Comprehensive system, they had no choice but to accept the public demand; above all, the 'Equal opportunities programme' already introduced was akin to the 'Comprehensive ideology' which the Tories again tried to overturn but failed.

In England, the education scenario concerning the children of the working class and immigrant communities was almost similar to the plight existed in the United States, where they had introduced the "Head start Programme" to make progress in eradicating illiteracy ensuring that every underachiever learns the 3RS before leaving the school. Similar social causes such as prejudice, discrimination and poor funding had effected educational achievement there. The success of the "head Start" programme was an example worth taking into account whilst preparing an underachievement programme for the children of working class and ethnic minority background in the U.K.

In Britain, under pressure, the government introduced measures to overhaul the educational scenario. With increased funding and other positive measures – the school discipline, career and the curriculum were first targeted and a lot for higher standard and better Exam results. The Labour government had already introduced 'the equal opportunities programme' in education which was extended to jobs, health and housing. This started melting down inequalities slowly but was still a long way to go. The project got into widening access to students of further and higher education as well specially for the disadvantaged students. The Race Relations Act dealt with issues of discrimination based on and faith in no time. All these opened the area of opportunities for those disadvantaged who could now see their bright future ahead.

The Tory Opposition to the 'Equal Opportunity's Programme'

The new right thinkers criticised the 'Equal opportunities programme' including the comprehensive pattern of education as expensive and wasteful because they alleged that no body could assure clearly what the outcome would be like. They picked on area where controversy could gain momentum. Such as, the 'mixed ability teaching programme' which confused teaching generally, so easily became a subject of severe controversy. This teaching method was still in the experimental stage – so time was needed to see it through. Main concern was that in the mixed ability teaching situation both the abler and lower ability pupils were taught together in the same teaching group based on same class work; teachers were busy helping the weaker ones who needed help most. The result was that the teachers' time was almost used up whilst the abler pupils got no teaching to help raising their standard. This became a serious issue when the abler pupils got bored because their abilities were not stressed and not sufficient academic work was provided to meet their potential. The employers were not happy either. Many lower ability kids left school without adequate basic skills and 3RS; so they remained unemployable. The investment in education was shared by the paticipatory private sector along with the education department. They were not happy that their investment was not delivering enough return as skill shortage still continued effecting the industry. The skills were supposed to come from the participatory schools.

Third, the economy promised by the government to grow also did not show signs of improvement. The Equality programme also failed to bring equality in society as originally intended. Meanwhile, the gap between the rich and the poor got further widened. The idea that more educated and trained workforce in the country would be a potential economic resource fell flat on its argument. The new right group began to question the viability of the Equal Opportunity Programme which they believed was fundamentally flawed.

The Tory Proposals for Solution

The answer to all this was the new right thinking group's series of educational measures including reforming the curriculum programme in a way to deal with the crucial educational issues. Besides, their priority was focussed on the requirement of industries plus boosting the national economy.

The new right thinking in their educational objectives hoped to create a competitive atmosphere amongst schools so that each school would try their best every year to scale the top of the League Table. The needs of the able and gifted pupils are to be adhered to and given education to meet their potential. They should not be made a scapegoat for the cause of others.

The new right, however, had extra plans for pupils who missed education in their early years for no fault of their own but because of family circumstances. Besides poverty, which prevented many to continue their educational pursuits, the language deficiency and effect of sub cultural environment also contributed to their under achievement. No education can be attained properly without adequate language capability and positive cultural impetus to back them up. In England, in the early eighties, the Tory government gave parents more choice to choose schools and asked the local educational authorities to publish school results nationally to show their positions in the league table. This was thought to be important for the failing schools to face up to the challenge and move forward. They could make more effort and compete to improve their places in the league table.

The government also put emphasis on all students to be properly skilled and educated before leaving schools. Not only for their careers, the requirement of the employers would have to be heeded as well, as stipulated in their specifics such as communication skills, numerals, literacy, manners, confidence, behavioural attitude and life skills. Lastly, the industry stressed the need for upgrading the level of voluntary education in order to bring them at par with other courses. This would bring their skill level commensurate to the requirement of the industries. According to Chubb & Moe, improvement would automatically follow if market system was introduced in to the education. The market forces are fundamentally economic forces which according to the right wing thought can be applied to the field of educational planning as well. In their article, 'politics, market and the organisation of schools' (1997), John E. Chubb and Terry Moe put forward their case for introduction of market forces as a remedy to cure serious educational underachievement in the U.K. which has been effecting the economy for some time and also other areas of social life as well.

According to them, there has been a 'long simmering discontent' about test scores, loose academic standards and lack of discipline in schools. Besides Britain, similar experience was felt else where in Europe. In the U.S.A. already several remedies were put in place namely, clear school goals, rigorous academic requirement, an orderly teaching climate, strong instructional leadership by the principal teacher and so on. According to Chubb and Moe these measures were still not good enough to bring in the required standard and to stamp out the appalling situation. Some improvement was made no doubt, but not enough to claim success. According to them, the results were just peripherals, nothing fundamental. Antiquated measures can only tinker on the surface – they don't go far enough to root out the problems. According to them, 'market forces' could deliver the right results. There should be some incentive for parents too for them to make their children work hard. It was suggested that there should be a 'voucher system' which would give parents more spending power and chance to choose better schools for their children. This 'voucher system' was a boost no doubt for both parents and children.

James Callaghan's Speech at Ruskin College 1976

In Britain partcularly, crisis in education worsened with deteriorating falling standard, teacher shortage, funding problem, lack of specialist facilities, poor exam results, discipline problem, increased truancy rate, inadequate curriculum offer, low paid teachers, crumbling school building and so on.

The Prime Minister, James Callaghan delivered a lecture at the Ruskin college Oxford in 1976, highlighting the declining standard and other related problems affecting education generally and the economy in particular. The 'multicultural education' he mentioned, was to be put in proper perspective in order to boost the morale of different multi racial groups in Britain, like the main stream groups, to enrich from diverse cultural stocks. He mentioned that Britain was now established as a multi racial and multi-cultural country without doubt, but multi cultural aspects are to be reflected as a matter of right in the curriculum.

There was confusion in some circles about what would be the consequences of multicultural education in the country as a whole on a long term basis. The multicultural education was neglected badly; many ethnic minority parents were concerned about their children's over all educational development with out benefit of their mother tongue and other heritage cultures. Many researches have shown that bilingualism is a skill which also helps learning of English language properly. Mr Callaghan called for a national debate as a priority on the whole subject of education in Britain. In response to that and amongst other things, the government under the labour control had ordered for the setting up of a Commission on the subject of 'Multicultural education' in England under the Chairmanship of Lord Swan. It was a comprehensive enquiry which produced a massive report in three years covering all aspects of the multi cultural educational issues. The report made a considerable number of recommendations supporting the cause of multicultural education in the United Kingdom. Unfortunately, many of these recommendations remained unheeded even to day.

Prime Minister Mrs Margaret Thatcher's Policies – The Market Forces

When Mrs Thatcher came to power in the eighties, she unleashed a full range of new policies pertaining to right wing thinking effecting not only Education, but also industries such as labour relations, trade union movement etc. First of all, sweeping legislation curbing unions' right to call strikes by teachers, railway men, civil servants and so on was imposed amidst uproar and stiff opposition. There was a large demonstration on the street showing their anger against losing the democratic right to go on strike in order to voice workers' grievances. Going on to strike was not completely abolished but restricted to stringent conditions such as overwhelming majority of the employees must agree to the strike proposal, their should be no picketing on the gates and unwilling members to strike should not be forced to absent from work. And the decision to go on strike has to be decided by the ballot. The result was astonishing. There had been no strike for a considerable period of time which proved beyond doubt that strike calls were manipulative and conducted by the left wing members of the unions. Mrs Thatcher's right wing policies were introduced also in other areas of national services such as the National Health service, Housing, Language learning, employment, immigration etc.

The market forces as mentioned was introduced in the National health service. The same thing was introduced in education where Kenneth Baker, Mrs Thatcher's right wing Education secretary who has put a package of market forces to change its Management system – transferring it from the Local education authority's control to the local management of schools called the governing body. Parents got their right to take out any school from the L.E.A's control, called the 'opting out' was the epitome of the new right education policy. The plan has been to replicate the grammar school spirit through the 'Opting out' provision. Then, a significant educational change of the century has been the radical reform of the Curriculum which was made as the 'National Curriculum' of the whole country. This introduced a uniform curriculum for all schools of the country including the private schools. So far, school curriculum content varied from one school to another which caused assessment and testing extremely difficult. Teachers taught what they liked and sometimes course was left unfinished. It was not easy to detect and to take appropriate action. This curriculum reform removed all these problems. Teaching was made skill based guided by the specific criteria and the course work had to be finished before the end of the term.

Hugh Lauder's essay on Marketisation of education as part of the new right thought, advocates a 'voucher system' similar to Chubb and Mo, for parents wishing a better choice of schools for their offspring – the system was already operating in the U.S.A. This voucher will pay the full cost of education of their children. Instead of the government choosing schools for parents which caused annoyance and the government was often blamed for not meeting the best choice for parents, the parents were now offered the right to choose for themselves the schools of their choice.

National Curriculum and the Technical and Vocational Educational Initiatives

The Technical and vocational Education Initiative (TVEI) was a pilot scheme for 14 to 18 year old students who have special aptitudes and interests in the field of technical and vocational subjects. They were offered this course to be taught in specified authority's schools and the idea has been to meet skills shortage requirement of the industries. This course was based on both theoretical and practical work experience to run concurrent with the conventional curriculum. Later, the TVEI programme was made available to all higher secondary schools, sixth form colleges, further education and tertiary colleges as well.

Later, another course named (CPVE): The Certificate for Pre-Vocational Education was offered to those who lacked basic skills including 3RS – for them to try to prepare for work. C.P.V.E. taught practical skills including work experience. But it failed to retain its status because it was generally regarded as a sub-standard course not suitable for 16 yr olds.

In 1986, having had studied the shortcomings of the TVEI and the CPVE, such as it did not raise the expected standard commensurate to other higher level conventional courses such as the G.C.S.E. and A levels. The government then set up the National Council for Vocational Qualifications to consider raising its standard to the level of general courses. This became the General National Vocational Qualifications (GNVQ) introduced in 1994. Its first job had been to standardise all the vocational qualifications and integrate them into the GNVQ courses which will offer practical vocational and skill education to those chosen for the course. It was decided that the National Vocational Qualifications would offer four year course to level 1 to 4. Level 1 is equivalent to the GCSE standard which would rise up to level 4 to make it equivalent to the advanced level general education.

Already changes have been made in the region of general education for 16 yr olds combining the former GCE, CSE and the CEE into the GCSE course with seven grades, from A to G. The first three grades A to C would be top grades required to qualify for the two year advance level course. The A level course is similar to the intermediate or the pre-university courses.

The New Right under Mrs Thatcher introduced more changes in further and higher education in the nineties. An Act was passed in 1993, which compelled further education colleges to become independent self – governing bodies with finance from a specially constructed Further Education funding Council. Fund would be allocated to each institution based on the 'formula funding' depending on the number of students.

In the same year the Act allowed polytechnics to become Universities. Third, the student grant was cut to pay for the funding of the colleges and to compensate for the loss of student grant, they were encouraged to take out low cost loans if necessary from the banks because, some well to do parents were willing to pay the cost of their children's education. But anybody who took this loan would have to repay it after their graduation or when they had employment.

Criticism of the New Right Perspectives

The 'voucher system' had worked well in the States though but when proposed to implement in England it was overwhelmingly rejected by the opposition, teachers and the unions on grounds that this would disadvantage a lot of parents who might not succeed making the right choice because of complexities involved in choosing the right one. Also many would fail to move out to the new site of their chosen school because of jobs and travelling problems. Further more, because of this system, if introduced, some schools would lose out quite a lot of good students and left with lower abilities only. Some specialist teachers too might think of moving out at this propitious time to seek for better careers.

This situation would leave some schools in desperate short of experienced teachers and bright students and thus might not survive for long. The fact is that parents with means and flexibility would benefit more from the choice and the voucher system than parents who lacked these means. Lauder argued that inequality in education was one of the main issues which would get worse as a result of the 'off out' system, because the worst hit would be the poor parents. The middle class parents would snap all the best chances before others even could try. In his considered opinion, Lauder found that the comprehensive system was a better guarantor of equality than the choice system.

The new right policies during their rule in the eighties and nineties included amongst other changes like cutting education budget by three and a half per cent which drastically effected the equal opportunities programme. The idea behind was to put more importance on teaching of classical languages like Greek and

Latin and also one more compulsory European language from amongst many instead of maintaining the equal opportunities programme. This plan deliberately excluded Asian languages to be taught at all. Many schools which taught heritage languages like Bengali, Hindi, Gujarati, were scrapped. Also gone was the English taught as a second language to ethnic minority children. This cut also gave a massive blow to those trying to get access to the main stream education through learning of English whose chance was now shattered. Many teachers from ethnic background doing the language teaching job were now found themselves out of jobs.

The Ofting schools out of Local education authority's control created a class of schools with selected bright pupils and fully funded by the central government. These are the privileged schools created by the right wing government in order to cream off the brains from the mixed ability teaching groups in Comprehensive schools. Actually, the beneficiaries were the middle class parents than any other groups. This system had created in fact a two tier schooling – one for the rich and the other one for the rest. This was against the spirit of the comprehensive educational policy and thus a body blow to the equality programme. Stuart Ransom indicates in his article 'Market or democracy for education' in Ahier et al edt 1996) that marketisation of education would do more harm than good to reduce inequality. It would create a group of 'instrumentally oriented, psychologically distorted, power hungry, egotistic personality' who would also develop anti-social values and exploit poor people.

Stephen Ball et al's study of the educational reforms in the 90s have found that the educational changes were showing signs of considerable effects on secondary schools. Both undersubscribed and successful schools were trying to make progress with increased provision offered by the government. The education League table also showed that some under performing schools, were making progress compared to their previous years. Some schools had started streaming and setting to give better chance to the hard working pupils. There was a noticeable change from students' need to students' performance. Stephen Ball et al believed that reforms had produced good values for education. There are others who have found that the educational reforms of the 80s and 90s have produced mixed results.

References

Ahier et al 1996, Stuart Ransom's Article – Market or Democracy for Education, 1996.

Stephen Ball, et al Market Forces and Parental Choice in S. Tomlinson (ed), Educational.

Reform and its Consequences, Rivers Oram Press, London, 1994.

John E Chub and Terry Moe Politics, Market and Organisation, 1997.

Part 10

20 Social Democratic Perspectives on Education

Introduction, The Tripartite System and its Drawback, The Open Entry, the Comprehensive System and its Drawback, The Functional Perspective and its Limitations, Labour Perspectives and Anthony Crosland, New Right Perspective on Education, The Labour Party and the Comprehensive System of Education, Evaluation of Social Democratic Perspective on Education.

Introduction

Social democratic perspective in education holds a middle ground in between the two extremes in educational thought, one is being the conflict perspectives dominated by Marxism and its offshoots – the Neo-Marxism and the other one is the new Right Wing Educational Ideology dominated by Toryism. Social democrats' thinking is reflected in the work of many sociologists like A.S. Halsey and Jean Floud, economists Like John Vaizey and some prominent labour and liberal party politicians including many educationalists. In the post-war Britain, one of the main concerns in education has been how to bring equality in education. As the existing system was deemed unfair caused by the selection of students using the questionable I.Q. tests', which had effected the careers of many good children, there arose great concern about how to end existing discriminatory system. The practice of inequality in selection and admission of students into the grant in aid schools specially the Grammar schools, was pivotal to secondary education. This was an age old issue introduced in the

Tripartite system in 1944 which generated failure to so many promising children from the working class background for decades.

Tripartite System and its Drawback

The I.Q. Test was used to divide children into three categories for three different kinds of education of which one particular group was put at an advantage over others in terms of educational offer. This group was the one selected for Grammar school education who would then go to the University followed by either legal or professional training; when they would obviously be put in to higher social status. The tripartite system had failed to remove inequality in education what it aimed to do. One of the other two groups chosen was for the Modern school education meant to develop students' potential, but in fact failed to fulfil the objectives and the result was that many left school without employable skills. Many lacked even the basic 3RS which cost them dearly in the employment market. The system engineered by the selection mechanism created social class division wider. The selection was culturally based, so it was socially and educationally unjust for the vast majority of children who were to attend the modern schools. The last was group was chosen for the Technical education – specially those who had a technical bent of mind. This group of course, did better than the modern school children because the industry preferred them. Professor Halsey and Floud believed that The Tripartite system's failure to develop the potential of the average pupils led to the short fall of skilled workers Britain badly needed for the industry. Secondly, the aim of the social democratic ideals for social justice was not achieved through the sort of education system that was on offer.

The Comprehensive System of Education

Later, changes came through the introduction of Comprehensive pattern of education in the seventies which as a first thing banned the selection based education and the result was a large the number of grammar schools gradually got absorbed in to the

Comprehensive pattern. The purpose had been to bring equality in education in schools and its eventual impact on the class system. Later, it was discovered that selection in the Comprehensive system operated in so many ways that escape from it was impossible. The ideal of equality was only a wishful thinking and some of it was achieved in a peripheral way though but the true equality remained as distant as ever. It was only an imaginary thought, nothing more.

A.H. Halsey and Floud were disappointed that the functionalist perspectives on education aimed offering better quality of life achievable through many of its educational programmes but which were not achieved. Truly, the Functionalist ideology was not aiming to abolish inequality in education completely. It desired to maintain what was on offer and not to dismantle the discriminatory practices in the sense the socialists wanted. According to the functionalists, rather, some form of inequality or disparity in education was good for society. Nevertheless, 'equality of opportunity' was to be made available for all; even though some would not make use of it on account of poor cultural background; but some would and proceed on to the educational career.

For a changing society, some radical measures were necessary to break with the past. The social democratic perspectives were trying to establish a 'Meritocratic' pattern of education which they felt was necessary to preserve the parliamentary democratic Government. It was thought that, every one had a chance to develop their potential in a Meritocratic system, which would benefit the society. This was a wishful thinking and soon it was found that their objectives remained obscure and inoperative before the Conflict perspectives made their headway in the form of the Comprehensive system. Regardless of the situation, much of the post war educational agenda centred round the social democratic concept of education.

Anthony Crosland, the labour leader of the 70s succinctly put forth some proposals in his book 'The Future of socialism' that fairer education system would also 'equalise the distribution of rewards and privileges so as to diminish the class stratification'. Class barrier stands on the way to achieve equality in education in society has been known since the end of the 19th century. Opportunities being made available were not enough to cover all areas of the problems.

Rather, the Social Democratic programme would continue to maintain the ability based education to promote quality rather than quantity. Even, according to their perception, inequality in society and particularly in education would do some good to those disadvantaged children specially from the working class back ground who having had realised their state in society would take the challenges offered and try to prove their worth, which was rather a healthy sign. It is true that some would not make it as said above, but some would make it which would be deemed as a success. In fact, there appeared to be only subtle differences between the functionalists and the Social Democratic perspectives in terms of ability based education, with the exception of special educational provision for slow learners, which was recommended by the social Democratic perspectives.

The Functionalist Perspective on Education

Under the functionalist ideology, ability based education was preferred to 'open entry' which would offer chances to those ambitious pupils who chose to go to the higher academic education. The system also advocated education for others with lower abilities in whatever capacities they could endear. Undoubtedly, there prevailed a right wing element in the functionalist perspectives which stressed that children of lower classes would have to work very hard to improve their future. This emphasis took no account of their poor conditions in which they struggled to survive on a daily basis let alone spend time and effort in learning in education. It is extremely difficult to progress in education with out proper amenities and positive home atmosphere – the key to success. The argument that just hard work could make you learn more for a better future falls flat for children under those circumstances. Social democrats also highlighted the issue that failing education on a vast scale costs the British economy quite a lot. They appreciated the fact that Britain had a desperate short of educated and skilled work-force which the present education programme would not be able to mitigate.

Social Democratic Perspectives on Education

Social democratic perspectives on education like the Liberal philosophy in education put emphasis on the educational development of each and every child – literally every individual is focussed regardless of their status and economic condition. The idea behind this philosophy is basically economic; even though political morality and social justice have been the main creed. Free market economy introduced by the Tory Government in Britain during the eighties and persistently followed by the Labour Government with minor changes no doubt, has produced a large number of skilled workers. This helped not only the requirement of industry but also its sustenance until next reforms were introduced.

But unfortunately, the requirement of education was not met because of unequal distribution of resources which failed to address the needs of the effected curriculum areas. The result was a massive failure in producing the required number of workers. Maximising skills of students of schools and colleges guarantee maximising national prosperity. This view was corroborated by the American economist, Theodore W. Shultz in 1961, who argued that knowledge and skills are a form of capital investment. Investing in human beings is as good as investing in the machineries in industries. Theodore Shultz voiced the social democratic perception of education saying that educated work-force could be more productive than less educated workforce which he corroborated with example from the American Agriculture system where educated and skilled workers were producing encouraging results.

British education policies have been dominated by the social democratic ideas since 1945, which included creating 'Equality of opportunity and increased investment in education' in order to placate underachievement, illiteracy and poor rate of growth. The social democratic spokesmen sociologists A.H. Halsey and Jean Floud decried the fact that the philosophy of the social democratic perspective was not implemented to address the needs of the children of poor families. Sociologists pointed out the fact that the education system had been failing to develop the potential of individual students. In this respect, the Liberal ideology of individual development coincided with the perspective of the social democratic ideal was not put in to practice either as envisaged.

Nevertheless, some of Social Democratic ideas were put into practice in Britain since the 60s. One of the objectives was to raise the school leaving age to 16 from 15, commensurate with the European standard. This will retain students for up to 16th year for further education. This would help particularly the kids of the working class and deprived minority groups in enhancing their career prospect. At the same time, compensatory education was provided to meet the special needs of under achievers. For many of them, equality of opportunity would be more meaningful, when they had attained the skills of 3RS and other subjects.

The New Right Perspective on Education

Increased resources were needed to deliver the expected output. New right policies of the Tories in the eighties and nineties have cut down the education budget by over 3 per cent on ground that equal opportunities introduced by the labour government in the 70s had failed to reduce inequalities in education despite massive injection of funds; so, also the class differences which remained more or less same. So there has arisen a case for cutting education budget for the sake of economy. New right has further insisted that only hard work could make children learn more and improve their career. This point has been critically opposed by the education pressure groups. The Tory policies of the 80s included education League table to reflect the performance of each and every school including the private schools to show their progress. The private schools had to follow the same curriculum and Exam system like the state schools. Schools performing better would get more funds than those performing less. This is a competition, according to the Tory policy, which every school must undertake in order to get more funds. This has been, the conservative government's recipe for improving standard and skills in schools.

But the social democratic theorists disagreed with the Tory education policy entirely. They perceived that better opportunities in education for all could actually create greater equality and higher national output. Cutting education budget mean shrinking educational opportunities which in fact would victimise those who were already disadvantaged by circumstances. The Labour party was of the same opinion. Their policy had been to invest more in educational opportunities, the only way to develop skills in new curriculum areas. It would expedite efforts to reduce poverty, class differences and discrimination – the recipe for economic growth.

The Labour Party and the Comprehensive Education

The Labour party's thinking in education during the sixties was rather confusing. Their comprehensive system of education had gone past the experimental stage in the 70s but no clear cut understanding was still known. Some comprehensive schools specially those incorporated from the Grammar schools had consistently done better in terms of standard and achievement than those converted from the modern secondary schools. Ironically, selection at the age of 11 had been removed officially, but lingered in different forms. For example, after free admission of children of all abilities into school, test process began later in the course once the children had been taught for a few months. These tests were set in English, Mathematics and science subjects for all pupils. According to the marks scored in the tests children were sorted out in to different streams based on their test results. Students scoring high marks were slotted into the top streams and those with poor marks were put into lower streams.

So selection prevailed later than earlier but continued in different forms.

The present labour Government's revised plan for reforms since the 90s appeared to be even more stringent and discriminatory. The Labour government was put under pressure by the opposition that the British economy was not competitive because the education system was not competitive enough compared to the trend in the world.

The labour Government since then proposed in their revised plan that a number of new technical schools otherwise known as the new technology colleges would be set up, strictly based on selection. The second category of change was to expand the existing 'Opting out' schools of the Local Authority's control of the Comprehensives which were to pass on to the 'opted out' system. The finance would be provided by the Department for education and science under the Central Government. That would again be based on the selection of pupils with proven technical aptitude and communication skills. The labour government of the 90s was convinced that in the age of competition and the surging economy of the Asian countries, the selective system was the best alternative to the 'Open Entry' system. All the big talk about 'Equality and equal opportunity' were then put on trial. The then British P.M. Tony Blair was the pioneer in overhauling the standard of education to face the challenges of the 21st century. The Equal Opportunities would still be provided for all; but it was up to the people to make the most of it.

Social Democratic perspectives understand that all the reforms in education since 1989 have helped many students but the central question still remained unsolved which could only be tackled by 'positive discrimination programme' for culturally and educationally deprived children. Educational psychologists also pointed out that deprivation occured primarily in the early years at home when negative characteristics were already internalised by children during the pre – school period. Also, this sort of problem could be tackled by the so called 'Head start 'programme based on the massive rate of 'pre-school education' meant for deprived and children of low income groups. Extra curricular activities such as music, sports, creative arts, painting, building work plus programme for raising self – awareness about their respective cultures and abilities must be introduced along with other schemes. This would reduce discrimination and increase confidence in their abilities. It is already mentioned above that greater investment in children is a greater investment in the wealth of the nation.

It is also understood that the benefit of all the educational programmes will take time to sink in to the values and culture of the underachievers. But it was also feared that any discriminatory action whether positive and negative would be backfired by the reactionary forces who would oppose this idea on ground of racial harmony. So, the idea was dropped.

Evaluation of the Social Democratic Theory

It is mentioned above that the social democratic ideas would eradicate inequality in education if introduced; but when put into action by both the Tory and the Labour governments, it proved otherwise; inequalities would not disappear so soon by piecemeal reforms. It is also understood that just a revised curriculum and introduction of equality programme would not be enough to tackle inequality fundamentally because there was a deep rooted educational and cultural underachievement which existed with many poor children. The question of 'Positive discrimination' was taken up for consideration too but found wanting on its merit as indicated above. Substantial investment of resources would be required with effective teaching method if a perceptible change was to be achieved.

The New Right group have criticised the Equal opportunities programme because it could not deliver the industry's requirement of skilled workers. That was one of the main reasons for the poor out put level. This proves the fact, according to the Right Wing group, that equality programme was not conducive to the interest of the economy. So a cut in the funding for the Equality of Opportunity programme was inevitable. It triggered off a debate which has remained as controversial as ever.

Similar tenor of discussion has also raised the issue of relationship between education and economy which has been discussed in the topic of the Conflict theory of education. Nevertheless, it would not be unwise to look at the issue here from recent evidence that some advanced industries in the world favoured highly skilled workforce than semi-skilled or non skilled workers employed by less advanced countries. It is also mentioned that skilled workers cost more which they could not afford. Some industries train their workers 'on the job'; they prefer this way than college trained workers. Randall Collins, the American sociologist has found that demand for jobs with high skills have been increasing in the United States jobs market than with low skills.

Besides, of what has been said above, sociologists are convinced that education is becomingly increasingly important in this competitive world. There is a crisis for educated and technologically skilled workers to meet the requirement of the manufacturing industries which try to produce new innovative products to catch up with the competitive market. The changes in the production system are creating new jobs all the time for skilled workers which the education system would have to deliver.

The Marxists find the educational offers so far have not solved the problems because their proposals were not consistent enough to warrant a perceptible change in the educational development. The proposals of successive governments have been contradictory and piecemeal. There have been educational cuts which in fact have caused the underachievement to persist. The Birmingham centre for educational Research, has acknowledged that the investment in education has gone up generally, but far more resources invested are to benefit the capitalist economy than the education of the working class children.

Therefore, according to them, class differences will persist, undercurrent recession in the economy will continue effecting inequality in education and its standard. All these add up to raise the question of the viability of social democratic perspectives in education which remains doubt ful for unforeseeable future time.

References

A.H. Halsey and Jean Floud.

H. Halsey, A.F. Heath and J.M. Ridge, Origins and Destinations.

Randall Collins, The Credential Society: A Historical Sociology of Education, 1979.

Birmingham University's Centre for Contemporary Cultural Studies.

Part 11

21 Sociological Theories of Education

Introduction, The Functionalist Approach, Emile Durkheim, Talcot Parsons, Criticism of Functionalist Approach, Conflict Theories of Education, Criticism of the Conflict Theories.

Introduction

Education is the first and foremost need of every child after food, care and shelter. It teaches them how to socialise and to behave with members of the family and those in the society. A child is able to feel pain and pleasure once he or she is born; learning starts then and there. There are many theories of children's education but our prime concern here is the sociology of education in which there are some outstanding contributions.

Amongst many approaches, at least four perspectives are imperative which need examination. These are the functionalist, Marxist, Social democratic and interaction approaches to education. The last two will be discussed in separate chapters. The key message of all is how to relate children's education to the needs of society and how to do that. Children's socialisation is the first thing which begins at home; having had spent early years at home and being equipped with correct attitudes which are the positive outlooks to immediate environment including the school; the children come to school with absolutely no idea about what it would be like, to begin their education which includes coming in contact with teachers, pupils, carers and importantly the head master or headmistress and the school security system etc. Home is where children got some sense of security and protection – important for developing self confidence and assurance. When come to school education begins with reading, writing and doing number. Part of the socialisation process involves the task of making children understand the need of good behaviour and how to respond to the immediate environment in school which include all the people involved in the education process. Care and concern will make them happy and they in return will respond to the people in school and outside in the playground.

Functionalist Concept of Education

The education of children is the prime concern of society. In functionalism, children are taught to develop value consensus and how to promote social solidarity. These things are taught both in social set up and in school.

In the school, the children begin to learn in an interactive way about different moods and responses of people along with skills and abilities. Both home and school work together to ensure a proper beginning for the children's education and socialisation which should continue throughout the school life. Correct language, manners and attitudes are learnt along the line of education. These will be essential tools for growing up in society.

To day's society is full of cultural diversities in which to grow and to learn how to cope with all the expectations. The school code presents common norms, values and beliefs for all pupils which are guidelines for forming correct attitudes towards other children, norms and mode of responses.

The school code enable them to gain social experience with one another. All approaches emphasise that the prime function of education is to turn pupils into good social being so that they can face the world ahead of them. They are expected to be well educated, ambitious and conscious members of society.

The functionalist approach is considered the most influential of all because in functionalism education is given a priority to play a transmitting role to promote society's norms and values to a wider society. The purpose is to ensure that various parts of society are to coordinate and work together for the good of the society. This offers a diversity of perceptions. To functionalists, education is a stepping stone to building a successful career of a student in life with an aim to build a stable and harmonious society. They believe in the primacy of educational values necessary to preserve all cultural heritage and to internalise them into their thinking. This is essential for developing a positive outlook as a recourse to prevent deviant behaviour. Functionalism also develops its relationship with other social institutions such as the economic system, the Rule of Law, and above all the education system. All these are prime ingredients of a healthy social system to which Emile Durkheim and Talcot Parsons have contributed a lot.

Both Emile Durkheim, the French sociologist and Talcot Parsons, the American professor are the two leading protagonists who saw education playing an important role in building a cohesive society. According to them, education in their system will be able to turn young people into successful adults who would play their appropriate roles in life. The fundamental idea of functionalism is to have a stable society within the framework of a well designed social system as proposed by the above mentioned functionalists and followed by many others.

Emile Durkheim

Emile Durkheim, for example, in the opinion of W.S.F. Pickering, who edited Durkheim's book 'Moral Education', cites that 'He was amongst others both as a founding father of sociology and the sociology of education, laid down a well designed functionalist view of education. He emphasised the need for having 'social beings' amongst ourselves with a commitment to serve the community'. To achieve the objectives, education plays a crucial role. To him, young people should be taught how to become useful members of society.

Durkheim insists that a society can survive if members are homogenous in their ideas and objectives and that their education is so designed as to perpetuate and reinforce the ideas of homogeneity crucial to the social solidarity. His objectives were to have a united people with a common goal for the preservation of society. Durkheim sees the individual as apart of the society rather than apart as a separate entity; the individual learns to be a part of the whole society, integrates and internalises the social values which are accumulated through generations.

Durkheim proposed a good deal of educational ideas such as, teaching of history which would develop an integrating force among young students and a common curriculum which also would instil shared norms and values to a diverse community of people. This was accepted as a part of the education curriculum in the U.S.A. The American values include a feeling of commonness, hard work and a desire to do better in life. His ideas have been to generate hope in the minds of the immigrant communities who have thronged into America from abroad and to feel a total American in the true sense. There is also a provision for a common curriculum which will help integrating of ethnic and diverse groups to the social cause and values. The teaching of the American history has been made compulsory for all because it brings to light the founding of the American Republic including the great life of Abraham Lincoln who preached 'equality of opportunity and racial unity'. (A full details of Emile Durkheim's ideas are discussed in the chapter Emile Durkheim). Durkheim's educational ideas have also influenced European nation in their bid to raise national consciousness, so they included his ideas in their educational programme.

Talcot Parsons' Ideas of Education

Talcot Parsons, the eminent American functionalist developed further the ideas of Durkheim. He saw the school classroom as a 'microcosm of society' in which to implant a concept of a social system. To him, the school is a training ground for young boys to grow from childhood to adulthood and into effective members of society. Parsons saw the family is an area where the children get a 'prescribed status' fixed at birth with values of cultures and social status already acquired by the family. But later, when they go to school and be apart of a wider society they acquire a status according to their achievement, for example, a child from a middle class background can retain parental class background or move down or move up to a higher status – all depend on their professional achievement. So this transition from the 'ascribed' to the 'acquired' status is a big step for the individual. Parsons saw the school playing a bridging role for the pupils in this transitional period. The pupils will be educated and their standard of achievement judged in order to allocate them roles to play in social life. The high achievers in schools and colleges will be selected for high status positions in the occupational ladder. Parson's idea of selecting and allocating future roles are in tune with the functionalist theory of stratification.

Durkheim's views and his educational objectives have influenced the modern sociologists and educationalists. As a traditionalist, Durkheim felt his values would help all sections to adhere to for the cause of communal solidarity.

Criticism of Functionalists' Educational Ideas

It is criticised that Durkheim's novel ideas were unrepresentative of the people and did not affect all parts of society. The curriculum put special emphasis on the study of national history of America but it did not put emphasis on the community studies, sports and individual initiative programmes. David Hargreaves, a British sociologist argued that many schools failed to produce a sense of dignity for the working class pupils. To lift pupils from their sub-cultural level, there should have been some extra curricular programme to enhance their all round skills. Once they had proved that they were equipped with up to date skills and standards worthwhile to face the needs of society then they would be ready to join the rest. Without special educational programme, the under achievers – most of whom were from foreign immigrants and children of the working class communities who would not benefit from the traditional schooling programme because of their language deficiency and lack of other basic skills.

David Hargreaves proposed that pupils should have some choice in selecting their fields of studies if they had.specific interests, aptitudes abilities in those areas. This will give them a chance to feel close towards their work rather than being imposed with some curricula. Secondly, community studies would give them a chance to see their fitting roles in society. In the collective role like the sports, community work, art and craft etc which also would give them a sense of self dignity and respect for others. They should also study normal academic subjects like others so that they don't feel left out from the rest.

Thirdly, functionalist approach to education is criticised as a right wing approach despite its being a credible commitment to a nation building force. The critics also believed that the education system with functional ideas would permeate in society in order to improve it further. The functionalists also recognised the differences in human abilities but accepted the fact that education could improve abilities. Playing proper role in the social system can not only eradicate poverty but also increase social status and strengthen social solidarity. Nevertheless, in their view they had not paid proper attention to all cultural groups and the working class families. It has appeared that the functionalists have not taken into account the ethnic cultural and religious values but they had concentrated on the values of the ruling class and also made a stride on promoting meritocracy.

Even though Karl Marx did not write any sociological theory of education as such; yet his sociological thoughts indicate that the education system under the capitalist set up only serves the interests of the capitalist power. It further points out that the school represents an ideology which is so organised as to preserve the privileges of the bourgeoisie and to ensure that the vested interests of the employers are maintained. Education is a reproductive system in which the working class is reproduced and substantial profit level is retained. There is a relationship between the school system and its effect on the career of children in employment. The system also reproduces inequalities in society.

Louis Althuser, the French Marxist philosopher points out that education has replaced the church authority as an agent of the ideological control of the school. The school has thus become a centre where the capitalist ideology is introduced to serve its purpose. The school has a programme in which children are told how to behave positively in relation to work and to remain docile. These requirements help not only to increase progress in school but also the level of production in the work places, which serves the best interest of the capitalist market. A docile hard working obedient worker produces more to raise the level of output in the industry than an expressive worker.

The curriculum too is so designed as to favour the interests of the capitalist forces more than any body else. Some part of the curriculum is meant to serve the children of higher I.Qs who happen to come from the middle and upper class sections of the society. The conflict theories clarify this issue elaborately to show that the education system is so divisive in which discrimination between the children of middle and working class families is made distinctly clear. This system ensures that entering into good schools guarantees better career prospects for these students but who will benefit from this schooling?; only the high achievers who come from the middle and upper classes backgrounds. The working class children would not get a chance because on the selection of pupils by the I.Q. Tests at the age of 11, most of them would get eliminated because of the poor educational background; so the device clearly favours the children of the middle and Upper classes. In this system, some people will benefit more than others. The education system is thus dominated by those who are already better off in society both materially and socially.

According to the conflict perspectives the education system serves the purposes of the capitalist societies which also maintains a correspondence between the school system and the workplace in a way as to reproduce a work force required by the industry. The school itself is hierarchically organised like the work place where the requirement of employers have to be met in lieu of wages and salaries. The school represents the capitalist interest much more than the education and career of the working class children.

This ideology is also explained through an uncharted curriculum called the 'hidden Curriculum' which means that pupils learn a lot more without being taught a formal curriculum. They learn to become a docile worker, well behaved, punctual and obedient. The school code becomes automatically the code of the work place where they will have to behave and work hard as they did in school. The two American sociologists Samuel Bowles and Herbert Gintis explain in their book 'Schooling in capitalist America' that the education system in the capitalist societies play a major role in the reproduction of labour power. Work caste a 'long shadow' over the education system. Education is instrumental to the needs of those who control the workforce. They are the owners of the means of production, in other words the capitalists. Like Karl Marx, Bowles and Gintis find work in America both exploitative and alienating.

Education needs a lot of change in order to bring equality in both education and society. Whether society depends on education or education depends on society is a debatable issue which continues despite considerable reform programme being implemented. The disparity in education is an age – old problem grown since long time that can not be eradicated so easily but what can be done is to reduce the inequality as much as possible.

Nevertheless, education has gone through radical changes during the last fifty years or so and most of these reforms are concerned about providing education to all pupils irrespective of class, colour and ethnicity.

The criticism of selection method is a valid one. The 'selection' of pupils by I.Q. Tests has been found at fault because it tests those skills which the middle class pupils have already acquired through their cultural background. This is a device used to select pupils for the grammar school education in which the pupils from the middle class had an advantage over their counterparts. The former had literary and language skills more than the latter. This had resulted in most of the places in the grammar schools were occupied by the children of middle class background. To eradicate this anomaly, the new reforms in education introduced the comprehensive system of education in the early seventies which abolished the I.Q. Tests altogether. This removed the most talked about grammar schools as the bastion of the middle class education from the system. Equality of opportunity was thus implemented to represent the spirit of the comprehensive ideology in the education system. (For further information please read a separate topic on the conflict theory of education).

Further Reading

Bourdon, P Reproduction in Education, Society and Culture, Sage, London, 1977.

Boules, Samuel and Gintis, H Schooling in Capitalist America, R.K.P., London, 1976.

Even, Illich, The Deschooling Society, 1973.

Paul, Willis, Education and Cultural Reproduction, 1977.

Part 12

22
Conflict Theories In Education

Introduction, Karl Marx's Educational Thought, Louis Althusser, The Correspondence Theory, The Capitalist Control, Education System in the Communist Countries, Evaluation of Bowels and Gintis, Ivan Illich: De-schooling.

Introduction

The conflict theories are multifaceted perspectives dominantly based on the ideas of Karl Marx and Frederick Engels. Other sociologists for example. Max Weber, Louis Althusser, radical and Marxist feminists, educationalists and socialists – all have contributed significantly to the development of these theories. Max Weber, of course belongs to both the conflict and the action schools of sociology; So his contribution has a different characteristics and flavour than others. Louis Althusser is concerned with the ideology of education which transmits values to suit the interests of the capitalist power. Radical and Marxists feminists are concerned with the gender division and their visible and invisible consequences in the field of education.

Karl Marx personally has not developed a sociological theory of education but his perception of sociology constitutes a considerable degree of educational thought purporting to conflicts in education between the educational offers and the providers of education – the latter serves the interests of the capitalist power. Schools are seen by him sometimes present sites of conflicts exhibited by strikes, pickets and working to rule.

The school system in the U.K. and other parts of Europe is a conglomeration of interests of right wing thought, private enterprise and socialist mode of comprehensive system which thus generate disequilibrium in the system. There is a lot of compromising situations in the system which can not be one way or the other but an amalgamation of both or more. The private system of education is selective based primarily on merit which favours the privileged group no doubt, but other considerations can not be overruled. The curriculum of the 1980s was designed to follow the national guidelines as provided by the national curriculum commission. This was accepted by the Education Reform Act of 1989 in the United Kingdom which was implemented for the whole nation without exception. The private system of education has to follow the same curriculum invariably as followed by the state schools. Democracy of course, permeates all types of provisions and the school curriculum reflects examples of such a system.

In Marx's words, the ruling class which works as an agent of the capitalist power "rules and think as well as producers of ideas" These ideas include the purpose of education, who it serves and by whom. Marx views the ruling class ideology as basically geared to offer education to people who would serve the interest of the vested groups, like the capitalists, the bourgeoisie and the privileged class of society. The curriculum is developed to educate students becoming skilled workers who can generate more profit for the producers, who are the owners of the means of production. The Wright Wing groups who believe that inequality is society is justified because people belong to different ability groups; so they deserve differential rewards. They ignore the fact that many people are born in disadvantaged circumstances in which early education was impossible for them and to improve ability is a distant possibility. If equal opportunities were offered many of them could have done better.

Schools represent ideology of the capitalist interests and education is so organised to benefit them. The school system establishes a relationship between the learners and the capitalist system of production; so quite evidently many leave schools without necessary skills and know how essential for a better start in life. Many go straight in to the factory jobs to do low paid unskilled work. The process of exploitation starts then and there. The owners of the 'means of production' would use them at their maximum capacity to earn good profit for them. This perpetuates inequalities and class divisions in society.

Louis Althusser

Louis Althusser, a prominent French Marxist argues that education turns hearts and minds of students into the ruling class ideology which is transmitted into the students' learning programme. The ideology informs students to comply with the requirement of work rules as set out by the employers for their benefit and also to remain docile and submissive during work and not to complain. In the work places they are further trained to work at their maximum level, so that their work yields high return. All the benefit are to be expropriated. The employers would not refrain from using coercive force if their interests were effected by non-compliance of rules. They want a high rate of return at low cost of pay.

Althusser has pointed out that education has replaced the Church authority as the main agency of the ideological control of the school. Previously, people learnt that the church taught pupils to understand their station in life. To day, it has been replaced by the ruling class ideology which educate them how to behave and to comply with the employers' requirement of production. So they would have to develop a docile nature to suit the working environment in the capitalist mode of production. According to Althusser schools transmit an ideology which teaches that capitalism is just, reasonable and fair and education is designed to make you learn the requisite knowledge and skills meant to serve the capitalist work system; no more no less.

He argues that schools teach the students their future roles to play in the work places for the requirement of the industries; and that profit making is a part of the work system which goes to the employers and that there is nothing wrong in it. In lieu of all these they would earn wages – weekly or monthly as pay packets. And for them there is nothing to grumble. That is the way the future managers, administrators and even politicians are trained to control the work force. The qualifications they receive at schools enable and legitimate the recipients to play the 'future role of exploitation and repression'. Althusser sees the educational processes as nothing else but ideological programme.

The conflict perspectives also maintain and accentuate class divisions in schools amongst pupils by a system of streams, bands, top and bottom forms etc. Also there exists grammar schools in which pupils are selected by the I.Q. Tests at the age of 11. There also exist the private and public schools based on the selection method. This is a discriminatory method eliminating those who could not pass through the tests and seeing them as ineligible for academic work. Those who passed knew the specifics of the I.Q. tests as taught by special coaching. Children attending these selective schools fortunately come from the middle and upper social classes, thus had an advantage in their early education whereas for others the background was not conducive to the required standard. The result is the difference between those who had higher abilities and those without has grown wider for ever for which the latter had been penalised.

To remedy this state of affairs there should be an equal opportunity programme for everybody to have an equal chance in life; whereas the education system do not do much to change the situation but rather permeates the society to promote the unequal system to continue. That is why, the system is reproduced year on and year off.

Correspondence Theory

Bowles and Gintis, the two American sociologists have pointed out in their book, 'Schooling in capitalist America (1976)' that there is a close correspondence between the social relationships in the classroom and those in the workplace. The major role of education in capitalist societies is the reproduction of the labour power. The correspondence between these two organs are vital for social reproduction which is the reproduction of the new generation of workers appropriately skilled to accept their roles in the capitalist society and also in the system of production.

Bowles and Gintis state that Schools are organised hierarchically as other social institutions. Teachers have to be obeyed by pupils who have no control over what works are given to do. The curriculum is developed by the higher authorities in consultations with teachers and their Unions; the students have to do the work as provided by the teachers. They do not have any part in shaping the curriculum. This corresponds to the situation in the work place where the workers have no control over what they do; it is all being set up for them to do. In the same way, rewards are being accorded for hard work, punctuality and compliance to rules and regulations. They are not expected to do something different independently which might effect the norms and specifics conflicting with what are set out to do. Many students lose out education because of the strict curriculum requirement which are not very interesting sometimes. External rewards such as qualifications motivate students to work hard in the same way as the workers in the work places to work hard for weekly or monthly pay packets. This is the nature of education and work relationship, which according to Bowles and Gintis is the correspondence that is reproduced again and again under the capitalist system of Production.

Bowles and Gintis explain the survival strategy of the capitalist system. Social inequality can not be eradicated completely. That is quite understood by the capitalists as well as by many social thinkers in whose view inequality is caused mainly by the inability and lack of perseverance of individuals. Ability differs in individuals across the social classes even when equal opportunities are offered to all. According to Bowles and Gintis, education legitimates social inequality; and at the same time, every body has an equal chance. The difference lies in the fact that those who are in a higher social background have better chances in life than those who are in the lower strata of society. Merit of the individuals are not all inherent, some of it are acquired as well. Good teaching, better educational environment and facilities are a guarantee for success in life. So education legitimates inequalities as it reproduces the class system. (Bowles and Gintis – Schooling in Capitalist America, 976, p. 114).

According to Bowls and Gintis, work in capitalist societies is both exploitative and alienating. The system in America has an unwritten structural mechanism known as 'the Hidden Curriculum' to achieve these objectives. The hidden curriculum is not based on set curriculum and exam result but things are learnt only by coming to school, such as punctuality, regularly, good behaviour, docility and to do what is given to do. In this way, the hidden curriculum shapes the future work force in America.

Education develops the future workforce in the way the capitalist industry would like them to be. In school learners are given credits for how one behaved and kept punctuality and regularity as much as academic achievement. They also find that students who show more staying power in the midst of despair and alienation are recommended for jobs than those who are timid but bright and lose patience. Students who remain uncritical and submissive are the favoured once for the work place. They also find that schools are organised hierarchically from teacher to the head keeping authority and control and the hidden curriculum expects students to abide by this structure. Development of individual personality and liberal ideas remain out of the question. At the end of the school period external reward comes in the form of certificates.

The employers' main motive is to make maximum profit out of their work. Development of individual personality and liberal ideas would be anathema to their interests. The work force is divided in a way that each has to deliver his or her quota unrelated to others. The overall knowledge of the work system is fragmented rather than integrated and connected to various subjects. The idea is to keep the system subdivided so that students don't get a comprehensive knowledge of what they do, similar to workers who don't know that others do. Knowing everything would cause a problem for the system to control every body in the work place.

Like functionalism, the conflict theories emphasise the importance of structures with in society. That is all they agree to. The conflict theories do not see harmony and consensus in the society but division and conflicts amongst groups – each pursuing their individual vested interests. The functionalists, according to Ralf Dahrendarf, set aside social conflicts and deviance as trivial matters which they believe would sort themselves out or would follow the consensus of the society. The conflicts within the society are endemic according to the conflict perspectives which are caused by the exploitation of the many by the few who also strive for power and authority, using discrimination and deprivation which are their main instruments. Ralf Dahrendorf criticises functionalism as a conservative oriented concept reticent to any major change in society.

Many conflict theories trace their views in the writings of Karl Marx specially his theory of class struggle. Marxism is predominantly based on the strength of economic determinism which divides society. Ralf Dahrendorf, the German Marxist sociologist argues that the economic factor is not the only important factor to cause a conflict in society. He identified authority and power holding by a person or a group also cause conflict in society. Feminism, sees the gender-based division of society as the main cause of the social conflict apart from every thing else.

Capitalist Control

The hidden curriculum has given a golden opportunity to the capitalists to control the work force; they are just quite made for the capitalists to exploit.

Bowles and Gintis have also found that the capitalist system prefer a surplus skilled work force in the market for them to choose the best hands from the many, a lot cheaper. This keeps room for them to intimidate, manipulate and extricate more gain from their work and if necessary to sack if any one is found not meeting their requirement. They know quite well that a surplus stock of workers is always there for a job; so replacement of a bad worker by a good one would not be a problem. According to

Demaine, (1981) the capitalist education system produces an 'alienated and fragmented' work force which handicaps building solidarity amongst workers. This is what the management wants in order to maintain their authority in tact by pursuing a 'divide and rule' policy.

Bowles and Gintis argue that there is a lack of clarity actually about what the education system in the Soviet Union and in the East European countries was like. Paradoxically, there are similarities between the Communist education system and that of the U.S.A. At first, education in the Communist countries is hierarchical and they also put emphasis on developing student personalities similar to the Western system. Bowles and Gintis argue that this was due to the failure of the Communist system to implement their full scale education programme. They state that, these countries have abolished the 'private ownership of the means of production' no doubt, while replicating the relationships of economic control, dominance and subordination – the characteristics of capitalism. In their view, genuine communist education system could develop only when the workers are able to take over the control of 'the means of production', otherwise, it would remain as a compromise or a go between the two systems – the system of the East and the system of the West.

Bowles and Gintis further indicates that socialism was established in the Soviet Union which theoretically abolished the social inequalities including the class system but best boys and girls are still selected for higher education and future state jobs, which proves that unequal opportunities have existed in the soviet system all the time. Again, theoretically, 'the means of production' are owned by the state only, no body else, but evidence is there to disprove this as some top state officials still had some vested interests while controlling 'the means of production'.

Evaluation of Bowles and Gintis

Even though the initial reaction was encouraging for this Marxist oriented report of Bowles and Gintis, but gradually it picked up criticism which are worth considering.

The correspondence theory has long been seen as a correct approach to explain the relationships between the schooling and work system in America but the critics expected to see appropriate evidence to believe in it and accept the findings. Enough evidence was not produced to make it credible.

Bowles and Gintis have argued that the major role of education in capitalist societies is the reproduction of labour power as a result of a correspondence between the social relationships in the work place and social relationships of the education system. Education thus feeds the needs of those who control the workers.

According to Mike Hickox these relationships could not be traced in the case of education in England. Research carried out by the sociologist has unravelled the fact that compulsory education in England has started long after the Industrial Revolution. Capitalism developed in England unabated even without the support of an educated workforce.

David Hogan agreed that the 'hidden curriculum' was actually influencing the pupils. But there was a need for more evidence to confirm every claim. There are rather evidence to say otherwise. Paul Wills found in some schools, in rural England where the lads did not like to conform to be the 'docile workers'. They behaved the way they liked with no inclinations for teachers' authority or school rules. As far as the British schooling is concerned, much of what Bowles and Gintis have said in terms of the influence of formal education could not be related to the ground situation.

Also, was found that the lads rejected educational success as defined by the school. They even mocked at boys who worked hard and conformed to the school rules. The lads in Paul Willis' findings actively created counter school culture. The kids knew well that they were cut out for low skilled job, so why bother work hard. They came to school to spend their time, 'to have a laugh' which was the best way to avoid monotony, boredom and authority. This is paradoxically the case with factory workers who took work lightly and sometimes enjoyed 'having a laugh' and mocking at each other – a way to avoid dreariness, boredom etc. This counter school culture contradicts the Bowles and Gintis' correspondence theory.

Ivan Illich – The De Schooling Society and Hidden Curriculum

One of the most controversial writers in the educational theory is Ivan Illich who argued that the compulsory education as it stood, for which people fought for so long should be discontinued. Illich studied theology and philosophy and worked as a Roman Catholic priest in New York. He criticised the liberal type of education as a formal education which is harmful to children and is rather unnecessary. His much acclaimed book 'The De – schooling Society' has caused a sensation in the sociology of education as it made a significant contribution to its study.

In his view, the school has become a custodial organisation which makes attendance obligatory, essential for the society to see children being 'kept off the street'. He further criticised the work in school which has little to do with the curriculum or job but has something which is required by the economic system of the authoritative mode of production. He calls it a passive consumption – an uncritical acceptance of the existing social order, to denote strict discipline and regimentation. What they learn is 'hidden curriculum' which teaches children that their role in life 'is to know their place and to sit still in it' (Ivan Illich, 1973). Illich advocates a 'de – schooling society' because there is no reason why formal education should be accepted as something inevitable.

He illustrates how the Hidden curriculum operates in School. The 'Hidden Curriculum' according to him, is something that is learnt being in school every day without being taught. Pupils have no control over what they learn or how to learn it. They are there to conform to rules. Conformity and obedience bring their own rewards implicit in school procedure and organisation. It is the 'hidden curriculum' which children pick up on a day to day basis being in school; that their role in life 'is to know their place and to sit still in it' (Ivan Illich, 1973).

Illich regards schools as repressive institutions, which indoctrinate pupils, smother creativity and imagination, induce conformity and coerce students into accepting the interests of the powerful.

According to Illich, real learning, according to him, does not occur from instruction, but of direct and free involvement in the learning process. Illich finds the education system at the root of the problem of a modern industrial society. School produce mindless and manipulated citizens who are educated to alienate, serve the society but oblivious of looking after the interest of the school. Illich is convinced that modern industrial society could not develop a mechanism to provide happiness to the society. Schools teach how to obey authority and at the same time get alienated from the system. The system does not teach children how to think for themselves but for the system.

Illich in order to rid society of the current repressive system proposes the abolition of the present system of education and replace it which he calls the 'De-schooling'. This is at the root of liberating human beings from a bad system. The de – schooling would include 'Learning Web' which consists of individuals with similar interests who meet around a problem chosen defined by their own initiative and who proceed on a basis of 'creative and exploratory learning'. Education, according to him, should learn specific skills, such as typing, wood work and speaking a foreign language. Education should be encouraging to explore, create, and freely develop their faculties and talents to the full. Illich has suggested a radical change of the system which only concentrates on copying, imitating and reproducing the programme again and again.

Criticism of Ivan Illich's Idea of Schooling

Much of what is said by Illich is true; change is taking place in the light of what he and other sociologists have been reflecting over the years on the situation but a wholesale or an absolute radical change has not been suggested by any but Marxists.

Marxists like Bowles and Gintis almost accept what Illich has said but deplore the fact that his solution has been misdirected; instead they argue "The social problems to which these reforms are addressed to have their roots not primarily in the school system itself, but rather in the normal functioning of the economic system" The de schooling would only do a piecemeal job of reform but what is needed is a wholesale fundamental change of the economic infrastructure of the society.

David Reynolds, another British sociologist claims that most schools in the United Kingdom do not teach pupils to be workers as such which is a job actually left in the hands of the school leavers to join the industry where many skills would be taught at the spot.

David Reynolds further comments that it is not simply possible for British capitalists to exercise detailed control over British schools. He argues that a lot of radically minded teachers teach in British schools who would hardly teach pupils to meet the requirement of the capitalists.

What is going on at the moment is the education planning which fosters requirements of *social, cultural, moral* as well as aesthetical matters side by side keeping in view of the economic needs of the country. Failing to do would mean the country would waste resources on courses if they were not being put into use. Lack of correct coordination between the Government planning and economic needs of the country could result in many graduates not being employed at all or being employed in low grade jobs. This would be a waste of the country's huge cost spent on planning, training and delivering the staff which the country could not afford to sacrifice.

References

Louis Althusser, Ideology and Education.

Samuel Bowles and Herbert Gintis, Schooling in Capitalist American, 1976.

Evan D Illich, De Schooling Society, 1973.

David Reynolds, Relative Economy Reconstructed, L. Barton and S Walker (eds) 1984.

Paul Willis, Learning to Labour, 1977.

Part 13

23 Power, Authority and Politics

Introduction, Weber's Theory of Power, Functionalist Theory of Power, Talcot Parsons, Marxist Concept of Power, New Marxist Concept of Power, Michael Mann's Concept of Power, Nordlinges' Concept of State Centred Concept of Power, Steven Luke's Concept of Power, Pluralists Concept Power, Functionalism and Pluralism Compared, Power and Authority, A Critique of Pluralism, A Critique of Power Theory.

Introduction

The concept of power is one of the most contentious topics in Political Science. Sociologically, power is related to societal relations with in membership and different institutions but politically, related mainly to the state authority, government, political parties, pressure groups, religious organisations etc. Sociological theories of power are predominantly shaped by Max Weber, Talcot Parsons and Karl Marx. But there are many others who developed quite a lot of theoretical approaches which can fall in between sociology and politics. Steven Luke's theory and pluralists' view of power are just one for example.

According to Anthony Giddens, power is an ever present phenomenon in social life. In all human groups, some have more power and influence than others depending on their social background, wealth, knowledge and political clout. In society, power is linked to the class structure. Those belonging to the middle and upper classes are in a position to generate more power through exerting their influence on the community in whatever capacity they can. Wealth also helps the rich to generate power by donating and spending huge amount on the development of welfare for the people. Power is therefore, both a social and political phenomenon. Socially, it is linked to the issue of inequality judged by the rights of people and the quality of life enjoyed by people based on their economic resources as distributed amongst people of different classes.

History shows, sometimes, the powerless can be very powerful when they are made aware of the condition they are in. If they realise that they are subjected to oppression and exploitation by the people in power such as an autocrat then they rise in revolt. It has been found in history that the exploited workers fought out to gain power from the rulers and exploiters. Also they have organised their powerful Unions to fight for their cause. The unions can inflict damage to the economy by destabilising the system, going on strike and forcing of the government accept their grievances. Some movements even can take ugly form like the bloody Bolshevik Revolution of October, 1917 in Russia. Earlier, the great French Revolution of 1789 is another classic example of what the exploited workers, peasants and poor people could do to unseat a corrupt and bankrupt Bourbon monarchy from power and to bring a historic changes in France including wars in Europe and reform movements in rest of the world.

Weber is well known for his theory of power. His view of power is "to realise their own will in a communal unlimited – it has its beginning and its end; it is not boundless"; Weber believed that "when someone holds power, others do not, because it is held at the expense of others". He calls power as a 'constant sum', which means that its quantity does not increase nor does it lose. Secondly, not every body can hold power all at the same time. If somebody has power others don't have. Weber's power is exercised either by a legitimate authority or by a coercive authority. The former is based on the consent of people for whom the power is used in order to meet their requirement. Coercive power is different; in which people are forced to obey the authority or else would be punished or victimised. Weber argues that some element of force is always associated with the legitimate authority in order to make people comply with the law, for example, when people refuse to pay the tax or disobey the transport regulations – they are punished.

Weber finds that in a democratic country, an absolute authority is rare; because democracy allows diversity of opinion and values to spring up which are essential for it to flourish and to generate different types of authorities. In a democratic system authority is not centralised but diversified even though the centre could exercise some important powers for the good of the whole country, the regional authorities would exercise their own for the administration of their particular regions. To him, out of the melee, the 'Rational legal authority' stands out dominant as a formal authority in the industrial societies. This form is backed by the rules and regulations which are needed to run the administration without being confused about what to do. Most functions of the government such as educational, industrial, political, defence, finance social and religious matters are run by the 'rational – legal authorities'. They are run by competent individuals or bodies who work in a structurally devised bureaucratic system. This is Weber's 'ideal type' authority and is reckoned to be the best amongst his other types such as charismatic and traditional authorities.

Charismatic and Traditional Types

Charismatic authority is a personalised authority since it is based on the personality of the individual whose natural qualities such as understanding of peoples' needs, his dedication for the cause of the country and above all a natural fascination people have for such a character which draw attention of all kinds of people without reservation. Mahatma Gandhi for example, had such a charismatic personality who moved millions of people to follow his path of non – violence for freedom struggle in India. There are also others in history who could be deemed as charismatic personalities such Mrs Indira Gandhi, Mother Teresa and so on.

The traditional type is mostly an inherited authority exercised by the feudal Lords of Europe and Maharajas of India who enjoyed enormous respect of people over whom they had ruled.

Weber's ideal type authority is estabilished by legal framework. Any breach of such authority would be penalised by law. A letter issued by a civil servant has got the force of law which can not be disobeyed. A decision of a judge or a Government official can not be ignored because that has a legal binding. This decision is not just legal but also is rationally decided having had taken into account all the aspects of the matter. Once it is backed by the law, the authority has the mechanism to realise the objective of the law. In other words, when it becomes a law it can not be ignored. Weber's view of power corresponds to the pluralists view of power.

In democracy, both individuals and groups have freedom of speech and rights to develop their views and to make them known to the ruling power. If the authority finds them feasible then these would be considered for policy making. Power is also measured by socially expressed wishes and views of different groups competing to influence the policy of the government. It is up to the government then, to weigh up the strength of their respective proposals of power sharing and also to consider which ones to accept.

The Functionalist Theory of Power

In contrast, Talcot Parsons' 'variable' power concept is different from Max Weber's 'constant sum' concept. Parsons' 'variable concept' increases and decreases according to the society's requirement or if the leader, he or she is a very capable person wishing to increase activities over the schedule, a lot more power would be generated to get them through the parliament; whereas Weber's 'constant sum' is limited by its fixed amount regardless of what a society's requirements are. Again, when a ruler is not an ambitious one, the amount of power to exercise would be strictly limited by its scheduled programme.

So Parsons rejects the 'constant sum' concept of power used by Weber and also disagrees with his view that power is used for the sectional interest of the power holder.

In Parsons' view, power is held by the society as a whole irrespective of who is in power and running the administration. Also that power is a variable sum which can increase if a greater amount of work is needed to be done for example, to improving the standard of living or for passing a lot of reform bills through legislative processes and so on. Fewer reforms require less power than more reforms. Also, in a developing country, more power is necessary to achieve the goal directed activities for them to pass lengthy bills containing difficult issues. In the course of the legislative process, difficult bills face obstacles, objections, opposition and delays. Therefore, use of more power is inevitable to get the jobs done.

Bills passed must ensure quality of justice maintained which should be able to solve the problems. Also bills passed must provide better health service, high standard of education, improved exam system and also better pay scale for the underpaid. Quality of justice should include protection of citizens from criminal gangs who must be caught and punished by the effective police force. Massive government programme of industrialisation and rehabilitation of homeless people require extensive power to process difficult financial bills through. Legislative processes take extra time to read lengthy bills introduced in the House of commons requiring more power – all these are for the benefit of the country.

Parsons' power concept is a collective power dominated by the 'value consensus' of society. Society's prime values are improved educational and living standards for the people. A society's power is evaluated by the achievement of the 'collective goals' in full. If all objectives are achieved, then the society is deemed very powerful. In Parson's view, 'power is a generalised facility or resource in the society'. With these resources, goals of the society would be attained as committed by the people. Since goals are commonly shared by all members of the society, so power will be used to accomplish the objectives. Every one has a stake in the society, so everyone has power.

Furthermore, according to Parsons, it depends on the quality and capability of the leader, as said before, how much work he or she could deliver and how much power he/she is able to utilise to accomplish the objectives. If the leader has the ability, imagination and ambition then more work could be done using more power. So the extent of power varies according to the ability and competence of the performer.

Parsons' value consensus of society is the sum total of the economic, material, educational, moral and cultural level of people achieved in a stable and orderly society. These collective goals when accomplished, would indicate that the society has generated more power than before. According to Parsons, society belongs to the whole community; so everybody should cooperate in building a social system in which to achieve certain social goals. An elected authority would be required for this purpose, whose job would be to serve the interests of all people efficiently. The authority can be vested in an individual or a group of people such as politicians with proven ability who would be allocated necessary powers to run the government. So the leader or the group will be responsible to exercise power to deliver all the services promised and if possible do more for the benefit of the community as a whole rather than a section. If they fail to deliver the objectives then they would be replaced by another elected body of the people.

Parsons' social system is based on the concept of co-operation and participation of all members. Parsons acknowledges the fact that not everybody can make it to the system but if a few members fail to adapt to the system, it would not be a big problem because the vast majority in accord, would be able to do the job well. In a democratic system, some may not adjust to as good as others. However, Parsons was confident that with help and support, negative forces would be succumbed to gradually integrate in to the society and to adapt to the system.

Parsons may be short sighted by the fact that political party or parties may not be able to deliver what they had been elected for. Or, it may be the case, that elected body serve their sectional interests more often than the interests of the country. However, Parsons' concept of power corresponds to the power of the Classical pluralists which ultimately rests with the whole society. Also that goes with the Parsonian view that democracy in the West in meant to serve the society as a whole which is a legitimate authority based on the consensus of people rather than the coercive power. However, classical pluralism also goes along with the Weberian view that power is limited by the fact of its totality, based on the 'constant sum' theory rather than the 'variable sum' as put forth by Talcot Parsons.

Marxist Concept of Power

Marxist concept of power, also known as Conflict perspectives apparently appear similar to the pluralist concept of power, the reason is both the concepts concentrate power in the hands of a few people elected by the votes of the majority in the party, even though ideologically they are different from each other. Both the ideologies are meant to serve the people at large, even though the Marxist concept is based on a single party rule whereas the pluralist view is based on a multi-party system. The pluralist concept allows different political parties to compete for power but only one party if it manages to win a majority would be allowed to form a government. When no such thing happens then, more than one party will form a coalition government together. This demonstrates that pluralism operates successfully is a true democratic system. But this is not possible in a Marxist type of election where only one party which is the communist party will be allowed to contest with in its own membership to choose the best candidates out of the many aspirants.

Elected members will then be in charge of governing the country and be able to exercise enormous amount of power.

In a multi-party democratic system based on different ideologies and social classes, power may be usurped by a few elite members coming from the upper crust of society, in which case power may be exercised by the few for the best causes of the upper classes. In the conflict perspectives however, the power holding group does not represent the class rule but all members of the society. Theoretically, the elite group is meant to rule for the best interest of the whole society than for a few as they are accountable to the community for their functions. Also they are to treat everybody equally without discrimination. It is no secret that the perspectives of the elite rule end up paying more attention to the benefit of the vested interests such as the bourgeoisie, the upper middle class and the capitalists rather than all people. In fact, the ruling class create the conflict of interests by a divisive policy denying and depriving the interests of the vast majority of people. Eventually, the powerless, being disgruntled and desperate confront the powerful ruling authority to oppose their oppressive rule which sometimes ends up in open rebellion. If they succeed then they would remove the ruling authority from power with a new authority. There are many instances where battles were fought and won against the rulers and then replaced by new governments.

Marxists see power stored in the economic resources under control of the capitalists and the upper class or the elite force who exercise power. Together, they control the political situation in the country. According to Karl Marx, economic resources create the economic superstructure which enable the capitalists and the bourgeoisie own the 'means of production' – the power house of the ruling group. Marx believed that conflict perspectives would expose the political state of affairs and predict when the powerless multitude would take over by overthrowing the bourgeoisie governments. This would lead to bringing the economic infrastructure under control of the community. In a communist society, power will be exercised by the community as a whole and every body will have an equal share in it. It will be the end of the regime of the vested interests and for people who held it for their sectional benefit. According to Karl Marx, at the end, the state as a source of all power will cease to exist ending the class rule under the autocratic control.

Engles has elaborated Marx's ideas of the state and the future of the class structure. In his opinion, in the primitive societies, neither the state nor the social classes existed but only communes, in which members shared power and benefits; no one accumulated wealth or tried to become rich. The future of communism is predicted to be a stateless and classless society. The views of Marx and Engels are embodied in the document called 'The communist manifesto' which became the gospel of the proletariat revolution to which Lenin made a significant contribution as well. During the First world war in 1917, the Proletariats also called the Bolsheviks proclaimed a Socialist government in Russia. This revolution spread when after the 2nd world war, communism trumped in to the East European countries one after another under Soviet Russia's backing, and later in the Far East under the leadership of Chairman Mao Tse Tung in China and Ho chi Minh in North Vietnam. Marxism has been criticised and interpreted in different ways and there are many versions of Marxism developed by latter Marxists otherwise known as the neo-Marxists.

New Marxist Concept of Power

Amongst the conflict theorists, there are two modern theorists whose work has been broadly influenced by Marxism. They are the sociologists Antonio Gramsci and David Coates.

Gramsci (1891-1937) was an Italian and also a communist activist who took part in the industrial workers' movement in Turin in 1926 in their attempt to seize power from the factory owners. His attempt failed but he was imprisoned by the Fascist government of Mussolini for his action in Turin for eleven years where he died. His contributions to sociological theories were jotted down in his prison note book which was a valuable document of his thought. Having had recovered the material, his followers compiled it and printed it into a readable form for the public.

His view of power was enshrined in his concept of 'hegemony' which is the ruling class authority. He defined 'hegemony' as 'intellectual and moral leadership' of the ruling authority. According to him, when the ruling class is able to maintain its control over the members of society through good behaviour and persuasion and holds its sway of authority for sometimes, then the power is known as hegemony. 'Hegemonic power' is something not enforced or imposed upon the people but introduced based on persuasion and mutual understanding with them This corresponds to Stephen Luke's 'Third phase of power'. Which is a power to influence people through the dominant ideas in society.

Gramsci differed with Marx's view that portrayed the ruling class as oppressive and unwilling to compromise. Gramsci felt this was a misunderstanding which could lead to social unrest and a recipe for discontent and eventual revolution which Marx believed was inevitable but Gramsci did not. His theory of revolution was different from Marx. Revolution, according to him, can take place only when the working class has developed their own intellectual and moral leadership to challenge the hegemonic rule of the ruling class.

Gramsci agreed with Marx that the society was divided into two broad based classes-one was the ruling class consisting of financiers, industrialists, landowners etc while the other was the subject class consisted of industrial workers, agricultural peasants and the working class people in general but disagreed with the Marxian view that the ruling class would not compromise with the working class, sacrificing their sources of profit, such as the 'means of production' and other privileges. According to Gramsci if there was no alliance between the two or other similar groups than 'the hegemonic rule' would come to an end.

Gransci argued that the power should be left both in the hands of the ruling class as well as the people. Power comes from the control of economy as well as from ideas, activities and experience of people. The ruling authority would not be able to monopolise power if people refused to give away their rights and experiences completely. As a Marxist, Gramsci liked to see a proletariat revolution to take place but not in the manner as Marx wanted. To Marx, the revolution was inevitable because of historical circumstances, but to Gramsci it is a possibility. He mentioned that in Czarist Russia, revolution took place fundamentally, because there was no ruling class in control as such and the monarchy was careless and incompetent. Therefore, there was no hegemonic control. That made it possible for the subject classes to take direct action in a head on collision with the autocratic Czarist rule.

David Coates, a British Marxist sociologist, agreed with Gramsci's views of 'hegemonic power'. In the context of British politics, Coutes states that most British governments have been able to maintain a high degree of 'hegemonic rule' because of public consensus which was with the governments' national programme. This enabled the ruling power to meet public demand for better provision for living standard such as the welfare provision, employment, national health service, good education and stability in prices and incomes. But Coutes could not guarantee that the hegemonic control could be taken for granted for long. Once public services are cut, and taxes raised – their consequences would be disastrous for the public such as, decline in public support and a gradual deterioration of the law and order situation. This was the situation in the 80s when Mrs Thatcher passed stringent laws effecting the tax system, curbing Union rights to go on to strike and cutting education budget etc; The result was the loss of hegemonic control and not long after, the Tory government under Mrs Thatcher was ousted from power. This proves one thing clearly that the hegemonic power is dependent on the consent of the people. Just using force would not be able to keep the ruling authority in power for long.

Power – Michael Mann – The Sources of Social Power

A new social theory of power has been developed by a British sociologist Michael Mann, which is still to take a firm footing. This social power theory conflicts with the major theories of power but sometimes coincides with them on common issues. Mann has tried to trace the root of the social power but ended up tracing the sources on common factors like the economy, ideology, politics and defence.

Initially, he has rejected the concept of society as an entity because according to him, the society has no unity nor does it evolve a unity. It is fragmentary and is like many other social institutions which do not last long. According to him, changes in society are so frequent that virtually no society can exist permanently. He confides that if he had power he would not hesitate to abolish the word 'society'. He disagreed with Talcot Parsons' concept of a 'social system' or sub-systems based on the 'value consensus' on the ground that no permanent social system can be achieved in the true sense of the term.

He defines that 'societies are constituted of multiple overlapping and intersecting socio-spatial networks of power'. (Michael Mann Sources of social power. Vols 1 & 2 '86 & 93) According to him, if sociologists would like to study society, they should first of all study the inter-personal relationships as nucleus to social fabric. Even in building these kinds of relationships, power factor plays a dominant role. Power is at the core of his social theory. Power in his perception can be conceived from both the individualistic as well as from the collective Points of view. Power is exercised for the vested interests either of the self or the group. According to him, power can not be anything except used over others.

As Mentioned Above, Mann's Sources of Social Power are Four Folds

Mann disagrees with Marx's 'primary' role of economic power as fundamental, compared to the rest of the sources. He argues that the following three sources are as important as the economic one. For example, ideological power provides philosophy and principles to the government; political power puts ideology in to action in the form of government functions and lastly, the military power which is concerned with defence, protection of sovereignty and maintaining peace and order, even if required to quell the rebellion in the country. Therefore, none of these sources are less important than Marx's economic source which is Mann's fourth source of power.

Mann's four sources of power can work independently or jointly in case if that should be necessary. If there is a coup for example, the military power would take over and dominate over other sources including the economic source. Similarly, if there is a socialist revolution somewhere and if it succeeds taking over power, then the socialist government would also override other sources and control everything including the military, political and ideological power. For example, owning the 'means of production' by the few, would then be replaced by the 'ownership of means' by ball.

In a democratic government, all sources of power work in cooperation and coordination with one another for the best interest of the country. Mann's approach to social power must embrace all these sources including military and economic power. Mann argues that depending upon particular circumstances caused by social change in a particular time, two or more of the sources of power can be used by a social group or party but rarely any group would be able to exercise and monopolise all sources for a long time. There will be a change of hands across boundaries which would aim to prevent a single group owning all power all the time.

Eric A Nordlinger, advocates a state centred power rather than a socially based power because, in a democratic system the state has the ultimate responsibility to generate requisite amount of power, also to use it for the good of people. He criticises the socially ingrained power as a 'pervasive grip upon citizens, journalists and scholars alike'. He believes that the state has an autonomous status of its own apart from people; it has distinct interests and takes autonomous action. The state has autonomy-enhancing capacities which have been overlooked. Nordlinger states that society centred approaches have been dominant for a long time, nevertheless, autonomy of the state must be recognised; at the same time he agrees that society can and does influence the state, similarly the state can influence the society. In his view, the state can act autonomously to change society.

According to Nordlinger, the autonomy of a democratic state takes three forms for example, a state has its own policies shaped by the wishes and demands of people. These demands are formed from a massive array of information collected from different sources, concerning the interests of the major groups of people. All facts gathered are sorted by the civil service in order to submit to the relevant government departments. Then, it will be their job to formulate proposals out of the information supplied for submission to the parliamentary groups for further processing and putting through the due process of law. Any opposition would also to be accounted for and any extra matter found useful would be added to the proposals. In a parliamentary system, it is even easy to pass them by the majority of the ruling party. State autonomy can thus be maintained without the society getting involved in the policy making process.

Secondly, the state is always in a position to persuade and to pressurise groups or opposition to accept its policy or the policy of the government and by doing so can enhance its authority.

Thirdly, the state exercises its autonomy understanding that there are major demands produced by the opposition or some other substantial groups, which warrant recognition and acceptance by the state. It would be wise to do so for the best interest of the country. The state would not go against them and create unnecessary difficulties for the government. So the sensible thing to do would be to keep the autonomy flying, and at the same time on occasions, accepting public demands without rejecting them.

There are sociologists who have conducted researches to find out that the state has enormous capacity to produce power independently. One of the sociologists, Theda Skocpol is emphatically advocating the role of the state in generating extra power and to use it in real politics. She demands that the state should be brought back in at the helm of power source.

Critics have found that the state centre theories are not perfectly clear whether they are fully independent of the society or they are partners. If they are, then the state can rise to establish a dictatorship of the state which could not be allowed in a democratic set up. They have also found that the state centred theories are exaggerating about their real sources of power ignoring the fact of politics in the country. On the other hand, the society centered power theories have to modify their standpoints by accepting the state's capacity to generate power whenever necessary to govern the country. The state must use their power for the best interest of the people. Therefore, there has to be a democratic solution such as a compromise between the state and the society about sharing power which is to develop through a dynamic relationship with each other.

Steven Lukes's Theory of Power

Steven Luke has developed a radical concept of power which in his view has three dimensions. The first dimension of power is the decision making power. He who can influence the authority to adopt a particular policy of their own against others then that person has the most power of all. For example, if the leader of the workers' union can pressurise the government to accept their proposal for pay rise or the right to go on strike rather than the government's, then it is clear that the unions have more power in this particular issue making decisions for the Government. This is similar to the pluralist view of power propounded by Robert Dahl and Nelson Polsby.

Robert Dahl argues that 'A has power over B to the extent that he can get B to do something that B otherwise would not do' (1975). Then it is clear that A has more power over B. Polsby argues that when sociologists study issues and submit their points of view for the policy making, then only those who have convincingly put their arguments forward, would be allowed to take part in the decision making process.

The second dimension of power does not concern about decision making; rather their concern is how to thwart and prevent others making decisions about certain issues. If a group have prevented other groups from tabling their motions for a successful resolution; then that is a non-decision making power. In a municipality or a local council, for example, if some group or groups are in a position to influence the decision making process of the council relating to budget cuts and successfully abort other's proposals, then they have the power over others. This co-relates similarly to what the pluralist view of power stands for. According to the pluralist view, if any particular group or groups within the municipality or council succeed carrying out their proposals in preference to others then they have the power.

The third dimension of power is held by people who have the ability to persuade and win over other groups into accepting their ideas. This is something shaping and manipulating the desires of others towards accepting certain decision already made. For example, in order to meet the desires of people, some pop group might like to hold a pop concert in a country areas which will affect peace and tranquillity of the local community. The local community would not like a noisy programme to go through their village. Besides, the area would be environmentally polluted by litters, remains of the food, digging holes for the tents and scattered rubbish. But the pop group would not give up. Through persuasion, they prevail over the community's feeling and get a permission for the show to go on even when it would cause discomfort for the villagers. This shows that the organisers have power over the community's. Steven Luke's 'Radical view of power' successfully survives against the strong contenders like the functionalists and Marxists; not forgetting the fact that Marxist sociologists sometimes, use the radical method in order to defend their causes.

Pluralist Perspective of Power

The pluralist view of power maintains that power is held by a majority of people in a democratic country based on political consensus which distributes power amongst different political parties or groups who represent their sectional interests. They try to bid for power to rule the country on behalf of the people. If any of them or a combination of two or more parties succeed winning the election based on adult franchise, then they form a government and rule of country for the interest of all rather than for individual sections. According to the pluralist view, competition between two or more political parties is an essential feature of a representative government. Not every group of people can exercise power all at the same time. Power can only exist in a democratic parliamentary system when ballot boxes decide who can rule and who can not. Pluralists see societies are made up of different groups pursuing different political aims. Such interest groups may combine into formal political organisation to promote their aims. Interest groups and pressure groups do not aim to take over power in the sense of forming a government but they can take part in decision making process even remaining outside the government.

Pressure groups do not take part in the decision making process which is the job of the government departments. Their main purpose is to influence the political parties and other state organs such as different departments to acknowledge their demands. When a group or a party comes to power with an over whelming majority then other groups who lost fight for power can only exercise their power in opposition. For them, a chance to obtain political power may come in the next general election which will be held in the future. Pressure groups under ordinary circumstances do not bid for power but they also have a right to form political parties or can join any of the existing parties to bid for power. Election will decide their political ambition.

In a democratic system, different groups of a society are important because these bring in pressure on the government to pursue on the main course of action and particularly on issues the government might have ignored. In the Western societies, the pressure groups are a vital part of a pluralist democratic system; not only because they can raise political awareness in the country, but also are constantly vigilant about what the government is doing on issues they had been focussing on. These pressure groups can be environmental, human rights, education of the backward classes, nuclear issues, animal rights, rights of women, pensioners, children and many more. They also work with trade unions and confederation of industry. They can bring pressure on the government in various ways such as by joining the picketing, demonstration, meeting and delivering petitions and wielding banners and posters.

There have been cases where the disgruntled party or parties or pressure groups have shown their power of disapproval of a ruling authority through demonstration and strikes. They claim to have 'peoples' power' which sometimes can force a government to resign or accept their demands. The pluralists see political parties and pressure groups are crucial to the democratic system because they are the means by which the views of sectional interests in the society are reflected. The pluralists also believe that decision making process belongs to all groups and sections. The democratically elected government of course have the right to implement their party policies adopted in the annual party conference which have to be given a priority; nevertheless, the government would have to take cognisance of those pressure groups, specially the trade unions who might have developed some sensible proposals worth considering.

Like Weber, pluralists reject the idea that democracy is possible in one party state since there must be opposition and pressure groups to represent the views of those who disagree with the government policies. Pluralists see the involvement of groups representing all sections of society is essential. Pluralism in strict sense of the term is effectively workable in a direct democracy also where every group is involved in decision making processes.

This view of power is some times equated with the classical or elite views of power. The pluralists also follow Weber's concept of 'constant sum' power which means power is limited and that when one group holds it other groups do not.

The pluralists deny Parsons' 'variable sum' concept of power and their all embracing 'value consensus' in democratic societies because according to them democratic system allow diversity of peoples' interests. The Pluralists see that even an individual has different interests when he or she it performing in different capacities. For example, he or she can be a teacher, a footballer or a political activist – all these different interests are associated with the same individual. According to the French writer de Tocqueville, a democratic political system requires individuals to have a large number of specific interests. If one section of society comes to power to dominate over others ignoring the wishes of others for over a long time this power will degrade into a state of 'tyranny' in which case democracy would not survive for long.

In pluralism, the essential feature is the representative government in which more than one political party must compete for gaining power. Periodically, there should be a change of government with a new party and a fresh agenda. The new party in power will have to prove that they have done better than the former party or parties when they were in government. On the basis of results, the party in power can claim a reelection.

Robert Dahl, the American political scientist as mentioned above who has developed the concept of classical pluralism was actually influenced by Max Weber. Robert Dahl argues that society is made up of many groups – each pursuing different political interests. In his book, 'Who governs? 1961', he has argued that participatory democracy like the Soviet Union is not adequate to represent all but only the representative democracy can be the real alternative to other systems.

Functionalism and Classical Pluralism Compared

Despite some disagreements with the Parsons' functionalist theory, classical pluralists accept Parsons' view that power is ultimately derived from the population as a whole and that the parliamentary system in the West is the best guarantee of a democratic form of government to continue with all people participating in it. But they don't accept Parsons' 'variable-sum' concept of power, although accept Weber's 'constant-sum' concept.

The pluralists also don't' accept Parsons' theory of social system which provides sharing everything with one another including the common value consensus. They rather believe that interests are divided by sectional needs and values rather than an all embracing common goal and common values. Different trade

Unions exist to promote the causes of different professional bodies and class differences also provide different aims and ambitions and so on.

Power and authority go together. Authority is assigned to a person or a group by the community who legitimise this with a mandate, empowering the authority to do the job for the community; in functionalism it is the collective goals that are to be furthered by the authorised people in power. Weber has found the 'rational legal authority' is most suitable for the industrial society; this authority is bureaucratically organised with best people at the top supported by trained and competent staff from the bottom of the structure.

The main problem with bureaucracy is that it becomes too authoritative and strict, causing hardship for minor or individual cases because they don't get a second chance. Then, reasoning suffers and fairness is ignored. Authoritative rule becomes 'iron rule' and repressive. Marx and Lenin hoped that the arrival of socialism would make bureaucracy work for the interest of the working class. But in socialism, sometimes it did work but other times it did not. Weber was also of opinion that democratically elected representatives might be able to prevent the unelected bureaucrats becoming extremely powerful.

In socialism, dictatorship of the proletariat is expected to melt in to the 'real socialism' which meant – the rule of the people would govern the country rather than the party. But in reality the party bureaucrats enjoyed more privileges and high salaries than the multitude.

A Critique of Pluralism

It is argued that the pluralists only accept decisions which are safe, and they like to stick to them in order to stay in power. They know quite well that other political parties are able to table alternative proposals for discussions and decision making. Pluralists are concerned about situation like this. For example, if Marxism, as a radical ideology takes views or use any other means to effect their decision making power, then democracy in the West would have a very difficult time. In democracy, many things happen which are unforeseeable. For example, sometimes, members from one party cross the floor to join the opposition or the party in power. This can cause imbalance in the House of parliament. Crossing the floor is most unethical in political scenario especially when the party is at risk of loosing its majority caused by crossing the floor. It would be harmful for democracy. This contradicts pluralists' view that power is distributed amongst parties in Western democracies.

Secondly, pluralists are also criticised for ignoring what Steven Luke indicated about the third phase of power which is a manipulative power of 'shaping desires' for the benefit of some groups. Sometimes, decisions are influenced by propaganda or false promise focused by the party machine or vested interested members to suit their purposes.

Thirdly, the pluralists' method of measuring power is not conclusive. The method and the empirical evidence taken in to account to measure power seem to contradict their claim that power is distributed and dispersed throughout the democratic system.

Power can be measured by the results of the actions taken to implement certain measures. It is often believed that justices can be done by distributing resources to benefit the poor. But in fact, their lot has remained same instead of the claim that resources had been allocated for this purpose. This shows that either resources have been misused or that resources were not enough to combat the problems because they did not produce the intended result. As a matter of fact, the pluralists' method of measuring power remains unsatisfactory.

Marxists argue that most people have been persuaded to accept the capitalist system even though it is against their interests. So a false consciousness is created. Even accepting the pluralists view of decision making process, it is true that some groups may exercise more power than others specially those who have wealth and status and educationally and professionally competent to exploit the poor and the disadvantaged.

Thirdly, Under the pluralist mode of government, many interest groups are not represented at all in the decision making process such as women as victims of domestic violence and children being abused at home.

David Marsh has modified his view of classical pluralism to be a 'fragmented elite model'. This is a departure from his earlier support for pluralism as a proper democratic model. Robert Dhal has also found some dilemmas with the pluralist thought. According to him, wealthy individuals and owners of large corporations have considerable power to effect the decision making power of the government.

A Critique of Power Perspective

Gender inequalities in the perspective of power has been an on going issue in sociology for some time. Dominance of male power over the society and control of women's issues by men have been criticised by women's organisations for over a long time. Areas in which power has been used to discriminate women from men are the work place, education, housing, employment and civil rights. Even in sexual relationship, legal power is used to favour men than women. Rights of women in terms of equal pay and standard of living have also suffered from questionable treatment. Feminist activists have put emphasis on the prevailing negative attitude and notion of men as well as the establishment against women. Men's relationship with women specially in married life is dominated by egoistic power play of men which has led to in many cases family break down, divorce and even suicide. Dispute over children's upbringing and education has also produced dispute in the family. Women's rights are undermined both in political parties and parliament as well. In India, women's representations in parliament and state assemblies are few and far between even when thousands of women leave college and universities every year with good qualifications. There is no encouragement and promotion of women to parliamentary career, rather they are seen as secondary work force and casual to their professional career.

In the West, women are increasingly being encouraged and promoted to take political responsibility in which they would have a great opportunity to fight for women's cause and equality. It is true, of course, that many, even capable women are abhorred to see the unusual nature of parliamentary work – sometimes finishing late night. This is feared to affect relationship and care of children. The parliament would not like to make special concession for women because that will raise the question of 'positive discrimination' in favour of women. Their domestic commitment is a special responsibility which must be recognised as important as any other job. It should not be treated as a hazard to career but contributory to the growth of a healthy society.

Questions

1. Is bureaucracy inevitable in Industrial societies. Give reasons. Describe the advantages and disadvantages of bureaucratic forms of organisation?
2. Describe the relationships between power and authority.
3. Critically discuss the 'rational legal authority' as the best form of authority amongst all.
4. Critically explain the theory of pluralism in democracy.

Further Reading

1. T.B. Bottomore Karl Marx.
2. Max Weber Politics as a Vocation – From Marx to Weber.
3. Maciver The Modern state.
4. Mills. C.W. The Power Elite.
5. Marsh. D. Power & Politics in Haralambos – Development in Sociology, Vol. 1, 1985.
6. Mann, Michael. The Sources of Power. Vol. 1 & 2, 1986, 1993.
7. Dahl, Robert. Who Governs? Yale University Press, 1961.

Part 14

24

Enlightenment, Modernity, Post Modernity and High Modernity

Introduction, Victor Seidler's Theory, Durkheim, Max Weber and Karl Marx's Concept of Modernity, Post Modernism, Criticism of Post Modernism, Marxist View of Post Modernism, Post Modernism and its Effect on Society, Anthony Giddens on the Effects of Post Modernism.

Introduction

Enlightenment is a movement that occurred in the Western Europe during the 17th and 18th centuries. It is an intellectual movement in which people were taught to reject emotion, superstition and prejudice in the day to day activities of life and instead use reason and rational judgement as a guide to all activities. In its perspective, knowledge can grow only from rational and scientific research than from supernatural objects. People have to detach themselves from emotional and prejudicial constrains in which they have been bound up for centuries in their way to understand the environment and the nature of things. According to Seidler, nature is an object which has no awareness and consciousness of its own, it can not guide us. Only science can guide us and through every problem we face in life and through science we can discover the intricacies of nature. Therefore, to study the nature and to find out its inner meaning we have to be away from it and study it from a detached point of view which is the scientific way.

Enlightenment movement has started from the ideas of the French intellectuals who cultivated rational philosophy embodied in their 'Encyclopaedic' literature. This book contained ideas which explains how a society should be run by rational way and made free from oppression and exploitation. According to the intellectuals, the scriptural law strictly based on the beliefs of the Roman Catholic Church was not based on reason and argument but based on moral dictates and guidance.

Therefore, the scriptural laws can not successfully run a state or a society because the society is made up of many mundane issues which should be dealt with differently by a temporal authority than by a religious institution. Besides, our society has different religious bodies which can not agree to major issues that concerns the welfare of all. The only way to run a society successfully is by man made political laws. These laws are made by debates and arguments based on reason through the law making process of parliament. The power of human reason should be applied to create a knowledge requisite to improve social conditions. This Enlightenment movement is a movement of reason through which changes can be brought in the cultural, social, educational, political and economic conditions of the country.

Enlightenment has helped the growth of modernity which has replaced many traditional customs and values by inculcating new rational ones to compensate the loss of the out dated ones. Modernism has helped the growth of capitalism together their progress continues unabated.

Many changes took place through enlightenment movement including the emergence of sociological concepts and theories. The age old belief that the society and its ethics were preordained by the unalterable laws of god has now been shaken up.

Victor J Seidler, who wrote about the industrialisation of Western societies and also other writers who explain that the Enlightenment thinking is the foundation of Modernity that has taught people how to think scientifically and fight superstitious notions that have engulfed peoples' minds from reaching right decisions.

Durkheim, Karl Marx and Max Weber

Durkheim et al – all took the cue from the enlightenment ideas. August Comte, the 19th century classical sociologist who is also known as the founder of sociology wrote that the scientific rationality was able to reform the society gripped by religious fear, superstitious beliefs and emotional approaches to life. Their Positivist stance has taught people to think rationally and calmly and overcome the impact of doctrinal influence.

The Enlightenment has enhanced the development of scientific approaches to enquiry such as the "deductive method of reasoning which led to the growth of mathematical science and the inductive method of empirical reasoning which led to the science of nature" (Dunthorne, 1991, p. 7). The success of the natural sciences encouraged a belief that "In the struggle of man against nature, the balance of power was shifting in favour of man". (gay, 1973, p. 3).

As mentioned above, Seidler and many others have explained that Modernity has released human minds from social constrains enabling them to reason and to use scientific knowledge to social progress. Modernism is thus a phase of enlightenment, in which people have more choice and freedom to do what they like. People have more time and resource to spend in luxury, in outdoor pursuits, in art, drama and cultural activities. People also feel that they are released from political bindings, excessive economic exploitations and social and religious obligations; so also their commitment to the community are now fewer.

Many have a feeling that they are liberated from repressions occurring from social taboos, rules of elders and community leaders to whom they were expected to remain obliged for ever. In modern society, families have become smaller, so women have more space to breath fresh air and to enjoy life and civic rights as men. Brigitte and Peter Berger have suggested that nuclear family pattern has helped to produce modernity as it has encouraged industrialisation. For example, many working class women are now able to go out to work as plenty of work is available for them which has improved their livelihood and lower middle class women are educated and trained to do office work including IT jobs. They are now in a position to raise their standard of living including developing leisure pursuits like music, sports, driving cars, going on trips with friends or families, join evening courses to improve career prospects, learning IT skills and partaking to social and cultural activities like men.

Thus, modernism has arrived along with the development of capitalism which has opened up industries and enabled people to choose their profession and earn more money and to enjoy their life more than before; side by side to work hard in order to get promotion in job which guarantees better pay and job security. Modernism delivers freedom of choice when people feel free to do what they like. This phase becomes intense when it meets with positive response in the post war period at a time of urban renewal. People's dress, fashions, style of living, their choice, outdoor pursuits, leisure activities etc. as mentioned above are changing relentlessly as new ideas cropped up all the time leading to new mode of life. Not only that, people's taste in innovative food, drink, art, music, literature and aesthetic sense have also found new dimensions as requirement has increased specially amongst middle class people. Each new invention leads to a new one which spreads as required. Many of these needs have been institutionalised once they have gone through the public approval.

Earlier, modernism had been better exhibited in the field of architectural development. Marketable new designed buildings, functional high rise flats – otherwise called the sky scrappers, new materials like sheets of steel, concrete and glass took over to build the economically designed buildings that has solved a long overdue need for affordable housing. The government in the West also has seen this being the best chance to house the homeless, the destitute and the newly arrived immigrants from the third world countries who otherwise could not afford to buy a decent place to live in one their own.

But it did not take long time to see the reality of the situation. At the dawn of the '70s, these huge complexes became unfashionable and also uninhabitable. They have become soulless structures infested with crime and vandalism. Many incumbents have left fearing that their life was at risk if lived in that precarious environment. Children were prone to abuse by predators, drugs and prostitution. These are also criticised as aesthetically unhealthy buildings and their outward view looked morbid like concrete jungles.

This phase of modernity has now been overshadowed by the impact of much improved concept of Post-Modernism.

Post modernity has come along to renew some changes introduced by the modernity, for example, changes in architectural styles and attractive designs although interesting to look at are not sociologically very significant in themselves. There has been outcry already against modern architectural designs which needed a thorough overhaul both in terms of their aesthetical characteristics as well as architectural purposes which must co-relate to human values and natural ideas. Big buildings must be nice to see if they could reassure peace of mind and social harmony.

There have been general theories of society which could not have found solutions for social issues because of their constant shifting the grounds. Also the status of science has been questioned in terms of sociology. Some writers have argued that post modernity has to be critically re-evaluated to find its social justification for all the changes that had taken place to far. Two of the post modern theorists Frenchmen Lyotard and Boudrillard have written enough to explain and to explore the current situation. Post modern theorists have argued that many people now do not believe in the inevitability of science and its power to solve all social problems.

Earlier, it was believed that our society could be run scientifically according to the Marxist laws. To day, in the aftermath of the collapse of Marxism they do not believe so any more. Marxism, as a grand theory has failed to deliver its prime objectives and peoples' beliefs in Marxism have now been shattered as a result.

In the post – modern phase of the industrialised society, people can see that one grand theory or a belief can not hold right for every thing happening in the society. There has to be a diversity of theories in the realm of ideas; rather than just one or two. As mentioned above the French post modern theorists have developed different views on society. They are Jean Francis Lyotard and Boudrillard.

J.F. Lyotard

Both Lyotard and Boudrillard used to believe that science had the answer to many complicated issues of natural science as well as of social science; so science was the source of knowledge for centuries. To day, as referred to above, that belief can not be taken for granted. Both the sociologists also believed that 'meta narratives' or big stories of society including myths, legends and tales – held and narrated by some old figureheads of primitive societies or tribal chiefs on which science and knowledge were based on for generations are now unacceptable as proof of the past. So, much of the details have now lost their credibility as a storage of information and knowledge. The main reason for their unreliability is that they are being told and retold by so many tellers and narrators that each had added something new to glorify their version to make people believe in them. The result is that they might have gone through many interpretations, effecting the, colour, characters and the nature of the content of the stories. Truth became a fundamental issue.

Moreover, these accounts are principally unwritten statements which can not be vouchsafed for their original as there is no evidence left to prove their purity. The science also have distanced themselves from unauthenticated stories because they became different over the years; the narratives are alienated, composed of opinions, prejudicial and ideological. So they can not be relied upon. On the other hand, Meta narrative stories about society or its issues can not be objectively proved either or rejected entirely. So scepticism about these material prevail which cloud the source of knowledge for a long time. Lyotard has admitted the state's "incredulity towards meta narratives" (Lyotard, 1992, p. 356).

On the other hand, Lyotard argued that science can not be totally free from the effects of meta narratives because social science has to depend on social facts some of which are anthropological. So the link between science and society can not be fully dismissed. Lyotard argued that social life is being organised around Language games which serve to justify the legitimacy of people's behaviour in society. But later in the post modern society, language games became replaced by scientific 'denotative language games'. In denotative language games statements are judged as to whether they are true or false by competing groups. Scientific statements are scrutinised and verified with evidence which have to pass through debates and arguments with other scientists and participants. Then, the selected statements would be approved and accepted which could not be made possible in ordinary language games. Later on, 'denotative languages games' are replaced by 'technical language games' which is appropriate to the technologically oriented society. Language here is judged by its effectiveness and usefulness rather than whether they are true or false. Truth is considered as less important than the needs of technological world.

Baudrillard

Baudrillard, another French Post modern theorist has introduced the concept of 'simulation' which reflects the image of something sociologically important. He argued that in the first stage of its development, the image of something has been a true reflection of the reality. What can be seen is exactly replicated in the image. But things changed through the passage of time when imagery continued to change to the extent that it assumed a different meaning – its true colour or character did not represent its original. Its image became distorted and meaning confused; when reproduced, it showed little relevance to its original image. Thirdly, it deteriorated further and finally lost its original image altogether. Boudrillard's simulation becomes 'simulacrum' when the image becomes entirely different from its original with no relevance to its former reality at all. He gives an example, such as the 'Disneyland', is a perfect model of a simulacrum. It is a copy of the imaginary world or a fantasy world which in realty does not exist but is based on stories told by travellers, sailors, pirates or fiction writers.

According to Baudrillard, too much attention is paid to unravel a particular object of importance such as the study of life of a primitive tribe. When under constant scrutiny and glare of camera people under spot light feel shy, or scared and loses their natural character. This hinders getting an authentic and original nature of their social life actually that is where they liked to film. As a result, the real life situation or the image of them changes. They become 'simulacrum' of primitive society.

Baudrillard and Lyotard agree that we now live in a post-industrial society. But Baudrillard argues that we live in a society when signs meant a lot to us but nowadays, they 'bear no relation to the reality whatsoever' (Poster, 1988, p. 170). Baudrillard argues that news reporting often involves simulation, sometimes, simulations can be more real than reality when reported with additional information or made it more sensational. The T.V. has gone into our life; nothing much we can do about it except that we can take what we like and reject what we do not like.

The post modern theorists have offered challenges to us by raising stimulating questions about the future of our society. Are the key features of the post modern society been fully unravelled or are we going to have a post modern culture to live by for a long time? According to Thomson, "We are clearly living through an era of massive social change" (Thomson, 1992). We have more diversity in thinking and a plenty of choice in choosing our life styles. Also we are left with questions like, our society is more fragmented than ever and life is more threatened by terrorism, violence and hooliganism than any thing like these we knew of. If these are the products of post modernism, then we have to do a lot to renew our life and secure our society from the clutches of these destructive forces.

The Marxist view of post Modernism offers us a different view than those of Lyotard and Baudrillard.

David Harvey, A New-Marxist View

According to him, changes in society have taken place no doubt but they are not that crucial to warrant a post–modernism age. He also believes that the meta narratives have not outlived their usefulness. Harvey, interprets Post–Modernism as a change caused by a new form of Capitalism which remains at the heart of the Western societies. Modern capitalism has increasingly become more dynamic, flexible and adaptive. According to him, economic factor still predominates over other factors such as social, cultural, scientific in terms of modernism. He finds workers still being exploited by the capitalist system in varying forms even with the consent of the Trade Unions and other socialist organisations and its extent is known when the gap between the rich and the poor is revealed by the economic reports. Capitalism too suffers from economic down turn and structural causes beyond their control, external factors such as international competition, technological innovations, emerging developing countries as economic force which offer attractive facilities for investment etc. When the crisis looms large, capitalist strategies take steps to adapt to changes by controlling the labour market in order to fit them in to their counter economic plans. Keeping in mind that the prime reason of capitalism is profitability, the owners despite economic decline would use different techniques, new skills and strategies to keep the damage to the minimum.

David Harvey stresses that Capitalism thrives because workers are paid less than the economic value of their products and the system is also dynamic because it is able to adjust to changes caused by innovation etc. In this way, the capitalist system survives. According to Harvey, period of crisis in economy is unavoidable so also the market economy which continues to do business. For recovery, in an economic crisis, according to Harvey, 'new mode of social and political regulation' should be the answer.

The capitalist economic system has to adapt to 'flexible accumulation' involving amongst other things reorganising the products and patterns of consumption. Reducing trade union rights by legislation, less job security for workers, increasing technological expertise and more employment in the service sector are other ways. Also, measures can be taken to invent new products in the computer games to attract middle class consumers and to overhaul the leisure industry. Furthermore, create a new trend in the lifestyles, outfits, fashion and revolutionise the film industry which could cause 'u' turn to the economy. These could bring cultural changes and herald a new era in modernity.

The new flexible economy of the late seventies and eighties embarked upon an exploration of opening up ventures hitherto unknown. As large scale industries with mass employment and consumption declined effecting the capitalist economy, so it required new ways and means to recover from the ruins of the old system. But how to do that is the question.

One way is to concentrate on inventing new techniques of production as indicated above. Secondly, to put emphasis on specialised quality products which middle and upper class clients would like to consume. Thirdly, to open a cultural diversity programme such as a large-scale tourism industry on inter-continental basis aimed to bring world cultures near your door. Fourthly, 'Time and space' become a big industry as holidays are being tailor made to suit your purpose – to enjoy ethnic food in the country of their origin, to watch world cup matches wherever they are held and also to see wonders of the world – all in a short space of time – in a matter of weeks and days everything in affordable prices.

This is the post-modern era which has come about during the stock market crash in the 1987s and economic turmoil in the nineties when more crashes occurred in the late nineties. The right wing Prime minister Mrs Margaret Thatcher in the U.K. and the Republican president Mr Ronald Reagan in the U.S.A. forged an understanding for reviving entrepreneurship in the period of flexible accumulation. 'Market forces' were introduced by which earning and spending were trimmed, in other words, no earning, so no spending was made the principal government policy –

based on 'cut your coat according to your cloth'. According to Harvey, post-modernism has not just affected government, it has also influenced the development of social and political movements worldwide. Issues like child abuse, sexual harassment in jobs, unequal treatment of women in employment, inequalities of all kinds including racial discrimination, and poverty in the third world countries have become serious matters which warranted immediate attention.

Effects on Education

Effects of Post modernism are numerous and varied as they are significant in terms of their positive and negative consequences. In the field of education, Robin Usher & Richard Edwards have produced a valuable work in their book, 'Post modernism and education', 1994. In their view, 'education is very much the dutiful child of the Enlightenment'. The implication is that education liberates whole humanity from ignorance and poverty with the help of rational and scientific knowledge. This helps people to free themselves from the clout of traditional constrains and superstitious indoctrination.

Under post modernism, individuals will be enlightened to realise their full potential so that they could become fully autonomous and capable of exercising their capabilities. Fully developed individuals would be able to take the society forward and to keep pace with the world. Post modernism also teaches us how to fight religious extremism as it is the modern day's enemy of democracy and liberalism. All dominant forms of paradigms whether political or social should be studied and their values extricated to enhance the movement of social change. Furthermore, it teaches us to know where is the single best curriculum in the world, if there is any, which can teach us everything we need to know. Education should teach different things in order to diversify our knowledge and truths rather than one set of truth. This will prevent one set of truth being made dominant over others.

Education should also cover current affairs and focus on all aspects of cultural, economical, political matters of society. There should be course on cultural pluralism to teach tolerance and the values of accommodating people of different cultures in to the society. Social exclusions should be avoided. Education should be based on modern, humanist and liberal ideology and the aim is to turn individuals into better people, able to fulfil their potential. Education should be offered on a life long basis as well so that no one is excluded from enriching their life at whatever age they are. Education system should also made special provision for marginalised and oppressed groups who are entitled to learn at their pace and abilities.

Effects of Post Modernism on Society

One of the effects is the diversity of social movements which occurred during the 2nd half of the 20th century caused by large scale modernisation of the urbanised societies. Societies in the rural areas remained stagnant for centuries. Modernisation programme did not cover the rural areas which needed urgent attention. Without their uplift no country can move forward. David Harvey, a Marxist, has identified good signs of growing Internationalism to fight Ecological disasters, hunger, apartheid, racism, Aid and terrorism which are killing millions all over the world. According to him, Post modernity has not just affected the Governments but also influenced the social and political movements all over the world.

Anthony Giddens on the Effects of Post–Modernism

Anthony Giddens, an eminent sociologist has acknowledged the positive signs of Modernity which have come almost in all areas of our life but he was also seriously apprehensive of the risks involved in those changes. He compares the modernity with a 'juggernaut' – a 'run away engine of enormous power which threatens to rush out of our control'.

According to Professor Giddens our society has become a 'risk society' in which we are constantly being watched over by some body we don't know, moreover, every one would have to carry an Identity card to prove where we belong to and from where we have come. Our privacy now is exposed to the extent that we have given away everything we treasure as private to those who are beyond our control.

It is now evident that, Post Modernism has unleashed more dangers to our lives but even more to the lives of the teen-agers than ever before. The teen population has increased considerably during the 90s and those born after are also exposed to the impact of post – Modernism. Taken together, they are now the largest consumers of the post modern age in the capitalist monopoly system. Their choice and tastes are being catered for by the monopoly market and the profit is going to the capitalists. Post modernism has offered opportunities to everybody to enjoy life with the benefits of the modern age but the dark side of the opportunities are now becoming strikingly clear.

The teen-agers and the young generation are misusing their liberty entitled to them to use for good purpose; any abuse of liberty is the big question. Many are living a trendy and expensive glamorous life style, watching violent movies which are crime related, romancing, dancing till late night with synthesised popular music. At the same time, they are also victims of unscrupulous gangs, drug addicts, loners, frustrated individuals, racists, fanatics and so on. Many of them are already in the dark side of life, drinking, smoking, drug taking, late night parties, shouting and fighting in the street. With money in the pocket and motley collected friends, teenagers feel they are some thing to be reckoned with. Post Modernism has become a cult of the young impressionable minds who are living a risky life in style without worrying about the consequences. The future is bleak indeed for many of them.

Our problems are also multiplied by the impact of serenes on the Ozone layer which is fast disappearing causing dreadful floods, big tidal waves, melting Iceberg and destroying the natural habitats of rare species, serene beauty spots and large area of forest and coastal regions. Nuclear proliferation is another danger lurking around threatening to destroy towns and cities; new members are even aiming to his targets and destroy everything. If these things happen much of our planet would be gone out of shape forever.

Action must be taken to at least minimise the catastrophes by organising world opinion to cut rich nations' aspirations for more power, wealth and control of the weaker nations. Answer also lies in redistribution of wealth to help the poor and those starving to death. Economic inequality is difficult to eradicate but plan should be devised to reduce the disparity as much as possible.

High salaried people must cut their claim for more pay which has no purpose in raising the standard of living which is already sufficiently high. Wasteful plans cost billions with no real benefit. No problem is insoluble if 'head on start programme' is undertaken by the world body to deal with the dreadful circumstances in which we are living. There are 'high risks' with 'high modernity'.

Further Reading

Sedler, V.J. Social theory, 19.

Dunthorne, H. The Enlightenment, 1991.

Lyotard, Jean Francis and Baudrillard. The Post Modern Condition, 1984, and 1992.

Thomson, P. Changing Theory – Changing Practice.

Harvey David. The Condition of Post Modernity, 1989.

Bell, Daniel. The Coming of the Post Industrial Society, 1973.

Boudon, Raymon. Theories of Social Change, 1986.

Nisbet, Robert. Social Change and History, London, Oxford University Press 1969

Ginsberg, M. Social Change, British Journal of Sociology, September 1958.

Gay, P. The Enlightenment: An Interpretation, Vol 2.

The Science of Freedom, Wildwood House, London, 1973.

Giddens, A. The Consequences of Modernity, Polity, Cambridge.

Robin Usher and Richard Edwards. Post Modernism and Education, 1994.

Part 15

25

Theories of Social Change

Introduction, The Meaning of Social Change, Nature and Causes of Social Change, Theories of Social Change, Theory of Evolution, Darwins's Theory of Evolution, New Darwinism, Uniliner and Multilinker Approach, Evolutionary Theory of Talcot Parsons (Evaluation), Karl Marx's Theory Dialectical Materialism.

Introduction

The meaning of social change

'Social change' in the words of Anthony Giddens, 'is difficult to define'. Giddens. A (2001), p. 42, because it is a complex issue and its perspectives keep changing along with social changes. When some fundamental changes in society take place in terms of different social issues like abortion, education, change of a constitution, immigration, divorce, age of consent, tolerance, integration, inter caste marriages, compulsory education for primary age group, women's rights, etc then life in society becomes different from before, even if they took place sporadically here and there still that would good for a society. At the advent of the modern age, however, Western cultures surged forth leaving behind the Asian countries which then were influenced by the Western values and cultures in the field of education, dress, language, food, music and political ideas. All this however took place slowly and gradually.

Also social changes in the West occurred following the scientific. The West developed their technical expertise required for their survival including conquering other countries in the way to expand their domination. Since the 17th century, Western colonisation of other countries took a pace, the nature of social change took a different turn. Having had seen the western societies changing faster than theirs in the field of material, scientific, educational and economic areas; the eastern societies took the cue from them even though slowly moved forward – first eradicating some of the old pathological superstitious beliefs including social taboos by instituting reforms. These superstitions held the society back for hundreds of years: the practice of human sacrifice in the name of religion, for example, the suttee-widow to die in her dead husband's funeral pyre, young widows not allowed to remarry, denial of human rights to women, child abuse and a host of other social abuses and injustices which plagued the society in so many ways. Generally, social backwardness was caused by the things mentioned above. Side by side, some urban societies followed the Western values in terms of material progress, human rights, education, language and social justice along with the British rule in India which continued to solidify their control in politics and administration. They were keen to help the indigenous reformers, who were trying their utmost to remedy the social pathos and felt the necessity of Western values to be implanted in changing the mores and thinking of people of the country.

Change denotes an observable difference specially in society over a time. Change must persist for some time in order for it to be a change in real sense of the term different from what it was before and should be in the social phenomena. According to Jones, variations or modifications of any aspect of social processes, social patterns, social interaction or social organisation mean a social change (Jones – Basic Sociological principles, p. 96).

Social change only takes place in any country when circumstances favour its inauguration in the phenomena whatever areas it could be – either educational, social, political or economic. Changes should be in the order of eradicating the old usages such as, abuse of children and women, bond between the peasants and landlords, social inequality caused by the caste system, so on and so forth. Social change is limitless; no society can boast of having had reached its limit. Every country has changed in some way or other but the degree and level to which they have is a matter of opinion. This subject is a puzzling one too because the criteria used to judge the level of improvement could be differing and thus be controversial. As there exists many differential theories to explain the pattern and degree of change, so there could emerge differing level of appreciations and methods in assessing the level of change. New directions too can break paths in which to forge new social changes.

Nature and Causes of Social Change

Social change in order to fit in the society for the best interest of the majority must be based on certain standard criteria. For example, there has to be some observable and meaningful social phenomena as indicated above, ready to undertake change or that such changes have already taken place, at least, to last for some time for people to appreciate, and to get accustomed to these. Some people would call something as social change if an old custom or a law is replaced by a new one either by law or without a law but under pressure from consensus of people of the country or from abroad.

The second criterion is the general readiness to accept a particular change and to legislate. For example, reforms proposed in the caste system, child marriage, women's role in society, child labour etc are issues which have been opposed by the conservative forces who argue that these are age old customs and practices and if disturbed by radical reforms that would shake off social fabric and upset the establishment including peace and order. Whether they like it or not, tide of change has come, it can not be held back or stopped, rather reform programme must go ahead. Introduction of free primary education, banning of extremist propaganda in religion and politics, abolition of poverty, improving farming system, introducing cottage industries, empowerment of women in politics and social life would not cause social unrest rather they would bring social cohesion and therefore be welcome and publicly acceptable.

Caste system in India has gone through many changes since 1947, but the system still persists which disrespects people of lower castes. The conservative forces do not like it completely eradicated. So opposition remains. Many social changes have been introduced during the last fifty years or so and they are all in the statute book.

In other fields of social problems in India, in particular, changes have taken place in the political arena which allows voting rights to all above the age of 18 including women and physically challenged people. But attack on children, women and old people in still rampant in society which the existing laws are failing to combat. So, new laws are necessary to deal with these crimes effectively. The crime must not go unpunished. It is also necessary to strengthen the police force by raising their profile before the public. The public must support the police force and cooperate with them. Adequate legal protection should be guaranteed against breach of human rights. Mugging, threatening behaviour, assault, abduction and all other crimes must be dealt with as fast as possible using punitive action and long imprisonment. Judicial delay hampers the seriousness of the crime. So there should be more law courts set up to deal with cases promptly. Standard of social change is judged by the standard of protection offered by the police – being made available instantly. Corruption in any form and in any place including bribery and deliberate delay in trials should be punishable by law. Also the standard of social change should be judged by the quality of judicial service both in terms of promptness and fairness.

According to Davis, social change can be understood and recognised when social organisations change their 'structures and functions' in order to improve efficiency and performance for the sake of the society. To achieve that level, improvement has to reflect new perceptions. Therefore, social change can take place when old customs and prejudicial and superstitious notions and practices in work and society are prohibited and replaced by rational and tolerant values. These are to be reflected and oriented in work programmes. Any change that promotes spirit of work, sense of fairness, tolerance and understanding of one another will be recognised as good values for the society. It will give a breath of fresh air and develop self confidence.

But there are people who would say radical change may be counter – productive which might effect the normal life of people. Moreover, radical change would force institutional changes causing more upsets. These things can happen; whenever, any change is introduced whether they are soft or radical, some people would be upset – this is a thing which is unavoidable. No change can take place without structural changes. People are not used to radical changes in society. Many people would be upset and not be able to cope with changes to take place one after another. It is absolutely true but the fact is that the society can not go on unchanged for ever which hampers economic growth and retards standard of living; consequently, people's life remains static and boring effecting everything, such as the cultural, scientific and educational growth of society. Therefore, social changes are crucial to country's overall development. Of course, there would be people who would remain enclosed with in their peripheries and reticent to change; the society can not wait for them, it must move on in a changing world.

Social change is caused both by internal forces and influence from abroad. Inevitably, every country experiences some sort of change either slowly or rapidly depending upon the nature of their material, social, cultural and economic circumstances. No society can remain completely static. Its inevitability is without question but when and how it would take place is arguably difficult to presume. But there are exceptions to rule, where any form of social change just can not take place because of the intransigence of members to any form of intrusion into their way of life at all. Change in the Trobriand and Andaman islands is so minimal that it is so depressing because circumstances would not allow any change in the society. The attitude of the native inhabitants was totally negative to change. This is caused by the fact that the islanders were scared to undergo change because they were susceptible to external influence.

Even the change in some third world countries is difficult to come by because of the age – old backwardness aided by resistance, superstition, scepticism, ignorance, religious taboos, bigotry, poverty, illiteracy etc. Those which crack, change slowly, because of the factors mentioned above. Also there are factors, for example, people with vested interests fear that change might jeopardise their profit making business. So they fight back against any thing that try to move the society forward. If any changes do take place they are not always consistent but haphazard and piecemeal. The level of change is effected by the level of economic condition, educational opportunities, socio-cultural and political circumstances which might border between the primitive and the pre-literate levels.

Countries colonised by the British and other western powers have comparatively changed faster than most others. Reforms introduced there removed a lots of barriers in terms of social taboos, superstitions, discriminations, ill treatment of women, etc which raised hopes and awareness for more reforms. Transport and communication system have been established with the railways and telegraphs on the way, new education system has been introduced, new laws and regulations have been passed to replace the antiquated old customs and laws. Changes like these improved social life; public services were freed from many red tapes, new law courts have been set up to deal with the rising cases of litigation and the local administration has been reformed and enlarged. Also laws have been passed to deal with the racial and communal hatred, social bondage of many lower caste people, lawlessness, torture and oppression of poor and destitute. Under pressure from the new laws things began to change for the better.

Theories of Social Change

Amongst many theories of social change, some are more convincing than others. The biological theories of social evolution propounded by Herbert Spencer, Emile Durkheim, Max Weber, Talcot Parsons and Charles Darwin were hailed as the pen-ultimate social theory being made available for sociology but which has now been discredited as unscientific and its credibility is left in doubt. We must also remember that the evolutionary theory has many variations and versions based on the expositions of individual sociologists and anthropologists; no doubt, each has its own rate of success and failure.

Development of the Theory of Evolution

The evolutionary theory is equated with theories of social organism, social Darwinism, unilinear and multilinear and Parsonian approaches. Evolutionism also is linked to the biological theory which has effected the social change. The term evolution explains how has social organism grown from simple to the complex organism. For example, the human society in its early stage was very simple and unstructured. Their ancestors were even more primitive – just learning how to use fire, flints and to curve stones to kill. When they moved to the next stage, which was the stage of hunting and gathering of food and water, life became complex and hard because everybody was busy struggling to survive in the state of nature. Thousands of years ago, in the Palaeolithic period, for example, the people like the Neanderthal men and women lived in the caves, there was literally no society at all; there were no norms of behaviour – worthy of mention; they had very little communicative skills – they were erratic, hot headed, temperamental, unpredictable and ready to attack. They wold not care for others, nor would they tolerate anybody posing a risk to their life. Uncertainty prevailed everywhere about what could happen next. Fury of nature, sudden attack from other cavemen, animals or strange things associated with no fixed material possessions made them insecure and apprehensive. Living as a social group was impossible; also there was no conscious understanding amongst them; every body looked strange to the other, fearsome and hostile. They were rude and rough and fighting was the only way to live and to prevail. Woman was under control of the powerful. 'Might is right' was the order of the day.

When tribal war broke out, things began to change; they felt instinctively to fight for their own group based on kinship. They also realised that without a leader, unity of the group would collapse; so someone was chosen to lead the group who proved stronger than others. The leader had to control the group, make decisions about what to do with rule breakers. This was just a start to the formation of a society in the primitive period.

Even in this period, division of labour was based on male going out for hunting, fighting and farming, women fending children and protecting them from intruders; they had also the duty of collecting wood and water. They domesticated animals, chipped flints, borers, and shaped drills, chisels out of stones. They made clothes from furs and animal skins, and ornaments from teeth and claws. Some of them left indelible mark on the wall by sketching, curving and painting the animals. Some kind of nature worship was in vogue. At this stage, they gave ceremonial burial to the dead and put his belongings in the grave with him believing this would make him rich in his next birth. So a lot of social activities had already started in a primitive social life.

The long Ice Age intervened and interrupted their growing up as social beings. According to Anthropologists and historians, there have been several ice ages in the history of evolution of mankind. Evidently, there were four 'Ice Ages' with three warm periods between them. This probably was the first one because this happened during the early Neolithic period when race awareness was still to take place. By the time, say about ten thousand years ago before the birth of Christ, the fourth Ice Age was coming to an end; the chief races of mankind were clearly marked off. Europe, Western Asia and the fringe of Northern Africa were occupied by the white race and the rest of the world was inhabited by the race with dark skin. Groups of wandering nomads from Asia began their way across to North America during the last Ice Age. They were known as red – Indians, because of their red skin and Indian origin where they had come from.

Nomads in Europe began their first agricultural life after they got accustomed to follow the basic rules of society set out by the tribal chiefs. Later, some sort of social structure was formed and necessary rules framed in which to live and conduct their business. Every body was accountable to the nearest authority in control. In this agrarian stage, civil bodies were formed whose jobs were to maintain the structure and law & order with in the society. At this stage, some sorts of political and legal institutions were also established.

The evolutionary theorists compare social development as a process with biological development of species which grew from the simple to the most complex form. For example, the simple amoeba as a species in its early life grew in to more complex being in the form of animal shapes. In the same way, human society grew from the simplest to the more complex form. As different organisms have more capacity to adapt to the more complex environment in their growth in which to survive against the most dangerous creatures, the evolutionary theorists, found in it the similarities between the biological development and the development of societies.

Both Herbert Spencer and Emile Durkheim were influenced by the nineteenth century idea of the biological evolution which was running parallel to the social evolution. Both used the concept of structural differentiation to explain the development of society becoming functionally more complex as it moved on. Spencer described his criteria in to four forms; such as a simple society which developed into a compound society in the form of clans and tribes. It took a long time for the society to move on to the next stage which devolved into the compounded form in the like of city states and kingdoms. Later, they grew into trebly compounded forms such as empires, modern nations and federations.

Durkheim's typology provided an increasing number of differential societies growing from the mechanical to the organic level which is fully explained in chapter on Durkheim.

Charles Darwin's theory of biological evolution: one version of it is otherwise known as social Darwinism. This is like the biological organisms in which human societies struggle for survival. Some societies fall behind others because of their failure to move from the simple biological mechanism to the more complex mechanisms of life. Their rate of adaptation is very poor compared to the rest which are more adaptable to the changing environment. Gradually, they moved into the next complex mechanisms of life. Western societies for example, have better adapted to the changing environment using improved mechanistic skills enabled by the lack of natural resources to easily to fall back upon. So they had to struggle for survival in the absence of plenty of proper arable land and other natural resources such as forestry, fishery and suitable monsoon climate to help fertilise the land to grow crops. Also the natural forestry endowed with wood and timber and mineral resources required to live easy life than with out. The Western societies in the wake of scarcity concentrated on developing material resources like digging canals for ferrying water into irrigating the land, building bridges to cross rivers, expanding domestic industry, developing trade with the neighbouring countries and inventing tools and weapons to fight for their survival. They would not hesitate to attack the neighbouring countries for food, metals and anything if they had to. Therefore, their development was quicker than other societies which had easy life with their natural resources.

What is a Biological Evolution?

According to Darwin, the development of the human species has come about as a result of random process; it is not dictated by the divine providence for any particular purpose; it is a random process of selection. Darwin calls it the 'natural selection' which hastens the evolution. The natural selection takes place amongst all species which struggle to survive with whatever means of survival available such as food, shelter and protection against extreme climatic and other circumstances. Different species produce different offspring with different needs and their number continues to increase. With limited resources, many of the weaker species get perished giving way to those best adapted to live, because some animals are more intelligent and alert and able to move faster to a safer zone with a keen eye-sight to see their surrounding clearer about what is going on. In the struggle for life, they had advantages over those less well endowed such as less eyesight. And these species will live longer, reproduced their genes to pass on to the subsequent generations. These are the selected species survived through the struggle. In the words of Darwin it is called the 'survival of the fittest'.

Natural selection process is unending. There is something called 'mutation' which acts as a changer of biological characteristics of some species as against others by a mechanical process which can eliminate weaker genes in order to help stronger ones to pull through. The mutated genes have more capability to fight the weaker ones and themselves advance into new forms of life which are new species. The giant reptile could not mutate into the new genes because of its small brain even though it had a large body which actually became a handicap; that's why it became extinct whereas smaller species had superior adaptive capability to transform into superior beings. In the process, our primitive ancestors are the products of superior mutated genes. Charles Darwin has thus found the continuity of development of species from the animals to human beings which is at the heart of his theory of evolution.

The modern evolution theory of Darwin is called the Neo-Darwinism which is about the science of genetics most people were unaware of including Charles Darwin until the 1930s. It is more scientific than Darwin's theory of biological evolution. This theory had been discovered by Gregor Mendel (1822-84) in the 70s.

Even though Mendel's theory is a new one, it co-relates with the main ingredients of Darwin's genetic inheritance. So, it can be said that the science of genetic is a synthesis of Darwin's biological evolution with Gregor Mendel's theory; in other words, an advanced form of evolutionary biology. This is also known as science of sociobiology.

Sociobiology

This theory primarily explains that the human behaviour is shaped by the genetic characteristics of the individual rather than by the culture of the society. This view departs from the usual sociological approach that the human behaviour is based on the cultural factor rather than the biological factor. But the biological factor explains that the human brain which has created the culture has increased in size through evolution and let the 'Homo -sapiens' to survive longer than any other species. Also it is proved that the 'frontal region of the brain' is associated with intelligence which has steadily become larger and a useful tool to survive against odds. The more intelligent a species is, greater the chance of its survival and to reproduce passing the biological characteristics to their offspring. Also, socio biologists suggest that certain biologically based differences in behaviour between the sexes will always remain same which can not be eradicated because of the genetic characteristics. This, then is the point of Darwinian evolution that those traits which evolve will be those which promote their own reproductive success compared to those who failed to succeed. The term 'reproductive success' is now used by many socio biologists to replace the more ambignous term 'survival of the fittest', in fact it is now increasingly believed that term 'survival of the fittest' was first coined by Herbert Spencer not by Charles Darwin.

Unilinear and Multilinear Approach

Development of society can take place in either of the two ways as indicated above or both working simultaneously. In the 19th century, the belief was that the social evolution could take place in the same way as everywhere i.e. in a single line of development in every country which is otherwise known as the Unilinear approach. At first, it starts as a simple way but gradually enters into the complex process. In the evolutionary situation every society has to pass through all the stages of development. No one can skip over others to reach the final stage quickly. There is another way known as the multilinear approach which has surpassed the single line approach in terms of its complexity. This theory recognises the fact that there are various lines of development of society to suit different types of societies as they vary from one another according to their environment, level of progress, differing standard of living, complexity, cultural differentiation and economic standard. (Lenski and Lenski, 1982). So a single path of change is not inevitable.

Evolutionists following the multi-linear approach see that increasing adaptation to environment is the most important mechanism of change to society. They also make a differentiation between progress and change.

Talcot Parsons views social change to result from the process of 'social evolution', that is to start from the simple phase to the more complex forms of society. He finds 'social adaptability' as a major driving force of social evolution. The history of human society begins from the simple hunting and gathering band to the complex nation state caused by factors of economy, migration, climate change, religious influence, cultural influence, adaptation etc, then the next stage starts with learning different languages, meeting, inter-mixture of races, wars, domination of weaker races by the stronger ones, inventions, exploration etc.

These have tremendous effects on the development of society which differs from one another due to increasing general 'adaptive capacity' of societies. Some societies do better than others because of quality of leadership, education, social ideology, purposes and planning. There should be specific societal targets to achieve through proper planning guidance, motivation and direction. While economic changes might provide a stimulus to start with, but in the long run, it would be the cultural impetus to decide the good values with which to determine the broadest pattern of change. Parsons identifies two sets of cultural values known as variable A and variable B. Variable A is typical of simple societies and variable B is typical of advanced industrial societies. According to Parsons evolution of society takes place when it has succeeded moving from pattern A to pattern variable B. Any society which fails to move to pattern B means it has stagnated.

Social evolution is an extension of the biological evolution. Both types of evolution, in the words of Parsons can be explained with the help of 'evolutionary Universals'. One of the Universals is the 'vision' of species which help them see their surroundings and to cope with life, move around for food and defence against risks to life such as killer species, whereas unsighted species or organisms would not be able to do so, so they would perish. The other essential variables are language, religion, kinship and technology – these are predominant factors for any evolving society. Even in the earliest form of society, without communication and religious beliefs no society could develop effectively. Kinship binds the blood relationship amongst the offspring which builds a family to help in need. Lastly, technology helps material progress of society which to move faster and to defend themselves.

Parsons explains that society evolves in a more complex direction to change its institutions and to adapt to becoming functionally more differentiated. For example, in a modern differentiated society, socialisation of children gradually passes from the responsibility of the family to the care of the formalised education system; in which to learn more skills and mature early in terms of spoken language, social skills and sporting acumen. Furthermore, they develop self confidence in an interactive communication and respond positively to behavioural situation. Education starts early through nurseries, child care centres, 'under five' schemes, toddler's group etc. Socialisation at home is limited by the absence of these diverse facilities.

Not only there are questions raised concerning the efficacy and scientific accuracy of the evolutionary theory but also their relationship to social development. The natural world linked to the evolutionary process and the social world. They are two different types of development. It is true that the climatic condition which is a part of the natural world can adversely effect the society's growth as well in terms of agricultural production, transport, communication and welfare of people including education, health and law and order. But that is only a part of the answer.

Adaptation, a core behaviour pattern in the biological evolution which helps certain organisms to promote their survival and genes transfer to another generation can not operate exactly in the same manner in social evolution. In the words of Anthony Giddens, "The concept of adaptation is probably of little value in sociology" (Giddens, 1984). Also there are considerable doubt about classification of societies based on their functions and structures because they do not uniformly grow and do not relate to one another where as biological organisms can be conveniently classified for useful purposes such as adaptation and survival. The nature of social and cultural change is more complicated than biological evolution.

Karl Marx's Theory of Evolution

Marx has argued that human society has passed through five phases of development in the process of social change; these are equated with the general theories of evolution even though Marx named these processes as the dynamics of Historical materialism. These five phases are, oriental or primitive communism, the ancient, the feudal, the capitalistic and the communistic phases. Each phase has its well defined characteristics but each was caused by the internal conflict between the forces of production and distribution. The primitive communism has been a simple form of hunting and gathering society in which goods were held in common and there was no class stratification. The ancient form of society grew from the primitive communism which disappeared stressed by tribal warfare for power and resources. The ancient phase of society showed signs of conflict for ownership and control. In Feudalism, few became big landowners who also were guardians of the ruling authority i.e. the monarchy.

Feudal lords protected their vested interests by controlling and exploiting people better known as serfs and peasants. Class conflict between those who have a lot and those have the least was deep seated in the feudal phase.

As the existence of conflict within the society brew up resulting from economic circumstances, the material forces of production continue to change to that effect, nature of conflicts too and the relationships with in the society. These had impact on the social institutions and the socio-economic relations, state and the government. According to Marx, conflicts are rooted in the material conditions of life. The mode of production in material life determines the general character of the social, political and spiritual forces of life. The social existence determines the consciousness of man.

Capitalism emerged with the rise of manufacturing middle class which dominated over the landed gentry. Class conflict, according to Marx, has brought the historical change of society. In his words, 'The history of all hitherto existing society is the history of class struggle'. The class conflict is the dialectic for social change. Social environment changes through economic transformation of society. Social development, in the words of Marx, occurs through the process of historical 'Dialectics' of materialism. Marx was a pure materialist and he developed the theory that each society is effected by its economic condition alone – known as the 'infrastructure' than by any other conditions. This economic base then helped the 'superstructure' to grow which consists of political, legal, cultural and religious institutions.

The 'dialectical process operates through the system of thesis, anti-thesis and synthesis. The dominant class is always the one that 'owns the means of production' and the exploited class is always the one that provides the labour.

The dialectical process of conflict continues until the proletariat revolution succeeds in abolishing the capitalists from power and establishing a communist order in which the conflict will be over leading to a classless society. This is the Dialectical process of history; originally conceived of by the German philosopher Hegel. The difference is that Hegel was an idealist visualising the rise of a nation through the Dialectical process under leadership of great persons like Alexander, Julias Caesar, Nepoleon etc., whereas Marx is a materialist visualising a society which advances into communism through the economic forces of production and of course proletariat trying to gain power through a revolution. This is a change which bring not only a new political order but also a structure of power with a new economic system. Social change does not come quickly say in the range of a year or two but slowly through centuries but the progress continues unabated.

Marx did not believe in the adaptation theory of the biologists; 'it is too mechanistic' as Marx thought. According to him, human beings try to master the natural environment rather than adapt to it. Thus his dialectical processes have evolved a new form of society otherwise known as 'modern' society which is a product of natural historical process.

Lenin

Vladimir Illich Lenin became the president of the Soviet Union in the 1920s. He was the leader of the Bolshevik party which organised a second revolution in November 1917 and overthrew the provisional government of Kerensky. In his document, 'Imperialism, the highest stage of Capitalism' Lenin concentrated on the internal dynamics of the capitalist society which generated imperialism. He argued that capitalist imperialism started in the later half of the 19th century. Its main purpose was to buy raw materials from the under-developed countries and use them to produce manufacturing goods to sell where their needs were the greatest. Profit accrued from the manufactured products was reinvested in the poor countries which multiplied the amount of profit because of cheap labour. This is a new form of Imperialism called the finance imperialism. Lenin argued that this gradually solidified into the monopoly capitalism concentrated in the hands of a few large-scale enterprises. The banks took over charge of financing the industries. Finance capital got bigger and bigger which spread its net all over the world. According to Lenin, this led to International companies but controlled by a few monopolists also known as multinational companies. They invest their capital which is nothing but the accumulated profit from the former investment and in this way exploit all weak and poor countries of the world and maintain imperialistic control. In Lenin's words, 'If it were necessary to give the briefest definition of Imperialism, we should have to say that Imperialism is the monopoly stage of capitalism'.

Theories of Social Change

Question

1. Explain the concept of social change.
2. Explain the Unilinear and Multilinear approaches of social development.
3. Explain Talcot Parsons' theory of 'social system'. Why this is criticised as a deterministic theory.
4. Why are Herbert Spencer's and Maclever's approaches to social evolution deserve special mention?
5. What is social Darwinism? Explain in the context of Charles Darwin's theory of evolution.
6. Why is Marx's dialectical interpretation of history considered scientific? How is Marx's concept of society developed by the historical process.

Further Reading

Maciver and Page. Society.
Ogburn. Social Change.
Raymond Boudon. Theories of Social Change, 1986.
Daniel Bell. The Coming of the Post-Industrial Society, 1974.
Lenin. Imperialism-The Highest Stage of Capitalism.
Karl Marx. Dialects of Historical Materialism.
Karl Marx. Das Capital, Vol. 1, 1970.
V.I. Lenin. Selected Works, London, 1969.

Part 16

26
Theories of Urban Sociology

Introduction, The Chicago School, Ecological Theory, Ferdinand Tonnies and Emile Durkheim's-theory of Urban Sociology, Talcot Parsons' Social System and Pattern Variables, Rural Urban Debate and the Loss of Community, Conflict Based Marxist and Weberian - Model of Urban Sociology.

Introduction

Urban sociology gained currency as a readable subject since the dawn of the 20th century. The University of Chicago pioneered the study of Urban Sociology covering the backdrop of the socio-economic scenario with in the city of Chicago. This was just a start which fast spread amongst cities in Western Europe including the U.S.A. In particular, life in Chicago presented a grim picture of decay of the inner city; its poverty, squalor, destitution, crime, violence, corruption which were rampant. There also prevailed despicable atmosphere of alienation, loneliness, insecurity of life, rowdiness, drunks, beggary, prostitution and so on. Shopping centres quite busy by day became ghost town by night with sights of thugs laying in wait to rob people coming home late from work.

Based on such a back drop of fear, hopelessness, and depression, a number of writers associated with the University of Chicago devoted to focussing on the issues of the time and produced vast amount of literature reflecting on the urban city referring specially to squalor, poverty and insecurity of life. Some theorists like Robert Park, Ernest Burgess and Louis Wirth made outstanding contributions to highlighting the issues. Some other countries like India had also areas of depression in which poverty and corruption were rampant but Chicago presented a different scenario in terms of insecurity, depression and hopelessness. Extensive researches into the nature and causes of conditions both pathological and physical have been carried out and in some cases action were taken to improve the situation.

The Chicago School and the Ecological Theory

It was realised by the ecological theorists that urban decay took place in areas where settlers clustered around in the form of ghettoes and who also tried to build a pattern of life different to other normal mode of living. They developed their means to procure livelihood with mechanism unacceptable to a civilised society. They depended on day to day living what ever way they could. Their immediate needs were more important than striving for future. This type of living gave rise to conurbations with appalling living conditions. When new settlers arrived without much means to fend for themselves preferred to join the melee regardless of consequences to their future. Living in over crowded accommodation often in filthy condition and supported by meagre help from friends which became obvious that life would be miserable and often precariously hostile.

The theorists of the Chicago School discovered that the origin of the urban cities scientifically compared to the Ecological system in the environment. The term 'Ecology' originates from the biological environment of the nature to explain the growth of plant and animal species which habitually cluster around certain specific locations such as lakes, terrain, river banks and valleys. These organisms select suitable space to develop their species and to adapt to the natural conditions to secure a balanced equity for survival and co-existence amongst different species.

But survival of the fittest becomes the order of the day there. Weaker species perish or retreat to safer zone leaving the area to stronger species. As what happens in the human ghettoes, the weaker ones suffer at the hands of powerful bodies who control life by extortion, intimidation, harassment and torture until law takes over.

The Chicago school theorists have identified the growth of urban towns and cities which can be explained by Ecological principles. Most urban cities and neighbourhood communities grew up along the river basins of the Niles, the Ganges, the Sind, the Volga, the Siene, the Thames and so on. The reason for this association is mainly the waterways, which gave life to the cities' business and commerce and to transport their products within disparate parts of the country and abroad as well. The dockyard of Bombay, Khidirpur of Calcutta and Haldia in North India are great examples of the life line of the growing cities which offered thriving social lives besides developing booming economy of the country.

According to them, cities become ordered into 'natural areas', through processes of competition, invasion and succession – all of which are the norms in biological ecology. For example, competition between the various species of fish, insects and other organisms in the natural environment of a lake, takes place which develop specific areas of settlement for each of them. The stability of these areas may not be all that permanent because battle for survival continues unabated as always stronger elements take over. No situation is tenable for long. Equilibrium of the area will be effected when invasion of a more powerful species would disturb the co existence and habitats around the focal centre which would be thrown in to disarray. This would make way for the new settlers to occupy the centre driving out the rest in to the peripheries. They become the successors to the former occupants. The uprooted species have to settle some where for safety and security – to survive and to procreate, probably, in the fringe area of the lake.

In the urban cities, pattern of location, movement and relocation follow the same pattern as the ecological system. Areas in the available space in the city are occupied according to the requirements of various groups of people – their business interests, vocations, social life and their affordability to stay on and so on. Neighbourhood grows from various instincts like kinship, ethnicity, fraternity, vocation, cultural interests, language, accent etc.

Concepts of planned new cities evolved much later after it was noticed that neighbourhoods grew from 'invasion and succession processes' which were disorderly and chaotically organised where life was insecure and unsatisfactory. Sanitary facilities, inter personal relations, corporate life, living pattern, ethics, behaviour, morals – all these were sub-standard and caused unbearable strain on the dwellers. The process of clearing the vagabonds, beggars, petty criminals, street dwellers, jobless and unclean people had to take place allowing corporate bodies to make room for more important and responsible people to move in and to settle down with in the inner city.

To develop a planned town and city, the corporate bodies had to organise to set up industries with in the city and to open up supply line for raw materials to flow in which would require space. The eviction of unwanted elements would open up space for development of business, residential accommodation and properties including space for pleasure and shops. So to grow the city's surrounding with workers from diversified skills such as carpenters, blacksmiths, servants, builders, cleaners, medicine men, nurses, teachers, priests, market stalls, butchers and fishmongers etc – all would have to be accommodated. Dwellers with means would survive and others would have to more back to remote areas.

Race for acquiring more land leads to price rises and for many families living with in the city area becomes impossible; so they have to move back to where they can afford to procure space and to set up their life. As a result, the city area is left open for aspiring developers to venture into opportunities for different kinds of businesses like pleasure centres, schools, shopping areas, hospitals and so on and for residents to generate work and living space around there. When pressure increases, the new neighbourhood spills outside the city. Process of invasion and succession continues whenever opportunities arise for new arrivals to settle in either within the city or in new urban areas and to see if business and property interests could be developed.

The ecological perspective explains quite a lot about the environment in which the nucleus of life proliferates which has given rise to a great deal of research work. This has helped in the thinking of town planning in many countries. Nevertheless, it has been criticised that no Eco system can be a perfect environment for a peaceful co-existence of any species for long. Even man made plan for co-existence can go wrong such as urban riots, communal riots-these are not rare cases. So what can an eco-system or an urban system possibly deliver even if consciously developed to meet everything that a community needs including peaceful Co-existence.

Louis Wirth is also a member of the Chicago school who has developed his theses 'Urbanism as a way of life' (1938). This has given us a view of urbanism as a form of social existence. According to Wirth, city as an urban area not only provides dwelling places, as well as workshops of modern men but also develops centres for economic, political and cultural life of the people. Wirth followed Durkheim closely who used the organic analogy to explain the development of Urban society. Wirth defined the city in terms of three fundamental features such as, size of population, density and heterogeneity which indicate that in a city with a lot of people, there is more chances of them contacting others than in a rural situation. But the contacts are casual in which emptiness becomes the characteristic. In a rural situation where the folk live have a fewer chances of meeting people than the urban city but have real contacts with even a few people when they sincerely exchange their views and communicate. Wirth recognises that alienation and loneliness in the city become more acute when life becomes more formal and are unable to meet in a real way. The contact is peripheral and devoid of emotional content. Urban city has opportunity to meet a lot of people but could be very lucky to get one of their kinds.

Whereas, that is possible in a rural set up. Most contacts between city dwellers are 'fleeting and partial', your relationship with people is casual and based on a few words like passing exchanges about weather or buses coming late or if there is an accident or a hold up by a gang.

The cause of weak bonds between people living in the city is their mobile nature. They do not stick to one place for long. There could be many reasons for that – Unemployment in the area, accommodation problem, crime and children not growing up properly and so on. It is true that 'pace of life' is faster in the urban society than in the rural areas. People are always busy and impersonal; contact with them is not just possible. Wirth agrees that despite loneliness and impersonality in the urban set up, traces of community life could still be found amongst immigrant population due to family connections and affinity in terms of language and cultures.

Wirth's theory is important because of its true reflection of what urban life is like in the American societies. This could also be true to many modern societies. Nevertheless, Wirth's theory has been criticised by many not being wholly true, or that its coverage is limited by the fact of its geographical locations. Herbert Gans (1962) has said that it is true that urban villagers' way of life, nature and behaviour are common in most modern cities not just in America. Wirth's work particularly demonstrates growing life in America's urban societies, even there it is not same at all times and places. Anonymity in the cities is quite a well known fact; nevertheless, it can exist in the rural areas too, even though its incidence may be few and far between.

Claude Fischer (1975, 1984) has come out in favour of urban life because according to him, urbanism tends to develop inner city communities different from those of the rural areas. He argued that those who live with in the urban complex can develop sub-cultural groups amongst people of having same interest and background who can join different political, religious, ethnic or cultural groups according to their likings. This diversity of multicultural atmosphere can only take place more in the urban cities than in the rural areas, where people are more or less confined to their same ethnic and cultural stock. Over a long period of time in the cities, people begin to know each other more closely which is a human nature. It helps to develop social nucleus based on their different interests and activities. In urban conditions people learn how to live in different circumstances because of the changing phenomenon. Urbanism represents complex social relations.

The Theories of Ferdinand Tonnies and Emile Durkheim have more implications for the Western societies than for the developing societies. Nevertheless, these have influenced the functionalist perspectives which have worldwide implications.

Tonnies in Gemeinschaft and Gesellschaft theses (1887) and Durkheim in The Division of Labour (1893) have clarified the nature of the rural and community social life in contrast to the life in the developing industrial urban society. Both have identified the community spirit, the oneness of feeling and the eagerness to help one another which are the hallmark of rural community society. On the other hand, the individualistic and impersonal nature of the urban society is evident more or less everywhere in the urban complex.

Tonnies explains that Gemeinshaft – the rural concept has changed to Gesellschaft which is a modern urban concept developed as a result of social change. Life is not same to both the types because of the nature of their economic activities. The former is agriculturally based with a few cottage industries whereas the latter is industrially developed, organised with modern technology and a mechanised system of production. This helps not only the domestic needs but also the needs of the economy as a whole. In the village, everybody knows everybody, so a stronger community bond develops which means that they are ready to help each other whenever that is needed by the community.

That is not the case with the urban town and city life where life is personalised, alienated and dispersed from the community; life is generally selfish and self centred. Relationship in the Gesselshaft society (urban concept) is formal and practical in nature with a few informal exchanges. On the other hand, relationship in the Gemeinshaft (rural concept) society is holistic that is everything congregates to the whole whereas in the Gesselshaft it is partial or segmental. Tonnies elaborates his concepts by applying to larger organisations like the church and rural or village gatherings for decision making processes where most people are involved. These traditional community institutions are morally and emotionally stronger than the modern societies which pursue practical and rational approach to activities such as big businesses, professional organisations, law making bodies etc. Casual relationship can develop during festival and political gatherings which may continue in the form of 'Hellow, Hi etc' for sometime. Durkheim's elaboration of his concept is more expressive than Tonnies. In his document 'The Division of labour' Durkheim has given a detailed account of the change of society from the rural to the modern phase.

Durkheim differentiated between the old or traditional society and the modern or industrial society in his 'Division of Labour' (1907), which he named mechanical and organic forms respectively. This shows transformation of old or traditional society in to the modern type. The mechanically characterised traditional society is uniformly accepted and strictly enforced homogeneous small community based on belief and personal contact. These are old and ancient societies traditionally and classically developed to uphold common religious beliefs, values and cultural habits. Members in this kind of society do not challenge or reject the religious beliefs and values. Moral consensus is paramount in the early communities. Identification with the whole group therefore is essential; individuality is not desirable. This is a holistic type in which all congregate.

Whereas, a more elaborate and diffused pattern emerged in the phase of organic solidarity after the society was passed on to the urban condition. Here the work system is diversified and broken down to specialised tasks performed by different people. This is a feature of modern society; the assembly line production is a typical example. According to Emile Durkheim, the name 'division' is organisationally divisive; nevertheless, it also makes people more dependent on one another. So, he argues, "Each organ, in effect has its special character and autonomy; and yet the unity of the organisms is great as the individuation of the parts is more marked. Because of this analogy, we propose to call the solidarity which is due to the 'division of labour", Emile Durkheim, Organic (1947).

Durkheim insisted hat for the organic solidarity to be successful, the society would need to find a strong new moral basis of solidarity in addition to practical interdependence, because with out a moral and normative consensus in society people would feel insecure, helpless, and hopeless and suffer from a lack of moral guidance to behaviour; which he called 'anomie'. In anomic state, a person's state of mind is fluid and is unable to think and act properly because he has lost his or her mental norm to stick to and follow up. This is a loss of personality completely. In that state of mind, according to Durkheim, deviant activities such as crime and suicide tend to occur.

Talcot Parsons' Perspectives of Social System – Better Known as Pattern Variables

Parsons has made a bold attempt to analyse the transition from traditional to modern society for which he is partially indebted to Emile Durkheim and Max Weber. He describes the transition through his 'pattern variables' as follows.

Pattern Variables 'A' and Pattern Variables 'B'

Pattern Variables in group A is represented by the characteristic traditional society and Group B is represented by the characteristic modern society. In the traditional society, a person's status is ascribed, which is given at birth such as one's own class or caste, whereas in the modern society, it is acquired; it has to be achieved through hard work; no body can give anybody an acquired status.

Pattern Variables

In the traditional society, people treat each other in a more personal way than in a modern society where relationship is businesslike and impersonal. In group A, affectivity is important which allows members to feel the satisfaction of expression of emotions such as punishing a criminal in front of them to see that the perpetrator is dealt forth with. Whereas, in the group B, which is a Modern society, affectivity is neutralised by the judicial system where the criminal will be tried in the courtroom which might take long time to get the sentence passed, even though the matter is very serious and dreadful.

Then, comes the collective orientation as against self orientation. In the first (group A), shared interests are most common which is important to them, for example, sharing interests with family and the community, whereas in the second (group B), the interest is self centred. The individual prefers to pursue on a course of personal success even if that means distancing himself or herself from the family, friends and community.

In more than one way, this diffusion of society in the form of pattern variables as presented by Talcot parsons replicate the Tonnies and Durkheim's typology. So what is important here, Parsons argues: in the modern society relationship between people is partial and rational, and people still communicate with one another to maintain normal relationship. This is an 'expressive element' people exercise as a requirement of 'functional imperatives'. Parsons says, this is evident in his kinship and cultural community sub-systems. It is also true that, there is a continuity of similarity of Parsons' model of societal types with those of Durkheim and Tonnies.

Conflict Based Model of Marxist and Weberian Rural – Urban Perspectives

Karl Marx's understanding of society is different from Dukheim and Tonnies' community concepts. Marx's has a class concept. It is the Marxist ideology, which believes in one day, national and international, community could be achieved when the communist society was established; that is under the Marxist banner, not under the capitalist rule. In the capitalist system competition between different ideologies and class conflicts prevents the growth of a genuine sense of community. Marx of course, agrees that under the capitalist class system, the ruling class would seek to develop a 'false sense' of community to minimise the class conflict and also for the sake of consolidating and staying in power. But that kind of community under the capitalist system would not last for long because the Proletariat revolution would crush the capitalist backed power and the community if there were any, would collapse along with the system.

Another contemporary Marxist, Manuel Castells who is also a member of the Chicago school broadly accepts Marx's critique of capitalism based on mass production using large work force to earn excessive profit. However, Castells accepts that the modern capitalism has changed greatly over the years allowing every body to have a greater share in the benefit of profit and to enjoy public services like schools, health, transport, social services and other infrastructure in society. According to him, mass production has led to mass consumption. In the same way, the rural – urban concept has changed a great deal.

But, there is a difference between the mass consumption under the capitalist system and collective consumption under the Welfare state services. These have implications on the rural-urban issues. There are also conflicts as a result of inequality in consumption and work place relations. Castells has identified a slow social movement occurring in many urban areas even spreading to the rural districts which is a new phenomenon – less envisaged by the Marxist ideology. Castells argues that the urban city area to day is an integral part of the processes of 'collective consumption' which has taken place slowly in the midst of industrial capitalism. In the Western countries, the Welfare system has brought wealth near to the needs of people. There is more distribution of welfare benefit amongst people of need than ever thought of. Even without communist regimes, collective consumption has now become a reality of life. In the words of Anthony Giddens, "The physical shape of cities is thus a product of both market forces and the power of government". Sociology 1993 p. 575.

Castells stresses the importance of the struggles of the underprivileged groups to alter their living conditions. The working class movements in the cities organised by the trade unions and pressure groups – most of them are mixed class people and workers who pat pressure on the government to improve their welfare and service conditions in jobs, housing and environment. So also is necessary to remedy the air pollution, traffic fumes to protect the green belts, park areas etc. Rural areas as well go changed with new infrastructure, technology and modernised industries. The developing countries, also change with expanding education, children's park and sports facilities. In the agricultural sector, mechanised farming and improved transport system for farm produce expedite transition to the urban stage. Agricultural produce today, has an international demand delivered from the products of the rural areas.

It appears that Manuel Castells' urban theory has produced a non-Marxist conclusion. Peter Saunders, a British Sociologist finds it agreeable with Castells. He confers that to day, the working class are consumer oriented who can afford to live in their own houses rather than council or rented accommodation and also buy goods and commodities they could never do. Transistors, mobile phones are now common stuff and there are many who could afford even television sets.

In the industrialised societies, they do even better. Any thing the middle class people could buy and enjoy, the affluent working class people could afford to do those things today, such as buying expensive cars, hi-fi sets including nice holidays; some of them even can send their children to private schools. Even the ordinary working class people are able to buy most of the gadgets like anybody else because of the distinctions between the rural and urban conditions have gradually disappeared. All this add up to one thing; radicalism and revolutionary ideas which once dominated the political atmosphere are unlikely to go down deep in to the minds of disadvantaged people because their needs are now being met with the help of democratic processes. The social movement, naturally would follow as a result of social change.

Max Weber argues that urban community must function as a trade – commercial community. In his view, the city functions as a market place and the community in the city should function both socially and commercially with the help of a local government and its effective law and administrative system. So the city life and commercial activities can be based on rational – functional principle similar to what has been envisaged by Tonnies and Talcot Parsons. There are views that the urban community life in most of the western cities is designed by policies of race relations which ensure fairness in distribution of housing facilities, employment, and educational opportunities. Nevertheless, inequality and racial discrimination exist in all forms of public relations and administration. They are enmeshed in ways difficult to be uprooted. They operate overtly and covertly in many fields specially in the rural context. Distribution and investment of resources in areas of needs do not match fairness and equality. The structure of social relations suffers as a result.

Whatever the circumstances, the time has come in an age of increasing consumption, to understand that the Marxists take cognisance of the fact that Urban growth is fastest in the third world specially in India, China, South Africa and others. The Marxist policies towards awareness and reappraisal of the changing circumstances in the current situation should be crucial and also that their policies are renewed periodically.

The scarcity of labour – intensive industry in the cities has encouraged rural migration to flow into the cities, fortunately or unfortunately, these migrants are young population in search of work, who also bring with them prospect of more births. Other resulting needs to include are better accommodation, education, health service, employment and business opportunities.

Further Reading

1. Anthony Giddens. Sociology 1993.
2. Robert Park. Human Communities: The City of Human Ecology 1952.

3. Louis Wirth. Urbanism as a Way of Life, 1935.
4. Claude S Fischer. Towards a Sub-Cultural Theory of Urbanism, 1975, 1984.
5. Emile Durkheim Division of Labour, 1907.
6. Manuel Castells The Urban Question, 1977, A Cross – Cultural Theory of Urban Social Movement, 1983, London.
7. Tonnies The Theories of Gemeinschaft and Gesellschaft, 1987.

Part 17

27 Empowerment of Women in India

Introduction, Concept of Women Power, Development of Women Power, Conflict of Values, Issues in India.

Introduction

Women in India are enjoying more power than ever. Socially, politically, economically and educationally women in India are striding ahead of many countries. Adult women are granted franchise like men and allowed to vote and compete in the general election and some are chosen as elected members of the Houses of parliament and also of the state Assemblies. Many women organizations have been formed with the fund from the central Government and run entirely by the elected representatives of women. The purpose behind these organizations is to help women come out of their estranged social position and understand their rights in free India and to take part in all forms of activities not only to help themselves but also to help the society where help is needed; many are unaware of their rights as free citizens. So, they should be educated to understand their values and to take interest in politics. Creating a sense of belonging to the society and their duties to develop the country they live and love is the job of these organizations. The signs are positive and they are succeeding.

Working class women – many of them are peasants, cleaners, helpers, carriers of bricks, and mortars, child minders, baby sitters and industrial workers are working more or less regularly and earning money to supplement their family's income. Economically, those who are working are in a better position than those who are unwilling to work. They need to be educated or made aware of the benefit of work which not only keeps them physically fit but also economically solvent and self-reliant. Economic power gradually paves the way to acquiring political power.

Women in the middle class constitute a different story. Lower middle class women are not well educated to take up office or teaching jobs who are also unwilling to take up working class jobs either because they are middle class housewives and have a pride or financially their husbands' earnings are sufficient to live comfortably maintaining a good the standard of living; where as the middle – middle class women are different, because most spouses are fairly educated and prefering to work, so their economic power enables them to send their children to private English medium schools, live in modern flats or apartments in the city and do cultural activities. Even though, many would not look for a political career. Middle class men exercise political power because they are interested in politics, knowledgeable and equipped with skills to handle intricate political issues. But middle class women despite being well educated are still less inclined to political career. There are many reasons for this. They like to live a trouble free peaceful life at home and leave politics to men who can take tough decisions. Secondly, women have a responsibility to bring up children, take them to schools, collect them, feed and help them with their school home work. These are important jobs they would not like to forego for the sake of political career. There are of course exceptional women who take interest in politics and involve in it. They are different.

Conceptually, power is abstract; the ability to take decisions is the proof that some one has power over others. In the parliament, the ruling authority holds power over the opposition, because the former has the power to pass laws with a majority vote even against the opposition parties; the opposition party or parties have no power to block or prevent passing the bill. So power consists of the ability to get your own views across even when others are opposed to it. Women power depends on their ability to get their way such as getting their bills passed in the lower house. The women have proved that they are no less powerful than men when they got their right of suffrage after years of movement for their cause.

Traditionally, in India as else where, power has been exercised by men as the custodian of authority and control, governing and defending the country against foreign aggressions. In particular, foreign invasions had been persistent for over many years in India. India's power had been dominated by foreign rule until 1947, when she won her freedom as an independent sovereign country and entitled to exercise power over her own affairs. Women did not have power to exercise until many years later. Her role was confined to domestic matters helping and morally supporting the men in their activities and in external matters. She had a responsible job of course, of bringing up children and getting them ready for schooling. But there are exceptions where women had also been in power and authority – ruling and defending the country against foreign incursions; For example, some women had heroic records of fighting the foreign rule, specially the Rani of Zanshi – who fought against British power in India in 1857 during the period of Sepoy Mutiny. Other than a few exceptions, the vast majority of women did not have power at all to fight for their rights.

Since the Indian independence in 1947, women have been forging ahead as a powerful force of social change. They have demonstrated their exceptional abilities in achievements in many fields. In the political field, Mrs Indira Gandhi had shown her tremendous statesmanship as a prime minister not only by bringing the Green Revolution in the Indian economy which fundamentally changed the economic condition of the country once and for all but also fighting extremism in the country for which she had given her life and had become a martyr, There have been several other women in the states as chief ministers and governors, who also have shown their great ability and power in running the government.

Now, there are thousands of high ranking women civil servants in the Indian administrative service in the foreign and police service and their number has been steadily rising. There is one exceptionally gifted woman, Dr Kiran Bedi, who worked as Inspector General of Prisons in the biggest national jail, named Tihar, in New Delhi. There, she introduced reforms to end the adversarial relations between the Police and the prisoners by adopting educationally oriented correction and rehabilitation methods in place of high handed measures and was able to bring change in the prisoners' attitude to life and the institution. Her work was recognized as outstanding for which she was rewarded with the "Ramon Magsaysay Award" comparable to the 'Nobel Prize' in Asia in 1994.

There are a lot of women judges, lakhs of doctors, teachers, professors, scientists and engineers up and down the country. Writers, lawyers, journalists, artists, sports personalities, women in fashions, music, acting, designing whose numbers are not few and far between.

There is an equal access of women to education. For widening opportunities for women, there are intensive educational plans being implemented in the rural areas. This will help women to understand the necessity of learning and earning in life by developing skills for their careers. There are other Programmes of adult education for women such as reading, writing and doing numbers. Also, Programmes for health care, employment, family planning, vocational training, social welfare study centers in which they would have to attend etc. As the years pass by, the aim is to raise the standard of women's learning to the level of men in all fields of activities. Without education no one can succeed in life, so women are no exception. Women must go to schools and colleges and make an effort to fulfill their ambition of life, believing in the principle of no education no progress. So emphasis must be put on the participation of women on all those educational Programmes being made available for them.

Development of Women Power in India

Women's pressure groups like the liberal, radical, Marxist feminist bodies have vehemently criticized the male domination of women all over the world. They have been vociferous in the media and wrote critical academic articles in the journals. They have conducted interviews and surveys and collected evidence to expose the nature of the male superiority in all spheres of life and exploitation of women in the society and suggested solutions to end oppression.

The repercussions of the women's movement in India have been very significant. Women's rights are recognized by the constitution of India since Independence specially universal adult franchise which entitle them to take part in voting during elections and also equality in jobs, education and also owning of properties. Racist and sexist treatment of women in jobs, education etc are strictly forbidden. Offenders are punishable by fine and imprisonment. Adult women are also entitled to contest the election to demonstrate their interest in politics of the country. But to participate fully in the political life is a different matter. Voting at the age of eighteen irrespective of educational and social backgrounds was granted no doubt but to take part in contesting a seat in the election requires a lot more qualifications than just age and educational qualifications, such as passion for politics, commitment to the national causes, proven record of trade Union activities and active party membership, ability to speak clearly and precisely, religious tolerance, patience, leadership, charismatic personality, professional experience, experience in social work and secular attitude to ethnic minorities etc. For women candidates proven record of working with women's organizations and projects will be considered as extra qualification.

Universal adult franchise for most men was offered since the Montago Chelmsford reforms of 1917 but women had to wait far longer for their entitlement to vote in the general elections. When finally, universal adult franchise was granted by the Indian constitution in January, 1951, the proportion of women actually who took part in the General Election was much less than the proportion of men.

The real obstacle to equality between the sexes was not the vote but according to Anthony Giddens, 'the deeply buried social divisions between men and women, which restricted women to the household and domestic tasks'. Many women thought that politics was not their kind of role, it is the men's business and that they would not be good at it. Rightly so, at that time; because many of those who voted for a candidate was not necessarily their choice but were manipulated to do so by the vested interested parties. Many young voters in the villages were paid to vote for particular candidates they did not want to. Threat and intimidation were used to acquire votes. These corruptions have been rectified by the introduction of identity cards with photos.

When things changed gradually to socially improving women's status in the public and their chances in education and employment, their interest in politics took a different dimension than ever; many became members of political parties and those who were able to lead got elected to municipal bodies, local and central legislatures.

As already mentioned, Indian politics have been dominated by men for over a hundreds of years. A general perception grew up that women's participation in politics would bring in fresh ideas by humanizing politics. But things did not happen that way for a long time because of the gender conflict accrued from men and women relationships, and because of women's dependence on men for help and support which enabled men to take an upper hand over women's affairs and as a result, women were controlled by men quite easily for a long time. But with expansion of education in the country in which women took a major part which helped them procure employment in different fields such as the teaching, training and instructing students in schools and colleges, in civil service, in the legal profession, in medicine, in scientific research, in journalism and also in administration. Once women became educated and employed things began to change for the better.

They enjoyed more social respect and economic freedom and learn to take tough decisions. All these gave them a sense of liberation from the control of men. The male dominated society however did not crack down immediately but noticed the thaw in the pipeline and the wind of change blowing to be reckoned with.

Conflict of Values

People educated and trained in traditional and conservative values had nursed amongst other things particular attitudes and stereotyped notions towards women and the social agenda formulated to serve people were not conducive to the needs and interests of women. Because, they were thought of as house keepers, looking after husbands, keeping the household tidy and bringing up children and also considered not good for power sharing. So they were left out of the general tenor of social movement. Women's movement for equal voting rights with men began only after the Suffragist movement in England in 1927. This opened up the horizon of women's vision of political rights and for society to renew their concept of women.

In India, it was realized that if opportunities were offered, women would do a better job to serve the country. Women were needed essentially in welfare, education, employment, child care and health services and so on. Gradually, it was also realized that women would also be good for politics. Women's promotion to higher posts would also reduce discrimination in women's employment and opportunities. Despite remarkable progress achieved in these fields by the women groups, their empowerment has been criticized by some conservative male opponents who thought that increasing participation of women to politics would not only trivialize politics but also damage family life and effect children's future.

These arguments are nothing new as they have lost their edge over the years. If women were to be confined at home, the country would be deprived of their contribution in which they would also be victims. There are many ways to bring up and educate children in modern days. Women can go to work when children start schooling at the age of five or so and getting domestic help with hired services is not a problem either. Women are of course, entitled to stay at home until they reach school age. Women can make great contributions to the economy essential to forge the country's development. In the teaching profession, the women are making tremendous contribution to the education service of children which was a dream earlier. As mentioned above, in all sectors of public life, they are contributing a great deal.

Women Power in India Since the Post-World War Period

In India, during the inter war period and after, perception of women's rights dramatically changed when they were called to serve in the support services. The traditional sexual divisional of labour between men and women's jobs disappeared as women were required to replace men called to serve in the army. Most of these jobs were in factories. People were proud that they had jobs but had to leave them with women because of the national emergency. Many legal obstacles were removed in order to make it easy for the new entrants to start work in to the jobs. Factory bosses had to accept them because they could not say no. This had paved the way for women to enter into in to career employment of production as well as service sectors. The trend continued throughout the sixties and seventies.

In the West, Women have made their mark in politics by participating in the Legislative bodies and in decision making processes within the corporate and government organizations. They have also made an impact in the political life independently. The Feminists have, for example, formed the National Organization of Women (NOW) to highlight the principal issues concerning women's predicament in society. The Feminist movement in Europe and the U.S.A. have also influenced the authorities to recognize their issues and to include them into the political agenda. The issues include equal rights at work, availability of abortion right, right to divorce and lesbian rights are some of them. Some of the issues are controversial and selective decisions are being given based on individual merit.

In Britain, progress has been made in terms of combating sex-discrimination at work where women used to get second choice against their male counterparts. Men had more chances of promotions in jobs than women even with similar qualifications and experience. Discrimination has also been practiced on foreign workers specially Indian workers who got raw deals against indigenous workers in jobs and promotions. There has been a slight let off recently after the Race Relations Board gave damning reports on the prejudicial treatment of ethnic minority workers in search of jobs specially those from the sub-continent. They were mostly offered jobs in temporary and casual positions where they were treated subjectively under persistent pressures to improve performance. Treatment tend to deteriorate as and when the economy continues to decline.

In the sphere of women's treatment in the family and society parliament has passed laws to protect women from domestic violence and against rapes, abduction and torture. Offenders and criminals are given heavy punishment including long prison life with no bail for sexual offenders.

Issues in India

Issues of Women in India have a different connotation than those in the West. The cultural factor in India has clouded the issues for over a long time which therefore requires a different solution; but it must coincide with the norms of modern society. The problems are not far to seek. Male dominance, caste, class and regional differences, child marriage, Purdah system, prohibition of widow remarriage and keeping temple girls – all these have been officially outlawed but in reality practiced behind the eyes of law. The general notion is that these malpractices or abuses of human rights will gradually disappear specially with the spread of education, social reforms and removal of poverty. Use of technology in schools, home and work places does a lot of good to understand and to realize that these superstitions, fear and dependence should disappear to lighten the burden of the government.

But unfortunately, superstitions, religious fanaticism, fear of being victimized and prejudice of caste and culture have not disappeared despite tremendous progress in the field of education. Mass educational Programmes have been put in place in order to broaden minds of people and to make them rational beings. In many cases, new problems and social evils have cropped up to threaten the very civilization of the country, They are the dowry harassment which is costing the country with the suicide deaths of many young wives, also there is a host of evil forces devastating women's life, such as rape, immoral traffic, oppression and exploitation of 'dalit' women and conversion of low caste people into other religions through bribes and marriages. These matters must be dealt with seriously if to rescue women from the clutches of the criminal forces. Action must be taken to effectively implement the measures so far undertaken or complacence would kill the purposes of reform.

In true sense, women are not free at all whether at home or in the outside world. Even when they are educated and working, they are not really free. At home, 'motherhood' is imposed upon them which is different from fatherhood. It is taught to them that motherhood is a women's natural destiny and happiness would only come from that. This deprives woman of their real power. Educated and working urban married women are thus torm in between the two worlds – employment and domestic duties. When she come home from work faces heavy domestic workload specially in a split nuclear family. Unless assisted by cooks and cleaners, they are literally bonded into doing every thing from cooking to cleaning, feeding children, helping them with homework and getting them ready for next day's school. So, they are not free. In the evening husbands may not be available for home help, because they are in office busy attending meetings or some thing else which usually runs late. What does a women do; wait for husbands to come for dining and relaxing. What happens if husband come home late then why not women? That sort of discrimination just could not be compromising because coming home late would cause serious problems for the children and possibly rows with him. So women are stuck at home but husbands are not. The women are not free but men are free.

So how to end this discrimination? There is no easy solution. No solution will be perfect. The feminists have suggested a lot of easy solutions for example, marriage system should be banned which would liberate women from the drudgery of the domestic responsibilities, because there in lies the root of the trouble. It is easy to say but difficult to do as the sociologists are not unanimous either solving that very delicate issue so simply because this action would create more problems than solve. Banning the marriage would gradually disintegrate the fabric of society.

Reference

Kapadia K.M. Marriage and Family in India, Calcutta, 1964.

Part 18

28
Sociological Methodology

Introduction, Different Methods, Scientific and Experimental Methods, Comparative Historical Method, Interpretive Qualitative Method, Symbolic Interaction Method, Phenomenological Method, Source, Primary and Secondary Sources, Questionnaire – Type of Questions, Interviews – Structured and Unstructured, Sensitive Issues, Disadvantages with Unstructured Interviews, Participant Observation, Secondary Sources, Social Surveys, Cross-Sectional and Longitudinal Surveys, Sampling, Representative and Non-Representative Sampling, Questions and Answers in Sociological Methodology.

Introduction

Methodology is an integral part of sociology which again is essentially a theory based subject. Sociology depends on methods to construct empirical studies of facts and phenomena of society which is transient. A theory enquires dipper into the facts and events: why they are happening. It is the job of the theory to examine the causes and effects of the phenomena and their co-relationships. A structural frame work is then developed to examine interpretations of facts and events which take the form of hypothesises. These will be given to the empirical study – an investigative process using both the deductive and the inductive methodology to test its scientific validity.

Different Methods: The Scientific or Experimental Method

The scientific experimental method is considered the most accurate of all to test hypothesises. Observation of the behaviour of things such as the phenomena is essential for hypothetical purposes mainly to produce a credible theory. Sociologists use more of the observation methods than the laboratory experimental methods. Natural sciences like the physics, chemistry etc are strictly laboratory based experiment which often uses the observation method as well. The kind of methods used by sociology and social science depend on the nature of the enquiries. If the areas are scientifically oriented, they use scientific quantitative methods with out hesitation, otherwise, they go for different other methods with particular reference to the methods of observation. After a hypothesis is formed it will be tested by the Empirical method to iron out its validity, in case, if found unworthy to prove its scientific value, it would be discarded. When a theory is developed by the above processes it becomes a law of science and can be used in further research purposes. (A full discussion of the relationship between Science and Sociology is done in a separate piece of work in part 1 in the book).

The Comparative Historical Method

According to Emile Durkheim, the Comparative Historical Method is most appropriate to the study of social development than any other methods. Historical method is a traditional method. It is also an objective method which can count every fact piece by piece and gather evidence from different countries acquired through excavations, museums, libraries, accounts of travellers and so on, which are valuable sources capable of measuring the level of progress in those countries. Historical evidence helps to assess social and economic life of people of different periods. Finds from the tomb of the boy king Tuten khamun, the Egyptian Pharaoh, and those collected from the excavations of the Mohenjo-Daro and Harappa in the Northern Province of ancient India are typical examples which to deliver evidence to study the social and cultural pattern in relation to the civilisations flourished long ago. The antiquity of the Indus Valley Civilisation of India can be compared with the contemporary civilisations prevailed in that period in the ancient regions of Egypt, Assyria and Babylonia.

According to Durkheim, facts and other phenomena can be objectively observed, classified and compared to other available evidence to point out the values of customs and institutions of people. Comparative Historical method can be studied both quantitatively and qualitatively in order to produce a fully picture of the life of different classes of people.

Contemporary sociologist, Ronald Fletcher stressed that a careful formulation and use of the 'comparative method' is sociology's only alternative to the experimentation', (Fletcher, 1981: p. 77), which means that except for small samples of 'group interactions' other aspects of sociology can not be put into the Laboratory tests. The comparative method compares facts and objects of similar nature such as the concept of poverty in the West but it can not be same with the concept of poverty in the eastern countries, because they are different but comparison helps to find out the causes of difference and nature of poverty in each, which can form a valuable part of sociological study. Even middle class standard in one country can not be the same in another country. Despite the fact that the causal relationships in terms of educational achievement and professional status may look same but in terms of earnings and standard of living it may not be the same. So sociology can involve into the comparative study of the diversity of culture and standard of living that exist between the developed and the developing countries.

Durkheim stressed the need for systematic comparison between similar types of society. He used comparative method to the study of 'suicide' explaining 'suicide' may be a personal thing, but is greatly affected by external factors which are negative social conditions. Durkheim discovered that 'social suicide rate' varies between societies but causes tend to be regular over time in a given country which affects the suicide rates. This demonstrates that there exists, social forces persistently operating in one country to determine suicide rates than in other countries.

Sociology is rooted in History or in other words, sociology is born out of History. Some writers like G. Von Bulow proclaim that Sociology is a kind of historical study. History deals with lives of people, social classes, human relations, social customs, development of social relations, education, mores, institutions, political systems, etc. which are also subjects of sociology. According to Max Weber, some of the important sociological analysis has been applied to explaining historical issues. Karl Marx's Dialectics of history explains the transition of society from the primitive phase to the modern phase which is an important part of a sociological study. So the comparative historical method helps the development of methodology in sociology.

Interpretive Qualitative Method

Scientific sociological method is not yet quite good enough to deal with all human aspects of sociology, as significantly, the behaviour is so varied and complex. It is a matter of qualitative rather than quantitative issue in which science is yet to perfect.

Sociologists agree to the fact that the Interpretive approaches are most suitable for interpretation of social action such as, meanings and motives of human behaviour, which require persistent observation and depth in understanding the meanings of their experiences, attitudes and beliefs. Qualitative understanding of people's social action and their interpretations are very important. People construct their social reality through their meanings and their consciousness which science can not explain fully – in laboratory conditions because that is not possible. Consciousness has to be interpreted first before it can be measured.

Causal explanation, a vertiable element in understanding meanings, which Max Weber believed but Phenomenologists did not believe in it because it was not important an element for their research work, rather a distant end product of sociological research, therefore, not necessary at all.

Max Weber, the social action theorist, emphasises that a sociological interpretation of human experience of their particular actions will clarify meanings behind moods and motives; such as, why do people read a book or why do people go to school?. There could be several answers to this question; to pass time because there is nothing worthwhile to do, or to know something of interest or reading to write an article or to meet a specific research requirement, and so on. To him, how to know why people behave in a particular way, is better known by being in the position of the person, such as the Verstehen method; this could help to unravel more clearly why a particular person behaves in a particular way in a specific situation. In the same way, you can answer the next question, saying that people go to school to learn skills, pass an exam and to get a good job. Some may say, 'I have come to school forced by law.'

Symbolic Interaction is the second of the Interpretive methods which unlike the phenomenology, accepts causal relationship to human actions as an essential element of sociological research. It relies on assessing and measuring the qualitative aspect of human actions. According to symbolic interaction, quality of a person's self-dignity and image dictates how he or she would react and take action in dealing with a particular situation. How to do that depends on the kind of experience and perception one has got-that acts as a prerequisite to the situation.

Herbert Blumer, an American exponent of Interaction concept, who coined the name of 'Symbolic Interaction' puts emphasis on variables. Variables are different kinds of evidence that helped Durkheim's study of 'suicide' but which could not be accepted by many interaction sociologists. To them, variables are in fact, arbitrarily created for sociologists to use for their particular research purposes. Blumer has stressed that human behaviour does not occur from a blind following of external forces, rather it occurs from how does a social actor perceives a situation and interpret its meaning. According to symbolic Interaction, Variables are required for the quantitative method mainly, the requirement for symbolic interaction is the qualitative method, not variable quantitative method.

Phenomenology

This is the third of the Interpretive methods which rejects cause and effect co-relationship as explanatory to human behaviour. It also rejects the objectivity of measuring the social world. According to the phenomenological concept, human beings make sense of the world by creating meanings and classifying them according to their qualitative values, which taken together make up the social world. Phenomenology depends entirely on the subjective nature of social life linked to the individuals' consciousness. It depends on the qualitative method of research, rather than the quantitative method.

Sociological Researches

Researches for sociology essentially involve collecting data by using interviews, questionnaires, observations and field survey methods. These data are divided into the Primary and Secondary sources..

Primary Data

The Primary sources of data are freshly collected or made; they are original in nature and never made and used before, so they are up to date and acquired by researcher on a day to day basis, it is generated by the ongoing research processes. This data is also obtained from the outcome of questionnaires, interviews, observations and field surveys.

Secondary Sources

Secondary Sources of the data already exist and have been frequently used. They are for example, historical records, official statistics, reports from official enquires, personal and official diaries, newspaper reports, memoirs, films etc. Sociologists use a lot of secondary data for reference.

One of the other research methods for collecting primary data generally used for natural sciences is by Laboratory based experiments, otherwise known as the scientific method. Sociology as a Positive science use mostly quantitative method and some experiments as well; it is also known as Positivism. Experiments require hypothesis framed from various facts and information. It is also called 'supposition'. Different facts are known as variable factors which are sorted out mathematically, also under laboratory conditions. To day, Computer science can do this job well using its numerical skills. The results can be verified and used for further research work.

Questionnaires

Questionnaires produce primary sources of information. Social Surveys can not be carried out without Questionnaires which prepare lists of questions asking about specific issues under survey. Questionnaires are also used in interview for both written and oral methods. Those who do well in the written test are formally interviewed orally.

The problems with questionnaires are the 'wordings' which can mean different things to different people; so answers can be different too. So, to avoid this problem, questions must be made simple but meaningful and unambiguous. To make interviews easy they can be made 'structured' interviews to avoid pitfalls, but the answers are expected to be same; they are thus criticised as being controlled and interviewer biased.

Type of Questions

Normally, there are only two types of questions used in the questionnaires – closed and open. Closed type o questions is also called objective type which offers several possible answers to a question. The researcher has to choose the best answer from amongst the many alternatives; or there may be several answers to the same question, from which to pick the top answer which can be number 1 in order of merit or importance and put the rest one under the other according to merit or importance. If there are seven alternatives, the last one say the seventh would be the least important of all. Each answer has a merit mark as well; the top answer has the highest mark or points and the least important one has the lowest mark or points.

Comparatively, closed questions are easy to answer and quantify but open ended questions are not. The respondent can use his/her own words to answer the 'open' questions but only difficulty would be to coding the answers whereas closed questions are pre-coded which the respondent does not have to do any coding. Researchers prefer closed questions to open ended ones.

Structuring interview questions have to be carefully constructed in order to avoid ambiguity; so questions should be straight forward. Words and phrases should be simple, relevant and meaningful. To check if the questions are answerable, a pilot study can be made to avoid pitfalls, ambiguity and doubts about meanings of the questionnaires. Pilot study is to test a small number of people; the objective is to find out the quality and reliability of the questionnaire. Rectifications can be made of any questions found dubious and confusing. The amended questionnaire then is passed on for structured interviews.

Structured questionnaire can be prepared on current local issues, for example say, smoking habit in schools and colleges in an urban area. Similarly, questionnaires can also be prepared on causes of suicide, street violence, treatment of women at home and employment, effect of T.V. on the viewers and so on.

Unstructured Interviews

Quite different from the structured interviews, which are formal and recorded for evidence, the unstructured interviews are pretty informal, open ended, flexible and more relaxing. The questions and answers are unwritten and the interview process continues for long. The objective is to see the performance of the respondent in a relaxed and free mind than being under tight formal conditions where the respondent may feel uptight and perform badly.

The benefits of the structured interviews are that they are direct and the answers are more or less structured too. The answers are factual and quantifiable, useful for verification and comparison. The respondents can answer 'yes' or 'no' like the objective type. So for research purposes they are time saving and less liable to errors and interviewer bias.

The benefits or advantages of the unstructured interviews as mentioned above are that they enable the respondents to feel at home when interviewed informally without any constrains and tape recording. It allows a trust and rapport to develop between the interviewer and the interviewee. The net result is that you know more about the interviewee, his or her personality and their reaction facing the interviewer. If the interviewee does not get nervous or stressed and feels free answering questions then there is a possibility that their answers could be better then the structured answers and also the possibility that he or she would be chosen for jobs.

Sensitive Issues

In the informal unstructured interviews, sensitive issues can be talked about without constrains, because knowing that these will not be used as evidence against the respondents, so they come out more frank and truthful answering sensitive questions, such as, marital difficulties, home atmosphere, kin relationships, sexual harassment of women in jobs and incest at home and so on. Unstructured interviews unearth valuable facts, which can open up new areas of information for further research work. Unstructured interviews also discover new meanings to stereotype issues and can shake off beliefs already taken for granted. These interviews throw new light into the perceived values and attitudes about race, beliefs and cultural hangovers such as, music, dress, food, education, language and so on.

Disadvantages with Unstructured Interviews

An interviewee may not like the interviewer personality – an implicit factor, when that is the case, then that may constrain his or her performance. They also may not like a particular accent, dress, mode of questions, class status, ethnicity and attitude of the interviewer, which may detriment the course of the interview. Nice and mild personalities, with of course, positive attitude to the interviewee are explicit ingredients of performing better than facing stern faced, seemingly trying to test intelligence with complex and dubious questions and attitudes which may constrain performance and may lead to a poorer result. Psychological state of the interviewer may be perceived as a non starter which can affect the responses. J. Allan Williams, Jr in his book (1971) has pointed out that greater the status difference between the interviewer and the interviewee, the less likely the responses will express true feeling.

The standard practice should be to enable the respondents do their way which can minimise the damage than expecting to follow a particular stereotyped method. Friendly atmosphere and a good rapport with the interviewer are important factors for a better start than facing an awkward situations; at the same time, it has to be remembered that the interview is a professional matter which has certain paraphernalia to maintain. But these have to be made known before the start of the interview; than for the interviewee to face them on the spot. Also, the interviewee should be kept at a distance from the interviewer to avoid any personal influence. This will help reducing the bias (Fielding, 1993, p. 141).

Participant Observation

When a researcher wants to know something about some body or a group of people, he or she has to observe the persons' or group's behaviour, nature of work, manner of speech, attitudes to others and inter-relationships with in the group etc, because seeing is believing, then you learn something about their life by observing them for some time. Participant observation becomes necessary when external observation is not enough to discern the intricacies of the pattern of life and behaviour of some group of people. So one has to be a part of the group at least for a reasonable period of time to see their mode of living, their activities, their attitudes and mode of behaviour to each and every body, who thus realistically is able to know and understand the group. Their culture, means of livelihood, beliefs, rituals, customs, etc.

are to be observed patiently and also to be taking part in their activities. This is an 'empathy' i.e. being on the shoes of others to know more accurately about them. This is also known as the Ethnography – one of the important methods of research in sociology.

Sociologists find this is an effective way of knowing the meanings of most of their perspectives and structure of the society under research. Participant observation has produced some very useful studies of ethnic groups, tribal groups, black and low caste people from all over the world. Living with tribal families, even painting the skin in black in order to live as a black person with black group and to know about their culture, religious practice, marriage system, medicines etc are quite well known already. Some of the studies are about the Italian American gangs in Boston and Chicago, tribal lives of the Trobriand Islanders of the New Guinea, Mbuti Pygmies of Zaire and aborigines of the Andaman Nicobar Islands in the Indian Ocean. These are a few amongst many others.

To be effective as a participant observer, one has to be accepted as a member of the group; the researcher has to gain some degree of confidence of the leaders and others in the sense that he or she would not be any problem to them. This becomes an extremely difficult job, because they would not like any outsider becoming an insider and becomes nosey to every secret in their life. They fear that any exposition to the outside world about their life would jeopardise their very existence as a nomadic people which they are very proud of; so they would hesitate to open up their private lives to researchers or even photographs taken on a regular basis. They would like to stay as 'closed society' away from the onlookers who could not be trusted at all.

Despite these obstacles, some manage to break the ice waiting over months and years to gain access into their confidential world either by bribing or even through a wedlock with some islanders. When they have collected enough materials for their purpose they leave. Some may have gone as far as the inner circle of their tribal life but some times had to sacrifice their life while returning or the search work being destroyed. There will always be an element of fear and risk to life, more importantly to their research work when trust had evaporated.

Secondary Sources

A lot of research work has been done based on secondary sources, because these are easily available from the records of the government's survey reports, Government Commission reports on education, unemployment, death from poverty, premature death of babies and children, suicides, robberies, murders and so on. Official statistics are the most important secondary sources of all. Most of the secondary sources are available in Libraries, Record Office, Reference books and journals.

One of the most important secondary sources is the 'National Census' which is a demographic survey of the whole population of the country. It was first started in 1801 which now takes place once approximately every ten years. For the first time in England, the Census asked a question of ethnic origin of individuals in 1991, a unique example of collecting identities of every citizen, with special reference to the commonwealth immigrants who settled in the U.K; because it has been necessary to compile immigrants' identities and profiles under changing social circumstances effected by the rapid rise of extremism and terrorism all over the world and Britain is no exception.

The faults of the National Census is that it had loopholes, by which many escaped taking part in the census count at all in order to evade paying the Poll Tax imposed on every head. The other fault was that there was no monitoring system to check out the defaulters and those who gave wrong information in the form. For Poll Tax – every adult in the family including the college students, who of course, paid at a reduced rate under the Tory Government had to pay this tax. This was a very unpopular tax and it had to be scrapped off after the Poll Tax Riots in London in the late eighties which had shown that it would not be tolerated. Under pressure, eventually, the Poll Tax system was abandoned and replaced by the normal council tax based on property valuation.

Social Surveys

National Census is the biggest form of social surveys which surveys the whole nation regarding its population, their economic condition including their earnings, births, deaths etc.

Because of some shortcomings of the national Surveys, Sociologists, who want to use accurate fresh original statistical data, usually conduct their own special social surveys which can target groups like the old age people, illiteracy amongst working class children, data on women's participation in politics and many more. Their objectives are to produce samples of data on a limited number but crucial areas as mentioned above which are the quantitative data based on questionnaire. The results are samples which can be turned into numerical data and used to generalise on a wider scale if necessary. Also the survey results can be conveniently used to refer to specific research purposes.

The Cross-Sectional Survey

The cross sectional survey is a survey of people taken from different social backgrounds to produce information about them during a specific period of time. It is a simple and economically cheap survey to do so where as the Longitudinal survey selects a group for a study over a longer period of time. The objective is to study variables of behaviour, attitudes, interests, abilities of the group of people over a continued or divided period of time. Cross sectional group of children are interviewed at regular intervals some times for months and years to gather their progress in 3RS, activities, behaviour, attitudes etc and to find out whether their social class backgrounds have cast any effects on their level of progress. These sort of surveys can also reflect on their regularity, punctuality, motivation and inter personal relationships with in the group during the survey period.

Sample Survey is a targeted group like strike minded teachers, miners or women's group fighting sex discrimination in jobs and representation in parliament or local government employees demonstrating for their pay rise etc.

Selection of people to form a sample group should be scrutinised to see if a cross section has been represented. Wrong selection may cause problems in decision making because it could not be applied to focus on the target group. Secondly, a pilot survey could show whether the respondents understood the questionnaire and able to answer them correctly.

Step one, a target group has to be selected; second, a 'sampling frame' can be prepared using local electoral rolls or school rolls and so on.

Representative Sampling

Selection of a sample group should be representative of the main group; for example, if the target group is a mixed ability multi-racial third yr class in a school, the selection should be made taking into account not only the abilities of all pupils from this third yr class but also the gender, ethnic and denomination issues of the individuals. Suppose, the roll has a strength of thirty mixed pupils from which to select only ten pupils, consideration must be made for all the issues in order to make it a representative sample. Also to be taken into account the issue of how many to be picked from each variable group.

Non-Representative Sampling

Non-representative sampling is the opposite of representative sampling. Some sociologists prefer the non representative sampling because it offers them a greater choice and freedom to manoeuvre the research technique as demand arises. They believe that to develop a good hypothesis requires rigorous tests which is more convenient with the non-representative samples. The fact is that it might not be as perfect as the other one in terms ethnic and ability issues; nevertheless, they believe that the non-representative sampling can be widely used on a variety of issues and subjects.

Questions and Answers in Sociological Methodology

What is a Longitudinal Research?

Sociological researches can be conducted on a group of people for a longer period instead of a short period. This becomes necessary when the value of research topic can be thoroughly checked and tested on a long term basis in order to get the perfect result, which can only be done if the topic is observed periodically at intervals so that all the variable data are scrupulously checked and verified. Such studies are known as Longitudinal studies. Longitudinal research can be carried out on a variety of issues for example, measuring changing public attitudes to smoking, dating, work ethics, racism, gender equality and so on. Longitudinal studies are used to collect primarily quantitative data in social surveys. Participant observation, for example, requires time to see the social life gradually unfolding as the observation continues. The Longitudinal research thus can deliver results worthy of an enduring value.

What is a Multivariate Method?

It is a research technique used by Emile Dukheim while researching on the suicide rates. This method tries to isolate the effect of a particular independent variable upon the dependent variables. Multivariate method tries to find out the effect of each variable on the other. The independent variable actually causes the dependent variable. Again, an independent variable can be influenced by another independent variable. To find out how much influence one independent variable has on the other, the multivariate method is used by which one variable is held constant till the other one is changed. Then the results of the two may be compared.

This method can now be used by computers with their statistical quantitative data to find out the relative importance of each variable and in particular their effects on each other; they can also be used to see which social class commits crimes, specially serious crimes, remembering the fact that all social classes commit crimes more or less of a variable nature and the question here is to ascertain which social class does what category of crimes. (Read also the work on Robert K. Merton's theory of crime).

What is Ethnographic Observation?

Ethnography is a method of studying the lives of people in their natural habitat. Usually, they are a small group of people who have their own culture and a structure of society with a distinct pattern of living as it interests the researchers. Ethnographic observers have to take part into the daily life of people they are studying and even to penetrate in.to the thoughts, emotions and actions of the people there. There is a storehouse of Anthropological facts and data collected from the study of primitive life of people covering many countries, most of it is done by Ethnographic method of observing, living and actively participating in the lives of those people. They had to learn their dialects and also their culture in order to develop an affinity with them. There is a classic case study of primitive people in a Andaman Nicobar Islands carried out by the Anthropologist, A.R. Radcliffe Brown, who studied the life of the islanders himself living in the Island for years. His contribution to unveiling the primitive life of this particular group of people is quite revealing.

What is a Triangulation Method?

No single research method in sociology is complete enough to produce a faultless result. So most sociologists have realised that, why not try combining different sociological methods into one comprehensive method putting all the criteria into the combined research work. This will minimise the pitfalls and maximise the accuracy of the result. This method is known as the 'Triangulation Method'. Already, in the social science research, the Deductive and the Inductive methods are both used in the same reasoning processes to get the best assessment. Earlier the research was done using either of the two. So, a controversy grew about their singular scientific values. This doubt was eliminated when both the methods were used together for logical purposes. In the same way, if the qualitative and the quantitative approaches can be combined into one unitary method that would substantially enhance the scientific accuracy of the research processes.

Unilateral Method

Unilateral Method will dispel doubts and controversies and pave the way for a satisfactory research result. Max Weber is a strong advocate of the combined methodological system (Read Haralambos, Sociology – Themes and Perspectives, 1995, p. 889-90).

Bryman has suggested ways and means for a combined method which is a 'Triangulation method' saying that, both the methods can be used to check accuracy of each other and the faults also can be duly rectified using the combined approach. Secondly, a joint approach can broadly focus on all aspects of the social group – the complete picture to be studied accurately and so on.

Triangulation also can take different forms, such as 'Investigator triangulation' which involves different observers and interviewers of different social backgrounds; each will be able to find the faults of the other and these faults can be rectified. The second form is the 'Data Triangulation' which verifies data collected from different sources at different times and cross-checked for validity.

Triangulation also uses other methods like 'open and closed questions', structured and unstructured interviews, participant observation etc. All data obtained can be checked and compared with each other. So, according to Denzin, Triangulation is a method to describe various ways of assessing the validity and reliability of research methods and data (Denzin, 1970).

What is Reflexivity?

Most of the research work done so far is done by the single social class which is the middle class, predominantly the white middle class whose perception of the social world is reflected in the studies of the society and various issues. This is called Reflexivity. So, the social world is reflected, shaped and influenced by the researcher's perception. The social background should be truly reflected but it is dominated by the white class perception mainly.

To remedy this problem and for the sake of reliability and validity, the researcher has to be self-critical as to see how much of the beliefs and values are coloured by class background different from the reality. The aim of the researcher should be to produce the true social reality as it exists not what exists in the class perception. Social reality must be studied without bias and prejudice. The researcher has to be rational, honest and fair minded in reflecting the social scene and also using empathetic method to get a clearer view of social scene.

Further Reading

Lynne Williams and Audrey Dunsmuir. How to do Social Research, London, Harper Collins, 1990 (Covers most aspects of basic research methods in sociology).

Bailey. Methods of Social Research (Chapters 1 and 3).

Arber, S. 'Designing Samples' in N. Gilbert (ed), 1993.

Gilbert, N (ed). Researching Social Life, Sage, London, 1993.

Part 19

29
Basic Sociological Concepts

Apartheid, Anthropology, Alienation, Altruism, Animism, Agrarian Society, Bureaucracy, Culture, Cultural Capital, Cultural Hegemony, Culture and Society, Conformity, Cultural Reproduction, Consensus, Community, Capitalism, Classroom Interaction, Deviance, Deviant Sub-Culture, Deskilling, Ethnic Groups, Egocentrism, Elaborated Code, Exogamy, Elitism, Feminism, Globalisation, Gender Differences, Hegemony, Ideology and False Consciousness, Institutional Racism, Kinship, Kibbutz, Language and Class, Norms and Values, Oedipus Complex, Race, Racism and Inequality, Restricted Code, Social Interaction.

Apartheid

Apartheid is a kind of racial barrier practised in South Africa which separated the Black people from the white people by way of making separate arrangement for them in terms of education, transport, sports, amusement, entertainment etc. Also they had separate toilets, bath rooms, railway carriages and busses where no whites were permitted to go. The Blacks had separate living zones such as the Neighbourhood areas in which only the Black people were to live. The blacks were compelled to live in their restricted areas no matter how well off they were.

The blacks, the mixed races and the coloured people had no voice in the government, because they had no votes for a long time; so they could not choose their representatives to stand for their interests with the Central Government. The Blacks were designated to live outside the urban areas in their native self ruled 'homelands', but controlled by the white rule; they had to travel a long way to the white areas for manual work. Mahatma Gandhi when practising in South Africa fought against the 'Apartheid system' by publicly burning the 'Identity cards' to be carried by all the non-white people wherever they went. Later, Nelson Mandela, the leader of the African National Congress also revolted against the Apartheid system for which he was sent to jail and given hard labour i.e. breaking stones. A few years later, he was released from the hard labour to spend time in solitary confinement with in the jail. He was treated as a political prisoner long after when he had finished going through all the repressive measures with in the jail. Over all, he spent 27 years in the jail and released only when the country gradually regained its freedom from the oppressive white Rule in 1991.

Anthropology

Anthropology is commonly associated with the study of primitive societies but can be occasionally used to study the traditional societies as well. Its dimension is important for Sociology because it tries to bring out the way people lived, their culture, how and where they lived and their means of livelihood etc. The more the anthropologists could uncover about the mode of living, including their beliefs, rituals, myths, marriage system, social life the better for knowing more about the life of the primitive people. This knowledge adds a valuable source of information for sociological studies.

The Anthropologist Marvin Harris has visited many regions where primitive people lived and found that their living pattern has not changed much over the years. Hunting, gathering, using basic tools, often clustered around hills and valleys like pre-historic people; or a gang of fifteen or twenty people wandering about not able to settle down or unwilling to do so. On the other hand, in some areas of North America, and jungles of East Asia, it was found that some people were living in groups like communities more or less permanently and cultivating land for food and domesticating animals for milk, meat, leather and also as beasts of burden. Some of these groups have already developed some nucleus of a functional society.

A classic example of anthropological studies was made by a British historian A.R. Radcliffe Brown and his colleague Bronislaw Malinowski, a Polish, and a co researcher – they produced important anthropological materials on the tribal life of the people in the Trobian Islands in the Pacific and Andaman inlands in the Indian Ocean. They gathered a store house of resources relating to their religious practices and cultural activities as well as their links with groups nearby.

Alienation

The word alienation was first used by Ludwig Feuerbach in 1841 when he wrote this in his book 'The Essence of Christianity' by which he meant detachment from God. Later Karl Marx has used the term alienation to mean detachment from work. Karl Marx had earlier accepted the view that religion represented human self-alienation but later he explained alienation as distraught labour force working for others i.e. employers.

According to Marx, workers get alienated from their work because they are not allowed to produce something unique of their own choice or different from set pieces. The employers have prepared designs for them which have to be used and delivered without alteration because capitalist market, they believe, has a demand for it. So workers loose interest in their work and get alienated and mentally detached from their work.

C. Wright Mills, the American sociologist has added besides what Marx has said that alienation also takes place with the White Collar workers too. In his words, Mills mentions that just as manual workers become like commodities selling their skills with things, a similar process occurs when the non manual workers sell their 'skills with persons' on the open market. This is what he terms as the 'personality market' in which every body has a market value of their own personalities; they sell it to earn money. A sales person sells more by his charm and communication skills, a manager or an executive is selected more by his or her personalities, knowledge and experience and the manner with which he or she manages the business than by their qualifications. A sales girl for example, working in a department store smiles, and shows she is ready to serve the customer – all these are for the sake of selling goods and to earn reputation as good sellers when she is diffident and self-alienated. At work she is not for herself but for others.

In this way, individuals become alienated from their true selves. At work, they are different from what actually they are. They all sell their personal qualities in pursuit of personal gain.

Karl Marx saw alienation distinctly and linked it to the 'means of production', system where the workers are seen not as a creative force but as drones which do not allow to control the production. They are not there as participants in the production but as one of the means of productions in which they will end up as chips. This leaves them alienated from the ethos and feelings of achievement.

Agrarian Society

Agrarian societies are rurally based small agricultural communities which have a long history dating back when people gave up their nomadic wandering life of hunting and gathering woods for fire and settled down for farming based on small plots of land as their main occupation. Even to day, these sorts of communities exist in remote rural areas in many countries. They also work in cottage industries in which to produce wooden tools to make fences, chairs, shacks and weapons to hunt animals until iron ores were found which could be melted to make roughshod tools essential for carpentry work. With these they learnt to build houses, make tables, wheel chairs, doors and boxes for storage. People in the agricultural societies also built coracles and small dinghies to sail around. To day, the agricultural communities are far more advanced than before as readymade tools are being made available for use in their daily activities.

During the primitive period, people also domesticated animals to use them for cultivation of crops. They had milk and meat from them, and skin for various uses. In order to supplement their requirement, they did occasional hunting, fishing and gathering of woods and water. They were not lawless breeds but are people who have certain rules to follow at least to maintain order in the community. They had chiefs either elected, or selected or based on patriarchal system. Some kind of social inequalities in terms of privileges and wealth were accepted as the norms of the agrarian societies.

Agricultural societies can also be pastoral, in that sense they settled near grassland, where animals could be found and fed but kept on moving according to seasonal changes. Some of these societies are peaceful but some could be warlike when trading with larger groups. They could be robbed and pillaged if found weak and not able to fight back.

Agrarian societies started their agriculture also at first in a small 'horticulture', a garden in which they could grow their requirement of vegetables and a few crops. This helped them with a regular supply of food without having to depend always on hunting and fishing. Later, community groups cultivated their land on a large scale once they had settled down; side by side other basic traits of a society such as ties with the neighbours and villagers had developed. They were peaceful but were ready to fight if nomads came to steal their cattle and crops.

Tribes in New Guinea for example, have division of labour amongst members of the family, each doing a particular crop in a specific area based on sub-division of farming land, such as some plots are meant to grow fruits and vegetables, and some for other varieties according to seasons. They also enjoyed measuring their wealth by the number of pigs they owned. Occasionally, they called neighbours to join pig feast which re-established their social respect.

Animism

Animism is a spiritual concept of some aboriginal tribes or communities of micro societies where people practise cult worship of supernatural forces like spirits or ghosts. They have thoughts of some invisible spirits who hover around with in the human society as if they still have some unfinished business. So they choose their victims; there is a widespread belief that some of these forces live in the souls of those persons specially women who are weak and suspicious. It is also believed that these evil spirits can cause harm to their minds and the effects can be felt by others as well in the society. The possessed persons are also known as sorcerers who are kept away isolated from the society.

Animism prevails more or less in many beliefs in the form of Tantric worship of 'high spirits' prevalent in some parts of Asia and Africa. Human sacrifice is made to calm down the 'High spirit' too. An elaborate discussion of 'animism' practice can be found in (E.E. Pritchard's book 1956).

Bureaucracy

Bureaucracy is an administrative system which operates in an industrial society. It is hierarchically organised where the structure is based on the ranks stretching from the bottom up to the top.

Bureaucracy has a history of its own. It is associated with an office, rules, red tapes and corruption. At first it was innovated by a French thinker named Monsieur de Gourney, boack in 1745, whose concept of 'bureau' was borrowed from a Greek word 'to rule'. According to Martin Albrow (1970), the word has been nicknamed as a 'bureau-mania', considered as an illness to indicate the rising power of the officials.

Bureaucrats are officials whose jobs are to oversee the work of their junior officials, who in turn do the same over the low grade staff below. Until recently, the volume of work the bureaucrats did was not enough to fill in their time. So, the spare time was spent in chatting, gossiping, moving around for no good reasons. It gives a negative impression of the officials; so to give a good show to the onlookers they pretend to be busy by creating unnecessary paperwork, copying them by the machine and dishing them out to junior staff who would find it hard to comprehend why; call staff meetings and ask members to

the past like a tradition. According to Ralf Linton, culture of the society is the way of life of its members which they learn, share and transmit from one generation to the next. "Culture is a design for living held by members of a particular society" as said by Clyde Kluckhohn.

So culture is how we behave publicly, because our behaviour can earn respect for us or disrespect, depending on how we communicate with people, if we do positively then we deserve some good response or else, negative response. Culture differs from group to group, faith to faith, class to class and country to country. Nevertheless, there has to be a public consensus about dealings whilst with the public whether as groups or individuals. Our social behaviour, manners and code of conduct constitute a significant part of our culture.

Culture and Manner of Behaviour

Bad behaviour causes tension; if a child misbehaves in school, it affects the behaviour of other children. Behaviour and manner are closely related. To cite an example, some people think it as a bad manner when one speaks loudly to some body standing or sitting near him, but when reminded of his loudness her or she would say that it is within their culture, no body would mind it in their culture. So they can't help it. This proves that manners also vary from one culture to another.

In the eyes of the Westerners, some of the social practices of the Australian aborigines would appear strange and cruel but actually that is with in their culture; rather these are sensible, rational and accepted part of their life. For example, during the days of famine and hardship in the aborigine's life, they would not hesitate to practise female infanticide, which is a killing of an unwanted baby girl rather than a bay boy, believing that a boy when grew up would be a supporting hand; he would go on hunting and earning a living whereas a girl would remain a burden in the family. In the same way, an old man would appear to be a burden in time of famine, so he would be pressurised to commit suicide and to relieve the society. It is known as

Geronticide. This shows that the human behaviour is decided by their culture.

There are other cultural diversities which exist all over the world. These exist in the food culture, religious practices, bringing up babies, life in old age, rituals in death and beliefs in life after death. Cultural diversity knows no bounds, so also the type of manners. Culture of tolerance should be practised by all, so that diversity does not interfere with freedom of conscience and rights of the individuals. It is also important to mention that in the name of cultural diversity any form of cruelty, violence, oppression, cannibalism, torture of animals for blood sports and sacrifice of humans for the sake of religious practices should be banned. Culture prohibits any kind of extremism and terrorism used to oppress and kill people.

Culture Industry

There is a development of 'mass culture' in the modern age. Culture to day, has become an industry. It is now carried out by the media industry like the T.V. advertisement, newspaper advertisement, which put on big pictures of attractive products for catching public attention. Producers use movie stars to publicise new products and manipulate people's buying culture of those products. The products for mass consumption develop into mass culture, such as fashions, perfumes, designed body, plastic surgery, organic food, tailor made life-styles, movie mania and many more. German sociologists Horkheimer and Adorno use the term 'culture industry' to refer to the products in which the consumers got used to and unwittingly promote the culture industry. According to them, culture industry produces false needs which are not true needs of people. Art and music have now been trivialised in the name of mass culture. In the name of mass culture a big business is in progress. They deplore the fact that there is no way out of this state of affairs.

Conformity

Conformity means abiding by the norms, rules and regulations generally accepted in a society. To live in a society, one has to learn either knowingly or unknowingly a host of norms and rules in order to be socially accepted as a conformed person. Social interaction involves a lot of nuances, manners and standard of behaviour such as good communication skills, control of manners, good voice and the ability to listen to others – all these norms have to be acquired if one has to be successful social being. To give an example, drivers are expected to follow strictly all the traffic rules, so that no one is injured on the road caused by bad driving; they should allow the pedestrians crossing the road and passengers in the car treated properly. Safety of pedestrians is paramount than the urgency of the drivers. Reckless drivers, cause hundreds of deaths on the road every year for no fault of the pedestrians.

Drunks, thieves and even drivers with licence speed away from drivers in front endangering motorists and walkers. Some are criminals driving with stolen cars, joy riders damage expensive cars while sporting with them, vandalising and killing so many people every year. There are reckless vandals who don't have even driving licence and so could not care for traffic rules; because they are not conforming to traffic rules. Some countries stipulate stringent training course for intending drivers, not allowing even a single fault in the driving test. This should be the norm for drivers in all over the countries.

The Society should strictly adhere to using sanctions against violation of conformity. Sanctions can be formal and informal. Formal sanctions are enforced by the law courts, assisted by the police who arrest the offenders and take them to the courts for trial; if sentenced, they are put under bars. Some sanctions are just imposition of a fine or a verbal warning if that was their first offence. This is informal sanction imposed without a trial. Motoring offences should not be treated leniently; if the offence causes a death, the driver should get a life ban on driving or imprisoned for a long period.

Informal sanctions are commonplace features for all social misdemeanours in which verbal warnings, or a reprimand for annoying women and others, or being a nuisance, or rude to people in a public place are just a few to mention. There is also non-conformity in terms of dress, hair styles, pattern of behaviour and bad attitudes which are usually ignored for the sake of public peace because definition of each is difficult to stipulate as styles are changing every day; so any sanction against these will be challenged. As a result, a large number of non-conformists are tolerated. Drunks wavering here and there, hooting out car horns at night, jostling near street corner, ignoring pedestrians passing by specially in the evening are all misdemeanours, but treated as minor offences and not punished. More Police patrol in the evening and at night on the street can cut down these sorts of offences a lot.

The concept of conformity is important for people if they wish to live in an orderly society. Non-conformists are called deviants who are a problem for society. Compliance with norms and rules must be accustomed to by all regardless of who they are. Life would be miserable if we did not abide by the conformed rules of society. R.K. Merton defines conformity to relate to 'culture goals' of society. In the U.S.A. and some other industrial societies material success is accepted as 'culture goals'. Any non-conformity with those goals will be considered as deviance. In the words of Durkheim, there are individual goals to contrast with social goals; if there is strains between them then individuals would have to adapt to social goals. Failure to do that would lead to deviants using their non conformed rules to achieve their objectives of life. Both Merton and Durkheim stressed that social norms must be made clear in order to prevent individuals becoming morally adrift.

Community

Socially, a community is a group of people having an organised mode of life in a particular area and doing useful activities. There are communities which have broad range of social and cultural functions variable according to the size of the membership. Rules are made to provide primary code of guidance dictating the norms how members should behave. Some rules are rigid and some are flexible. It is expected that a community maintains a bond of friendship, understanding and a spirit of unity with in the membership. According to Nisbet (1970), a community is the most fundamental of sociology's unit ideas. Many communities are well organised and peaceful but some are not, which have difficulties in maintaining harmonious relations with neighbour communities having different cultures.

There is no agreed definition of the concept of a community. Sociologists vary in conceptualising the meaning of the community; but everybody agrees that members should have to live in peace within the community. Despite the tricky situation, Sociologists have formulated a set of norms for a community to follow as mentioned below:

That it has a social system, which promotes peace, it has a fixed locality which can be geographically identified. Some sociologists regard these aspects of community as interlinked. But, Newby insists that these are distinctly separate units, the presence of one does not necessarily guarantee the presence of the others.

Again, living in the same locality does not automatically promote a warm spirit of community. According to Newby (1980), a community is a communion of people in which to develop a spirit of quality relationship.

Other characteristics of a community can be shared values, institutional ties and regular social interaction. A community indicates commitment, solidarity and emotional bonds. Cohen (1985) suggests that a community is best understood in terms of symbols, meanings and identities. Feeling of an identity is most important because it gives a sense of security and belonging – a foothold in which to develop a community spirit. Large scale community develops anonymity and impersonality in which to keep warm personal relationship becomes a distant issue. But with commitment, involvement and a bit of flexibility that can make community life different.

A community exists in different forms according to the requirement of the members. Even within the metro cities, community spirit can exist despite anonymity and impersonality. Those who are involved in social functions, community activities like educational matters, senior citizens' development, sports etc, anonymity and impersonality disappear. Some people of course like to live in seclusion too. Personal freedom to live in peace must not be tempered with interference by others. Cultural activities, religious festivals etc are all community based programmes which can be structural and functional. So a community never dies.

Grouping with in the community can spoil the community spirit, specially those are from political, ideological, class and religious based groups. So, a community should be well aware of the elements which can cause disruption and disunity; so that necessary actions can be taken to deal with the recalcitrant forces.

Capitalism

Capitalism is an economic system which had existed long before Karl Marx wrote the Communist Manifesto and the Das Capital. He criticised the Capitalist system of production along with its mechanism of the 'means of production' and the concept of 'surplus profit'. He also predicted that a socialist system of government would follow when the capitalist system was brought to an end. He exposed the exploitative nature of it which used workers to produce excessive profit for reinvestment in industries in order to earn more profit.

The means of production included land, labour, capital and organisation – these are owned by the capitalists. Marxists argue that the work in capitalist system is meant to make profit from the labour of the poor workers depriving them of the benefit of it. The whole machinery is controlled and managed by the capitalists without involving the workers in the management. This resulted in the capitalists becoming richer and richer at the cost of the hard labour put in by the workers.

One of the faults of capitalism, according to Karl Marx, is its mode of production, which alienates people from the work they do. The system turns them into just wage earners, nothing more. The workers don't feell proud of producing something on their initiative because they were not allowed to do that. That is why they feel distraught and alienated. They work like robots i.e. putting things into slots, they are not needed to use their imagination and thinking, as a result turn into worker drones, their potential is thus debased and gradually destroyed; there is no satisfaction and no fulfillment of work. To Marx, alienation is the main evil of Capitalism.

Consensus

Consensus is related to views, opinion and understanding of people to any social and political issues. Consensus is known by public opinion, media report, Gallup poll or agreement of people. Consensus can be known by the voice of people as well whether or not there is a public support for the government on certain crucial issues like going to war, the devolution of power or joining the E.E.C. etc. When a government realise that they have little support for their policies and also that the public consensus is fast eroding, they rethink about what to do – modify the policies or face an impending defeat in the election. Consensus can dictate what action should be taken to turn the tide against the government by moulding public opinion. To give another example, the functionalists give importance to the 'value consensus' i.e. agreement and cooperation for social integration. To them, society is regarded as a system made up of interconnected and interrelated parts which are to correlate to one another to be functional. If there is an agreement of members for this system, it is consensus.

Interpretive approaches to education focus on small scale interactions between the teacher and the taught and between groups of pupils within the classroom. These interactions show the meanings which the lads give to their actions and by doing so construct their own social reality. Quite contrary to the functionalist and Marxist approaches which tend to show behaviour is shaped by the social system, the interaction way is different which focuses on the individuals' reactions to different stimuli with in the classroom atmosphere and by doing so they show their social reality and their individualism as persons.

Classroom interactions reveal not only students' background, but their attitude to work, teacher and other fellow students also the interests shown, as well as motivation, intelligence and ability to invent and to learn. All these add up to diagnose who is an 'ideal type' student and who is not. American sociologist Howard Becker 1977 and the British sociologist Paul Willis 1977, p. 11-12 have studied kids' attitudes, behaviour and performance in the class room interactions on a long term basis. Their findings indicate that the lads quickly form their groups, give meanings to their actions and that teachers have to negotiate with the kids what work they would do or would not, essential to keep order in the class room. Sometimes, the kids are given a bit of responsibility of the class under the conscious eyes of the teacher to see the difference in kids' attitude to work and sometimes negotiated with the consensus of the pupils. The pupils and teacher work out a teaching and leaning relationships with in the class room.

David Hargreaves (1975) examined that it is not a straight forward teaching and learning matter. Kids' behaviour would gradually deteriorate if understanding was not established. Teachers would have to use a few ploys to 'get their way'. They might, for instance, make excessive demands and then compromise. They also offer 'reward and punishment' ploy such as if you work hard now, you may be excused doing homework to night.

Pupils are constantly being assessed and classified which help to determine their own curriculum and the sets they would benefit from and the type of exams they would sit for. The studies reveal that teachers could easily identify middle class pupils from the rest in terms of ability, behaviour, interests, motivation etc and pupils who did not meet these requirements could be termed as working class kids.

Interactions with in the classroom also reveal that gender differences exist. Teachers pay more attention to boys than girls resulting in better results for the former. Michelle Stanworth (1983) in a college of further education found that girls were at a disadvantage in the classroom even when they were doing the same course with the boys. Michele concludes that girls' experience in the classroom indicate that they were undermined and only had to accept a second place in the class. Dale Spender wrote in 'The Schooling Scandal (1983)' that school reinforces gender inequality in the wider society. Social relations in the classroom, the content of the curriculum, the attitude and expectations of teachers are all biased against girls and favour male predominance. Dale Spender concluded that in mixed education, the dice were loaded against the girls.

Deviance and Deviant Sub-Culture

Deviance is a multifaceted concept which can not be simply defined. It needs a fully explanation. It can take varied forms within societies as it is practised both secretly and overtly. There can be collective deviance existent in government offices and there are deviant groups like the New Age travellers or skin – heads in contemporary Britain. Deviance is wide spread and not confined to a particular country or to a particular group in a society. Generally, when people deviate from norms of standard of behaviour they are called deviants. So, deviance can simply be defined as non-conformity to a given norm or standard of norms. Deviance is also generated by cultural factors as different cultures have different norms of behaviour and values which may not be common to one another. For example, in many cultures drinking alcohol is prohibited but not declared punishable by law except for under – aged children. But still people including children drink flouting the official ban. They can be termed as deviants. We are here mainly concerned with the socially accepted common patterns of behaviour and value system prevalent in societies and any breach of these are deemed as deviance.

Sociological research has found that a particular behaviour may be termed deviant in a particular situation but not in another; for example, smoking in restricted areas is treated as a deviant act but outside it is not. Plummer, 1979, has pointed out that there is a difference between 'societal and situational deviance'. Societal deviance is commonly known as rape, murder, assault, abduction etc which are serious crimes and punishable by law. 'Situational deviance' is offensive and should be reprimanded. It is like construing the normally accepted rules to suit their self made rules when deviants are with friends and colleagues. This is a deviant behaviour which contradicts the normally accepted social rules.

Deviant sub-culture is predominantly a culture of the minority social groups who make their own rules and values of life to follow by ignoring widely accepted social rules and values. In Western societies, sub-cultures are spread across all social classes – each developing their distinct norms, attitudes and values to conflict with the main stream social classes. Some members of the lowest stratum in the stratification system develop a negative attitude to life if they had failed to acquiesce to opportunities offered to improve their social status, but blame others for their predicament and sometimes their own fate as a reason. This becomes a part of their sub-culture.

Sub-cultural theories explain that there are splinter groups who formulate their own ideology of life in contrast to the main stream cultural thoughts. Their aim is to live and to enjoy life the way they prefer even if it is a deviant way. They think that the values of stereotype society are boring and not worth accepting.

Albert Cohen (1955), has developed a sub-cultural theory to explain the working class deviance. He agrees with Merton that adherence to the dominant values creates problems for the male working class adolescents in the inner city areas because the middle class would not accept them in their groups, clubs and associations. So, they have no choice but to develop their own groups and ideas.

There is a deviation in the working class sub-culture as well as they have different groups based on their particular types of behaviour and cultures. They are generally delinquents but divided into groups like the Mods, punks, hippies etc, whose hair styles, fashions, and living modes are distinct from each other. They understand that they are different as characterised by their behaviour patterns and, so they prefer to stay away from each other. They choose street life, drinking, playing, smoking, sometimes singing and forming groups. They prefer inner cities and cluster around street corners. Others form racist sub-groups like the 'skinheads' who gained notoriety by calling Pakistani immigrants as 'Paki' and verbally swearing at them. It was offensive to target Pakistanis in particular, living in the East End of London in the sixties, later they abused calling 'Paki' to any Asians they came across. They were stealing from the Asian corner shops, mugging and swearing. They felt that they should be recognised as a social group and not ignored.

Deskilling

According to Harry Braverman, an increasing number of non-manual workers have lost their jobs since automation, which work faster and more efficiently but which causes deskilling. Their skills are not required and allowed to rot when the automation took over. Work task gets fragmented into simpler routines which the computer does more efficiently than manually. The existing qualified and skilled non-manual jobs are expensive to maintain; so a lot of them were laid off or forced to do semi-skilled or unskilled jobs letting their skills to waste. Those who refused to do lower grade jobs were made redundant or given early retirement but with compensation which were not be that handsome. As a result, these non manual middle class workers have become deskilled and 'proletarian'.

Harry Braverman has argued that most routine white collar jobs have become 'deskilled' to such a degree that they now differ little from manual work. This has led to the rise of Proletariat class than the expansion of the middle class. Braverman has argued that high skills used in the 19th century by the middle class workers are not in use to day because new skills developed by technology are sweeping the market. Some jobs have been deskilled by new technology which has led to the creation of jobs suited to the IT trained.

But many sociologists disagree with Harry Braverman saying that he has over stated the case because some occupations have become re–skilled rather than deskilled, such as typists and office clerks now do word processing and record keeping on the computer.

According to Karl Marx, skilled workers have been replaced by machines which reduce them to the job of machine minders. This happens in a capitalist society which gradually deskills them to the level of unskilled workers. According to some sociologists, the workforce rather than becoming homogeneous is becoming more diverse, with a growth of white collar, managerial and professional occupations. This version is strongly challenged by Harry Braverman (1974). Friedman describes what he calls "responsible autonomy" whereby workers are allowed limited freedom to control their own methods and pace of work. He says that workers are often required to exercise greater skills and initiatives than before. This differs from Harry Braverman's version.

Ethnic Groups

Ethnic groups are a minority people identified as different from the main stream groups in terms of cultural, racial and linguistic points of view. The ethnic groups belong to small communities of their own; in Greek version, the ethnic groups are tribes which have less power and culture and also significantly different from the majority groups. The ethnic groups may also be the break away groups from their original home communities and by doing so have settled down abroad and developed their own distinct social culture including separate religious faiths or cults. They can still speak the languages of their mother communities but now treated as outcastes. It is the political and economic pressures which made them leave the country of origin and becoming ethnic groups in a foreign country.

Features of the ethnic groups have been elaborately enumerated by the House of Lord's judgement in a case 'Mandla vs Dowell Lee, 1983' which is as follows: That an ethnic group has a long shared history and a cultural tradition of its own; that it is a minority which has a status of an 'oppressed group'. The people in this group have an origin of a common descent, a common language and a literature. Under these criteria many minority groups can be identified as ethnic groups; the Sikhs for example, constitute a viable ethnic group, living abroad in England or so. Minority groups; for example, the Hindus, the Muslims and the Buddhists who have mainstream statuses back in India are ethnic groups in the U.K, U.S.A. and other European countries and their faiths and cultures are different and followed mainly by their own people. In the same way, if a group of English or French people, settled in India and lived there they could be called as ethnic groups as well.

With the development of sociological studies during the last half a century or so, ethnicity like many other important social issues has become a serious sociological subject with scope for further researches. Western countries for example, shoulder ethnic influxes from the former colonial countries and also from East Europe. But they have brought with them their respective ethnic cultures, values and norms which sometimes conflict with the indigenous values and norms. Mostly, the disagreements amongst them are about their cultural preference facing the impact of the mainstream cultures.

Sociology is now rich with matters and issues concerning the life of ethnic minorities living in Europe. Racial discrimination still exists in terms of jobs, housing, education, sports and social life. Their cultural impact also has a bearing on the indigenous population. Sociologists share views concerning effects on learning and imbibing western values necessary for national integration. There is no fixed boundary between cultures which can even disseminate into the cultures of the world. Multi-cultures have now become a fashion in the West as people like ethnic food, music, dress, ideas, films, work of art etc. Literature too produced by the Asian writers is increasingly becoming popular material with discerning readers.

Ego-centrism

In a symbolic stage of a child' growth when he or she has reached the age of four to six, their imagery is capable of describing some objects in the way they like. This is 'ego-centrism' according to Jean Piaget, a Swedish educationist whose pioneer work on child development has put forward that a child at this stage has a language mastery to represent objects and images in a symbolic fashion, with a few chosen words which may not be all that clear. What they see outwardly is only described in their best acquired language. According to him, this is 'pre-operational stage' when a child is ego-centric, would not like to accept that they were wrong. They are too confident and so dislike being criticised even though being imperfect and inconsistent. The child fails to see or appreciate the object from others' points of view.

At this pre-operational stage, according to Jean Piaget, a child is also unable to relate to thought processes and to co relate to a rational point of view. He or she speaks from egocentric state of mind which is bereft of a clear concept of objects or events in the environment. For example, if a child sees water poured from a tall jar into a shorter jar but fat, he or she will react to say that water is less in the fat jar than it was in the tall jar even though the volume of water was same.

Margaret Donaldson has questioned Piaget's view of a child's 'egocentrism' as it has come from an adult's point of view saying that egocentrism is equally characteristic of adult behaviour in some situations. Also Piaget is criticised from the point that his observation is based on a small sample which should not generalise. On balance, it can be said that Piaget's study is stimulating as it evokes interest and opportunities for further research work.

Exogamy

In ancient societies, clan system divided societies into different clans and members were obliged to obey the rules of the clans; if anybody disobeyed the rules were excluded from the clam, in other words, made out-caste. One of the rules was known as the 'exogamy' by which no member was allowed to marry some one from within the same clan or kin.

Similarly, in Hindu society, no one is allowed to marry one from the same Gotra that is from the same kin grouping, but has to marry some one from a different Gotra or kin of the same caste. Different Gotras with in the Brahmin caste can marry from different Gotras but must belong to a same caste. For example, Brahmin is a caste which has different Gotros. Marriage in the same Gotra i.e. kin is not allowed but they can belong to the same caste. Exogamous marital relations do not take place between close blood relatives. The exogamous marriages between different Gotras or kin are necessary for the existence and functioning of the family system. This kind of marriage between different kins' is regarded as one way to develop social solidarity.

Ideology and False Consciousness

Ideology is a set of ideas, values and beliefs identified in a dominant group which holds power over les dominant groups. Ideology is essentially a political concept but it can be used as a religious concept as well. Here we are concerned with the former when the concept is associated with a ruler or a system of government which aims to maintain its power over others, sometimes against their wishes. In Marxism, ideology is a part of the conflict theory which aims to replace capitalism with a socialist ideology. Capitalism represents a ruling class ideology; according to Marx, this ruling class ideology is a part of the superstructure developed from the infrastructure which is based on the 'economic relations of productions' and the capitalist system is run by the economic relations of productions.

Destutt de Tracy, a 17th century writer, used the word, 'Ideology' for the first time. He used it to mean, 'a science of ideas'. Later, it was used by religious groups to keep control over their devotees. Karl Marx regarded this ideology as a 'false consciousness'.

According to Thomson, there is a neutral concept of ideology as opposed to Marxian concept. He writes that neutral ideology is one representing independent views but not aligned to any particular group or party to represent their values and beliefs. It is also different from the critical notion of ideology which can be negative. In fact, it leans towards the interests of the dominant group over the weaker groups to maintain social order. Thomson, 1990, p. 53-54.

Thomson stresses that media does a lot of ideological work through their various programmes; it is not interactive with the public, but is more or less like the one way process.

Members of the ruling class produce a dominant ideology for the society advocating its goodness, utility and benefit that every worker and member of the system would derive from. The ruling class ideology conceals from the people – the oppression and exploitation that go with their ideology. Workers are not aware of it. Under capitalism exploitation is disguised under the cloak of equality and freedom. However, the members are conditioned to accept what is granted to them. Marx calls this a 'false consciousness' when workers are content with the system and as long as the programme is paying them their living money regularly they don't bother much about exploitation and oppression.

Marx explains that the ruling class ideology is a distortion of facts when it gives a false picture of the society. He believes that this ideology can only camouflage the real state of affairs for a short period but later it would be gone when the disintegration of the capitalist system was completed.

Hegemony

It is a Marxist concept used by Antonio Gramsci, an Italian neo-Marxist who explains how do the Bourgeoisie continue to maintain their hegemonic power over the subject races. Hegemony means a class rule, such as, the Bourgeoisie ruling class seek to maintain its domination by persuading people to follow their rule because it is beneficial to their needs. They are told that their rule is based on fairness which offers equal opportunities to all. Hegemony is a control system by which the authority likes to stick to power as long as possible serving the public interest. So they carry on a publicity campaign to popularise their cultural and ideological preponderance over others parties. They believe that this propaganda would convince people who would support their cause. The public are not coerced to accept the hegemonic rule but influenced to believe in their cultural and political superiority over other parties. They influence the media and the education system as well and make these their publicity mouthpiece. Furthermore, hegemony is a male dominated ideology evident from personalities involved in it. The rule is also active in sports, public life and movies which also enhance the hegemonic image. Now-a-days female models, politicians and academics are also used to speak out for them.

Cultural Hegemony

The Neo-Marxists believe that in the capitalist system, the culture of the class rule is reproduced through the mass media. This is the cultural hegemony. Gramsci stresses that the popular culture is now partly dominated by the youth sub-culture. They aim to get their trendy culture recognised by the society as well as by the ruling authority. They have a culture of good popular music as well as modern fashion which have a marketable value. Also they have developed their ideology which if not recognised could put up resistance to ruling authority's domination of the society.

Oedipus Phase

According to Sigmund Freud, a child develops an intense sexual urge for mother when he or she is about four to five years old; sometimes this urge lasts up to the teen age. If the child is a boy he continues to remain attached to her mother longer than if the child is a girl who transmits her affection for her father. The boy finds father as a rival and so develops a hatred towards him. According to Freud, he picked the term Oedipus' who happened to be a Greek mythological figure, not knowing who he was, fell in love with his mother and married her, later, he realised that his father was no other than her husband – a rival to his love, so he killed him. Freud termed this as an 'Oedipal phase, when the child' attachment for their parents had an erotic element.

This phase can turn into sexual relationship if not inhibited by parents' rejection of their close attachment. According to Freud, the children under pressure from parents, begin to learn to repress their erotic desires towards their parents.

Gradually, they learn how to be their own persons rather than remain dependents on parents' care and affection. They develop their autonomous self and the 'Oedipus complex phase' has left an impression on them such as how to grow sexual relationships with members of opposite sexes when they mature as adults.

Freud's theory has not gone without a controversy but on balance, has left a powerful influence on the development of the growing adolescents' future relationships specially of sexual nature.

Positional Theory

This view is corroborated by the French sociologist Raymond Boudon who (1974) argued that inequality in education is inevitable in a class ridden society; because students with varied social backgrounds start from varied social positions with differing intelligence levels. For example, a student from an unskilled working class background and a student from an educated middle class or professional background will have different educational aspirations leading to acquiring different social positions because their purposes of education are not same. The former aimed to pass an exam, assured of a job and a fresh start in career; that would be a road to escape poverty and build a future.

Whereas, the latter have to go to the University for higher education to see if at least can reach a similar status of their parents. Children of the middle class have already got a good base of culture and education. They like to maintain it and if possible enhance it. According to Boudon, they would work hard to maintain their class position. Lack of a university degree would affect their position to the detriment of the family; it may also affect the educational attainment of their children. But the students of the working class background rarely aspire after that but be happy to have a start in life even though would have to struggle moving for higher ladder into the career. Working class children generally have a poor economic and cultural background which could effect their attainment in education; and to go to the university would be an uphill task. So, unequal social positions are reproduced with of course exceptions for some, who could break the poverty trap by scaling higher into social positions by working very hard.

Polygenetic Theory

Polygenetic theory is a race theory about the origin of mankind. Michael Banton has developed a theory to state that human beings do not come from the same racial origin and therefore there is no common ancestry for all human beings. The humanity is divided into distinctive groups; it has several origins; so it is polygenetic. Originally, race was determined by the physical characteristics like face, colour of skin, type of hair and height of people which constructed the biological theory of race. The Monogenetic view is that all humans originate from the common species. They have become different caused by the effects of migration, different climatic and environmental conditions.

According to Banton, racial differential had existed since the dawn of history when people were born in different parts of the globe at different times. Darwin has developed the concept of human species as a result of biological evolution.

The concept of sub-species grew when species were constantly changing and selecting in different geographical locations and evolving species of different characteristics which can be classed as sub groups or sub species. Darwin found turtle and birds varied from one island to another; they were animal sub-species. So sub-species grew from the main species effected by modifications during the biological evolution. Some of the subspecies were extinct from further development because of poor mating which produced infertility.

When sub-species evolved in different ways they could eventually become distinctive by their own characteristics.

In the same way, different human races could have evolved like different sub-species of animals. So distinct characteristics of human beings are the outcome of a combination of factors like the natural selection, sexual selection and variations in genes selection etc – all produce distinct human groups. So, there is a case that all humans have a common origin in the beginning, but later, branched out in to different races or sub-racial groups.

Language and Class

Basil Bernstein both as a teacher and sociologist has acquired considerable experience on the subject of link between language skills and educational achievement. His teaching experience in the East End of London schools showed that working class students' form of communication was not adequate enough to cope with the formal education. They spoke at the level at home which was a restricted code below the level maintained in school, as a result, their understanding of the subject contents was limited precluding adequate learning.

Bernstein (1961) has identified two forms of speech which exists such as the restricted code and the elaborated code. The former is only the basic code like short speech spoken informally with friends, meant to convey a limited message to small groups of people who already have a wink in the subject. Sentences are short, simple and unfinished generally without a subject or a predicate.

By comparison, the elaborated code gives details of speech explaining the content of the subject and maintaining grammatical sequences. The speech is meant to be understood formally by all rather than by a few.

According to Bernstein, working class children speak one language only principally – the restricted code whether at home or with friends outside but the middle class children are able to speak both. At school they learn through the standard speech which is an elaborated code but whilst with friends they normally get into the restricted code. But they don't find it difficult to follow the teaching language at school because teachers teach and speak in the formal elaborated code.

The working class pupils on the other hand, have a language difficulty, this and other potent causes combined with such as the cultural and economic factors continue to retard their progress in school. When taught, the children of this category fail to follow the teaching process and thus remain disconnected to learning. This issue is sometimes interpreted as lower I.Q or lack of required rate of I.Q. Bernstein insists that he was not implying on their ability level or intelligence input in their code, but stressing on the language structure necessary for learning which is not with them. The elaborated code gives detailed descriptions of objects, facts and events which to build analytical relationships between things. That character is lacked in the nature of the limited code.

Most sociologists agree to the fact that there is an element of cultural and economic deprivation of these children which preclude their educational achievement and their language pattern is not helping them either. According to Bernstein formal language structure is an essential part of learning. Those who have not got it would not make it in educational success.

Racism

The concept of Race is about the colour and culture of people, their genetic roots and biological characteristics. The subject is interesting, complicated and controversial. To add to its depth, there are several race theories, each is significant in its own way. Race is also based on superiority and inferiority complexes, prejudice and cultural difference between people. Some people think that it is the size of the brain which makes the difference between different racial groups. A Philadelphian doctor, Samuel James Morton argues about the measurement of skull sizes which is the yardstick of the quality of race people. He claims that the Caucasian people inhabiting in England, India, parts of North Africa and the Middle East had the largest cranial capacity which is the size of the brain, capable of intellectual development. His five race theory includes the Ethiopians who have the smallest cranial capacity.

Hitler believed that the Germans belonged to the Aryan Race which was the superior of all races and argued that the Aryan race had been corrupted by coming in contact with other races, such as, the Jews and the Slavs. In South Africa racism was practiced by a system of 'apartheid' which segregated people according to their racial origin.

Biological theories of race identify people according to their physical characteristics, such as hair pattern and colour of skin which is called phenotype. Afro – Caribbean and black skinned African people belong to this type. The genetic differences between groups of humans are known as genotype. Recently, thinking of genetic theory has changed. At first, let us look at the concept of genotype itself.

The geneticist Steve Jones has found that there are 50,000 genes in each human being and these genes determine the differences between humans. It is found that changes in fewer than ten genes determine skin colour. Ultra – violet light and climatic variations make a lot of differences in skin colour. Ultra – violet light from the sun produce vitamin D in the skin. Dark skinned people do not manufacture vitamin D as easily as the light skinned people. Sunny climate favour the dark skinned people more than the white skinned people. Scientifically, genotype is a controversial issue. Genetic differences to determine race does not hold water for long. Steve Jones does not believe that there is any genetic justification for distinguishing races. He also believes that many attitudes towards race have no scientific basis. Richardson and Lambert doubt that there is a Race superiority. They argue that there is no clear connection between biological differences and differences in behaviour and culture is groups of humans.

Michael Banton has found that biological differences in human beings occurred as a result of climatic and geographical variations in which people were dispersed and influenced to produce different types of human beings. According to Banton, race can be conceived of three different origins of humankind; either as a common origin, or several origins or sub species. The latter has emerged from Charles Darwin's theory of evolution. Each has its good reason to back its claim.

Now a days, there are three perceptions of racism in practice: one is cultural, the second is scientific and the third is institutional racism. The cultural racism is about peoples' attitudes, values, beliefs, their ideologies, art, music, craft, literature etc. The cultural racism has a long history but it takes different forms depending on where and when it had taken place. The scientific racism has its root in the 19th century which is described as 'racial stocks' based on 'superiority and inferiority' complexes.

In 1839, as indicated above, doctor Samuel James Morton has classified race into five categories such as Caucasian, Mongolian, Malay, American and Ethiopian. This concept has been further developed by J.C. Nott and G.R. Gliddon in their book Types of Mankind, 1854. They were trying to show that historically there existed the superiority of the white races. They have shown that the Caucasian being the white skinned people 'have in all ages been the rulers'. They sincerely believe that there are distinct biologically different races who also have different behaviour patterns. Some of them remained pure and superior to others. The racial thought of the Nazis is close to these views.

Institutional Racism

Racism in Britain is enmeshed in the institutions in such as way that it can not be separated as a distinct issue. Efforts have been made though to lessen its impact on the society by goodwill practice and general guidelines to improve attitudes of people towards different racial groups. Some sociologists hold the view that racism is a basic feature of Britain's social institutions such as the legal system, the housing, educational, and above all the employment policies. They believe that racist assumptions are built into the rules and routines of these institutions; even though there are individuals who do not support racist attitudes and behaviour in the system, yet they are helpless to combat the racial force – it is internalised into their psychic condition and the system is continued as if it is a normal day to day business. The victims of the racial practice are the ethnic minorities who suffered discrimination from institutional as well as individual prejudices in jobs, sports, housing, education etc.

Racism to day is discussed openly both academically and in real life situations which was not possible earlier due to fear of backlash and more subjective treatment. Now-a-days, People believe that laws have redeemed the impact of racism. So, severity in racial practice is difficult to maintain. Some think Britain's immigration laws are a living example of racial discrimination specially for those immigrants who came from the Asian sub-continent than those coming from the Eastern Europe.

In 1987, E, Ellis Cashmore, published a study of racism in England based on in-depth interview, with 800 white people in the English Midlands. This unveiled 'The Logic of Racism' from the viewpoint of the English working and middle class people. Without going into details, Cashmore found that racism was present in all classes and in all age groups. He found that racism is a product of the 'a type of natural conservatism'. It can be unequivocally said from his point of view that racism in Britain exists in different forms in different sections of society, but everywhere it has the same root-the racial prejudice.

According to the Marxist view, the state in Britain serves the interests of the capitalists by ensuring that the immigrants are to work cheap to generate maximum profit for the private entrepreneurs. Racist policies are designed to this effect and to supply labour through the immigration laws; exploitation of the immigrant workers persisted and they are also blamed for going on strike. Several reports on racism in Britain have shown that current events have slowed down the racial practice, most importantly in jobs and the result has been caused by the establishment of a Commission for Racial Equality. This gave hope of change but was soon dwindled by the fact that so far no culprit was given a sentence. The fear was that any radical measure would rather damage racial harmony for which the Commission was set up. No legal assistance was given to those victims seeking to fight their cases in the law courts. There has been a Race Relations Act which had gone through several changes to adjust to the changing situation, but it made no reckonable difference to alter the situation. In fact, the commission has largely become a debating chamber rather than an executive body.

Values

Values are abstract ideals acquired from social and cultural traditions. One man one wife is a value system of marriage relationship prevalent in most societies.

Most families value children's education as a supreme duty of parents because an educated boy or a girl is an asset of the family as much as society. Other values are human rights, tolerance for people of different races, peace and harmony in society.

Values of society are expected to be adhered to and also embodied in the constitution of the countries as a matter of guidance. Some values are to be strictly followed by all for example, tolerance of different faiths and cultures is absolutely necessary for maintaining peace and harmony in the society. Any breach of tolerance should not be ignored or condoned. Values and norms go side by side as one without the other could have only limited application.

Western countries value accumulation of wealth as very important which can make people rich and happy. Modern societies to day follow the Western values for achieving material prosperity; also many countries including India put spiritual values side by side the material values as major values of society because one with out the other would not be complete.

Values also are a set of beliefs people observe as guidelines. An individual value is strongly influenced by the specific culture in which he or she happens to live. If a society has a multi-culture, it will generate different values: some many not be same as others. But, for the sake of maintaining harmonious relations in society these are to be tolerated. Those who disagree and are harmful and distressing have to be identified and excluded from the general value system. The question of the majority and minority values come with in the same principle of tolerance. The General International values embodied in the U.N. Charter for example, the 'human rights' have to be complied with without exception, so there should be no confusion about their usage.

Norms

According to the American Anthropologist Edward Hall, norms and values are a silent language. A value is translated into behaviour by a range of norms. Norms vary according to a particular situation. In a wedding reception, for example, people present themselves in their best appearance in order to be noticed and treated warmly; so also in the funeral, people wear black suits, black ties etc in order to make the occasion sombre and grave. Norms about dress is important in a posh society such as, dinner suit is a must in a ball or in a banquet and no entry with out it. People approve of the good manners with a smile and bad manners with derision. Manner as a kind of norm is also valued as a courtesy. A good manner is a part of the same value system.

Kinship Relations

Kinship is a blood tie between members of the same family who can also be distant relatives. Members from mother's and father's families are all related to by kinship bond. Father and mother have no blood ties between them because they come from different families; after their wedlock their children are knit by kinship. Step brothers and step sisters are also related by kinship. Uncles and aunts either from mother's or father's sides or of both are also blood related but treated as secondary kin even though shown same respect as others. So the basis of kinship is the relationship established through marriage and descent.

After industrialisation and specially with disorientation of the joint family system in the modern days, nuclear families have been growing in numbers and the kin relationships have become increasingly a disappearing issue specially the secondary kin relationships which are in turmoil. Where joint family system still exists, kinship relations get active during occasions like marriage, Anna Prasanas, funerals etc. Grand parents of both father and mother's side are also treated with great respect specially when their services are required during family occasions. In most nuclear families, occasions of these kinds are kept as private with in the close kin and a few friends. When two people marry they become kin to one another; the husband and wife are called the affinal kin who set up a family and the children born of them are kin to one another and their children start the line of descent.

In some respects, kinship issue becomes complicated once anthropological and biological analysis of descent are unveiled because different cultures produce different kinship relations. Some sociologists discover that in some traditional societies kinship goes beyond the extended family relations. For example, a clan as a closely knit group believe that they have descended from a common ancestor. They find within themselves a common identity and affinity to be distinguished from others. They are bound by certain obligations with in the clan such as religious faith, economic ties, marriages, duties, moral obligations and so on. The clan can be a small and a big one depending on the size of the membership. There are clans in different countries with different rituals and cultures. The clan members feel that every member should be treated as a biological kin as a father and mother and brother and sister and so on.

As mentioned above, after industrialisation and modernisation, the kinship ties are losing their grip on the family. Nuclear families get further split when children get married off and settled independently either in land or abroad. Parents have now just become only parents and nothing more. The traditional pattern of kinship spirit is now beyond recovery. Economic domination has squeezed the families smaller than envisaged. Disparity in earnings and living standards have further divided even the most closely knit nuclear families.

Sociologist, Talcot Parsons has argued that despite the loosening effect on the family, kin relationship still continues in the form of care for the elderly relatives and offering optional financial help to distant kin who are in distress. The British sociologists Young and Willmott have shown that the extended family networks in the East End of London are still in existence in traditional working class communities in 1950s. The study of Bethnal Green in the East of London, shows that there exists a strong extended family network which supports members whenever help is needed. Mother and daughters in particular have close relationships long after the daughters were married off. Daughters visit their mothers several times a week for advice and help when children are born.

Young and Willmott have further researched to find out that when the young families move away from the proximity of their parental home, kinship ties gradually decay. Families become more adrift, self centred and dependent mainly on husbands for support and companionship. Husbands also get more involved in domestic activities. The Feminists of course have attacked Young and Willmott's view that husbands get more involved with domestic work. Ann Oakley, for example (1974) suggested that housework was still predominantly done by women with minimal assistance from their husbands.

The social Anthropologist Murdock has concluded in his book 'The social structure' 1949) that amongst 250 societies he studied, although there are wide variations in the kinship relations of these societies; there exists a family system which includes two adults of opposite sexes having a socially approved sexual relationship and having one or two children either born of their relationships or adopted. It also appears that traditional marriage as a bond between man and woman did not exist in some of those societies.

Murdock found that nuclear family was the basic unit around which all family systems grew. Some societies had nuclear unit as a part of the larger kinship group. Some of the societies permitted polygamous family system to exist allowing individuals to have more than one wife or more than one husband, known as polyandry.

Kibbutz System

We can say that comparing human societies, there is a tremendous diversity in family and kinship systems. One example is the Kibbutz family system in Israel where the normal family does not exist; the family's functions are overtaken by the state and the responsibility is lodged with the Kibbutz. A Kibbutz is a community of families whose main responsibility is the child care who are educated and brought up there with state help but without involving the parents. The children in the Kibbutz are brought up by the trained foster parents away from the care of the biological parents who are only allowed to visit their children for a short period a week. So, the normal family system with natural parents has been done away with as the children are under care. Diversity also exists in the kinship pattern in some societies in Burma, Tahiti and Ashanti in West Africa.

Globalisation

Globalisation is a multifaceted and a dynamic concept; it is hard to conceptualise it without incurring controversy. Areas it covers are many; each area is Multi-dimensional, and conflicting; any attempt to process a uniform system of the global issues could end up in complexities.

Globalisation involves all developed and under developed countries irrespective of their cultural, economic and political systems. In realty, it goes deeper than that when it effect the life of all people. McGrew defines globalisation as the process by which events, decisions and activities in one part of the world come to have significant consequences for people in quite distant parts of the Globe 1992.

Globalisation has developed International trade, Transnational Corporations and global communications network. The multinational companies increase their wealth manifold every year outstripping annual earnings of many small countries. America is the home of many of these companies; others are spread throughout the world. Giddens (1990) has found that globalisation has developed opposed tendencies such as some countries are trying to develop centralising all functions into one system, whereas others are devising decentralisation; some go for integration and others for fragmentation. Some people see globalisation as a sinister attempt to dominate the poor and the weak countries by the powerful West both ideologically and economically. There may be some truth in it, but the greater truth is the benefit it yields to the underdeveloped countries whose needs are overwhelming.

The world has developed faster during the 19th and 20th centuries caused by the rise of nation states, democratic and parliamentary systems, dictatorships and constitutional monarchies, side by side political and economic imperialism. The world has become vastly different with growing affluent societies on the one hand and many poor and destitute countries are becoming more self reliant on the other. This is a new thing which is encouraging. At the same time, gulf between the rich and the poor has got wider and getting worse.

The growth of wealth is welcoming because every country – rich or poor should become richer and no country can prosper without sufficient wealth of its own. Wealth helps to reduce poverty and prevent large scale starvation and devastation left by the natural disasters. Not a week passes without a catastrophe being unleashed by the effects of global warming and the changing eco-system. The whole planet is being disturbed by the emission of carbon dioxide and the Ozone layer being thinned year on year as a result. Scientists are increasingly convinced that there are holes in the Ozone layer through which sun heat directly hits the planet earth and disturb the balance in the environment. As a result, the Iceberg is melting to cause terrible flood. That coupled with the changing climate bring the tidal waves devastating the lives of thousands of people and their coastal regions which get engulfed every year. The wealthy nations are not exempt either. The rich and the poor alike are victims of the global catastrophe.

Effects of Globalisation

Globalisation has marginalised the national and local products by bringing the standardised products of the multinational companies for consumers. They have particularly influenced the middle class consumers with products like beauty treatment, fast food, drinks, trendy modern music, with top Hollywood movies, fashion products, computer games, mobiles, books, magazines, attractive world wide holiday offers and so on. They have a powerful media to back their products which have removed small local shops and small manufacturing enterprises out of business. Again, these products have been modified into cheaper versions to cater the craze of the young generation and the working class consumers. Profit from this lower grade market is colossal which has now outstripped the profit earned from other groups. Mobile phones are now owned by even the illiterate people and their sale is increasing all the time.

There is also an effect on local cultures when transmission of international programmes are produced providing exotic interests like dramas, soaps, music, sports such as football, cricket, wrestling, boxing, gambling etc. Local cultures are now being promoted to develop interests in those areas for discerning consumers.

One thing that has affected most is the development of insecurity in life. People feel empty even in their own homes not knowing what would happen to night or to morrow.

Lastly, because of large scale industrialisation of countryside and world wide deforestation of many green areas, the environment is left in a state of beyond repair. There is an unlimited damage done already to the animal population. Emission of carbon dioxide from millions of cars and smoke released from the industrial production round the clock has caused growing heart diseases all over the world. The future generations will no doubt inherit a defective planet with hordes of unimaginable problems emerging to which no solutions have yet been found.

One of the terrifying developments is the massive growth of terrorist attacks on the important installations obviously to hurt the economic nerve centre of the countries. Extremism, fanaticism and blind belief are causing havoc to the society for which there is no reasonable justification. Meanwhile unfortunately, thousands of innocent lives are shed every year by senseless killing.

Bibliography

Ralt Linton, 'Present World Conditions in Cultural Perspectives' in R. Linton (ed), The Science of Man in World Crisis, New York, 1945.

Clide Kluckhohn, 'The Concept of Culture' in D. Lerner and H.D. Lasswall (eds), The Policy Sciences Stanford, 1951.

Horkheimer and Adorno, The Culture Industry.

R.A. Nisbet, The Sociological Tradition, 1970.

R.K. Nerton, Social Theory and Social Structure Enlarged Edition, Free Press, New York, 1968.

Newby, 1980.

Michelle Stanworth, Gender and Schooling, London, 1983.

Albert Cohen, Delinquent Boys, Free Press, 1955.

P. Thomson, The End of Bureaucracy, 1990.

Index